AF560277

THE GREAT UPRISING IN INDIA, 1857–58

The Great Uprising in India, 1857–58

UNTOLD STORIES, INDIAN AND BRITISH

ROSIE LLEWELLYN-JONES

MANOHAR
2025

Cover illustrations: Two scenes from the near-contemporary murals of the siege of Jhansi, in the Lakshmi Temple at Orchha, near Jhansi (photographs Rahaab Allana, Assistant Curator, Alkazi Collection of Photography, New Delhi).

First published by The Boydell Press, Woodbridge in 2007

This edition (2025) for South Asia is being published by
Manohar Publishers & Distributors

Licensed edition with permission from
Boydell & Brewer Ltd
Bridge Farm Business Park, Top Street
Martlesham IP12 4RB, Suffolk, UK

ISBN 978-93-6080-542-5

Published by
Ajay Kumar Jain *for*
Manohar Publishers & Distributors
4753/23 Ansari Road, Daryaganj,
New Delhi 110 002

Printed and bound in India

CONTENTS

ILLUSTRATIONS

This book is dedicated to all the victims of 1857 and 1858

ACKNOWLEDGEMENTS

The first acknowledgement must go to Professor Huw Bowen, editor of the East India Company series of books published by Boydell & Brewer. It had seemed impossible, in 2005, to generate any interest at all in Britain in the 150th anniversary of the Great Uprising. Museums were completely ignorant of the event, publishers didn't want to know, and the only activity seemed to be in India itself, which was promising an ambitious programme involving Pakistan and Bangladesh. A phone-call from Huw in April 2006 said delightful things to an author's ear, like 'we are interested in your book', and subsequent meetings have simply reinforced this first impression of a sympathetic, imaginative and thoughtful editor. Peter Sowden, the general editor, also gave me useful pointers that have helped in shaping this book.

Nothing in the National Archives in Delhi would have been possible without the help of Jaya Ravindran, who directed me to the indexes needed, smoothed my path in requesting records and was always someone I looked for on entering the Reading Room.

Staff on the Third Floor at the British Library, London (whose department is so frequently renamed that any reference to it may already be out of date), were invariably helpful, and took the trouble to phone me when requested books had arrived from off-site locations.

Lieutenant General S. L. Menezes read all the chapters in this book at an early stage, and subsequently proofread them again, and made very helpful suggestions.

Captain Timothy Ash, who first told me about the Kotah Residency murders, read the draft chapter and made helpful and encouraging comments.

My friend Veronica Brinton sat with me during Christmas 2006 while the last amendments were being made.

To all the people named above, my most grateful thanks. I am sorry that my old friends Peter Taylor and Nick Shreeve, both Indian historians, are not here to read this book. Their comments would have been invaluable.

Any errors in this book are the sole responsibility of the author.

PREFACE

This is an unconventional history of the events of 1857 and 1858. It attempts to integrate the military events of the Uprising with the breakdown, and subsequent restoration, of civilian administration that took place across northern India during that period when the 'Wind of Madness' shook the foundations of British rule. It places particular emphasis on many of the previously unnamed Indian participants in the Uprising. Men and women in northern India were suddenly caught up in dreadful events which many of them had not wanted, and which they had not sought. Others embraced the opportunity to rise against the British in different ways, not only by murdering them (and the Indians who worked for them), but also by destroying British encroachments like the electric telegraph and the new railways. The sepoys of the East India Company Army rose against what they saw as efforts to destroy their caste or their religion through the increasing influence of Christian preachers, some of whom were Army officers. In the ensuing conflict, churches were deliberately destroyed, and printing presses, used to print religious tracts, were smashed. Other people simply wanted to redress old wrongs which were not to do with British administration, but which had been festering for a long time. Land records, held in the district headquarters, were often burnt, in the hope that the land revenue tax would be lifted, or that land-grabbing would pass unnoticed.

The British reaction to the crisis, though initially hampered by lack of troops where the outbreaks occurred, was to recapture the towns which had been taken by the sepoys and their supporters and to restore order in the surrounding countryside. Both these aims were largely achieved by the end of 1858 but at a terrible cost to the Indian population. After the recapture of Delhi in September 1857, British officers boasted about killing terrified civilians who were found hiding in their own homes. The remaining inhabitants were evicted and forced to spend the winter in the open, outside the city walls. Gallows were erected in city centres where men were hanged in batches, with no discrimination made between the rich, the poor, the civilians and the sepoys, or indeed frequently between the innocent and the guilty. In the countryside, villages were burnt and the villagers, fleeing for cover, were picked off like wild animals and shot. The routes along which the British troops marched were marked by the corpses of Indian men hanging from trees, sometimes after the most cursory trial, but more often than not without any kind of justification for their deaths.

The intention of this book is not to repeat familiar stories from the Uprising, but to shed light on previously neglected areas. The determined efforts of the inhabitants of Lucknow to defend their city against the British during the winter of 1857; the reasons that led up to the murders of the British Agent at Kotah and his sons; the official depredations of the British Prize Agents; the varied punishments visited on the Indian population, and the way in which both Indians and British memorialised the 'Mutiny', are among the topics examined here. After the Uprising and the subsequent assumption of Indian rule by the British government on 1 November 1858, the East India Company was abolished. Its story, beginning on the last day of the year 1600, when Queen Elizabeth of England granted a charter to the Company, is being told in a series of books published by Boydell & Brewer. Thus, in chronological terms, this book is the last in the series and it shows why the world of the East India Company came to an abrupt end after 258 years.

In spite of hundreds of books on the subject, there is a huge amount of documentation connected with the Uprising, which has never been published. Much of it is contained in the India Political Consultations at the British Library in London, and the Foreign and Home Consultations in the National Archives in Delhi. This is the raw material of history – the nightly reports written by candle-light in a tent at an army camp; telegrams transmitted by the electric telegraph and transcribed by hand on printed forms; a proclamation in Urdu by the Nana Sahib, printed on thin, glazed paper; the pencil-scribbled comments on an official memorandum. There are dozens of pathetic letters from women who were widowed during 1857 and 1858 and who sought a small pension from the Company coffers. There are dignified petitions from Indian merchants listing their possessions which had been stolen by British troops and the dreaded Prize Agents. There are pleas by petty officials, British and Indian, for their back pay during the months of unrest, which were met in an extraordinarily unsympathetic way by central government. When Charles Elliot, a head assistant in Jalaun District, asked for payment of his monthly salary of Rs 100, he was told to produce his last pay certificate. He replied

> I regret much I am unable to produce my last pay Certificate in consequence of my being compelled to flee suddenly from the station on hearing of the outbreak of Jhansi which was only 36 miles from our Sudder station. Had the other European residents taken the same precaution and acted as I did, very likely they would all have been in the land of the living today!!! I and Mrs Elliot are the only survivors from the ill-fated District, the office records are destroyed, and the officers killed renders it impossible for me to produce one. I am quite a stranger in Calcutta, and living in one of the Refugee houses

> supported by the relief fund and if government would grant me my arrears of pay due, it would be of great Service.

This kind of letter is just as much a part of the history of the Great Uprising as the well-worn stories of the siege of the British Residency at Lucknow, or the horrors of the Bibighar at Cawnpore. Yet we are almost completely ignorant of the way ordinary people had to carry on with their lives during this traumatic period. If this book throws a little light on an 'alternative' history of the Uprising, then it will have succeeded in its purpose.

There are a few points to note in reading this book. The term 'rebels' is not used in a derogatory sense. It is simply a description of Indian men and women who rose up against British rule, and who were literally rebelling against the existing order. Many of yesterday's rebels are seen today in India as freedom fighters, and British readers should acknowledge that Indians will always see the events of 1857, rightly or wrongly, as the start of the movement that finally shook off British control of their country in 1947, when Independence was won. Similarly the term 'mutiny' is a technical description of soldiers disobeying their officers, although it is widely used, both in India and elsewhere, to refer to all the events that took place during the Uprising and not just those amongst the sepoys.

Indian place names and proper names transcribed into English always present a problem for the historian. Different spellings are used, sometimes in the same document, because there were few standardised spellings of such words in the mid-nineteenth century. English pronunciation has changed too, and the long drawled-out 'a' which gave us 'pawnee' for *pani* (water) has gone. Wherever possible, the invaluable *All India Directory of Postal Index Numbers* has been used to identify today's spelling of place-names. The only exception is Kanpur, which I have retained as Cawnpore. Proper names are given wherever possible in their modern form, using dictionaries of Hindu and Muslim names. Even though this means at times altering the text, it seems important to me that these men and women should be dignified by their proper names, and not by the often misheard or misunderstood English versions.

Rosie Llewellyn-Jones
London, 1 January 2007

TIMELINE

1856

7 February	Annexation of Awadh by the British
21 August	Queen Mother of Awadh arrives in Britain to petition Queen Victoria

1857

26 February	19th Bengal Native Infantry troops at Berhampore refuse to use greased cartridges
29 March	Mangal Pande, 34th Bengal Native Infantry, wounds two British officers in a failed mutiny attempt
8 April	Mangal Pande hanged at Barrackpore
3 May	Sir Henry Lawrence confronts mutinous troops of the 7th Oudh Irregular Infantry at Lucknow. Leaders of the revolt are imprisoned
6 May	34th Bengal Native Infantry disbanded at Barrackpore for striking their British officers
10 May	Sepoys at Meerut mutiny, kill British civilians and officers and ride to Delhi
11 May	Meerut sepoys arrive at Delhi, and are joined by the garrison, Europeans murdered or flee
12 May	Sir Henry Lawrence holds a durbar at the Lucknow Residency for loyal troops
24 May	General Anson, Commander in Chief, leaves Ambala for Delhi, dies at Karnal two days later from cholera
28 May	Troops mutiny at Nasirabad cantonment in Rajputana
30 May	Lucknow garrison mutinies
30 May	First 'Mutiny' Act (XI) passed by Legislative Council, Calcutta, makes it an offence to rebel, or conspire to rebel against Queen Victoria or Government of the East India Company
31 May	Supposed date for the Bengal Army to mutiny
31 May	Sergeant Major Gordon (Sheikh Abdulla) begins march to Bareilly with 28th Bengal Native Infantry who have mutinied at Shahjahanpur

6 June	General Wheeler and Europeans are besieged at Cawnpore by the local garrison
8 June	Battle of Badli-ki-Serai allows British troops to establish their base on the Delhi Ridge
12 June	130 Europeans escaping from Fatehgarh murdered at Bithur by Nana Sahib's men
13 June	Act XV attempts to stifle the English and vernacular press
27 June	Europeans massacred at Satichaura Ghat, Cawnpore, after false promise of safety by Nana Sahib
30 June	Sir Henry Lawrence and troops defeated by rebels at Chinhat, and retreat to the Lucknow Residency, where the siege begins
5 July	Birjis Qadr crowned King of Awadh, in Lucknow
15 July	Third massacre at Cawnpore, 200 European women and children killed by Nana Sahib's men
15 July	Khan Bahadur Khan proclaimed as the King of Delhi's Viceroy at Bareilly
17 July	General Havelock enters Cawnpore
13 August	Sir Colin Campbell, newly appointed Commander-in-Chief, arrives in Calcutta
14 September	General Archdale Wilson begins the final assault on Delhi
20 September	Delhi captured by British and Indian troops
21 September	Bahadur Shah Zafar, King of Delhi, captured at Humayun's tomb by Captain William Hodson
22 September	Three Mughal princes shot by Captain Hodson at Khuni Darwaza, Delhi
25 September	First relief of the Lucknow Residency by General Havelock and Sir James Outram
15 October	Murder of Major Burton, Political Agent at Kotah, his two sons and two other men
17 November	Second, successful relief of the Lucknow Residency by Sir Colin Campbell
24 November	General Havelock dies from illness at Lucknow
31 December	Government Agency Committee established at Delhi to investigate actions of the Prize Agents

1858

2 January	Lieutenant Frederick Roberts captures rebel flag at Khudaganj
2 March	Sir Colin Campbell begins the recapture of Lucknow
14 March	Looting in the Qaisarbagh Palace, Lucknow
16 March	Lucknow is finally recaptured after fierce fighting

21 March	Government Commission to apprehend rebellious sepoys established under John Cracroft Wilson at Allahabad
30 March	Kotah city captured by General H.G. Roberts and the Maharao released from imprisonment by the rebels
3 April	Sir Hugh Rose recaptures Jhansi
17 April	Lord Canning issues printed list of rebel names and descriptions
17 June	The Rani of Jhansi killed by British troops at Kotah-ki-Serai, near Gwalior
1 November	Proclamation by Queen Victoria read throughout India announcing that the Crown has assumed authority for the country and issues a pardon for all rebels except murderers

1860

3 February	Distribution of prize money from the capture of Lucknow

1. Map of India

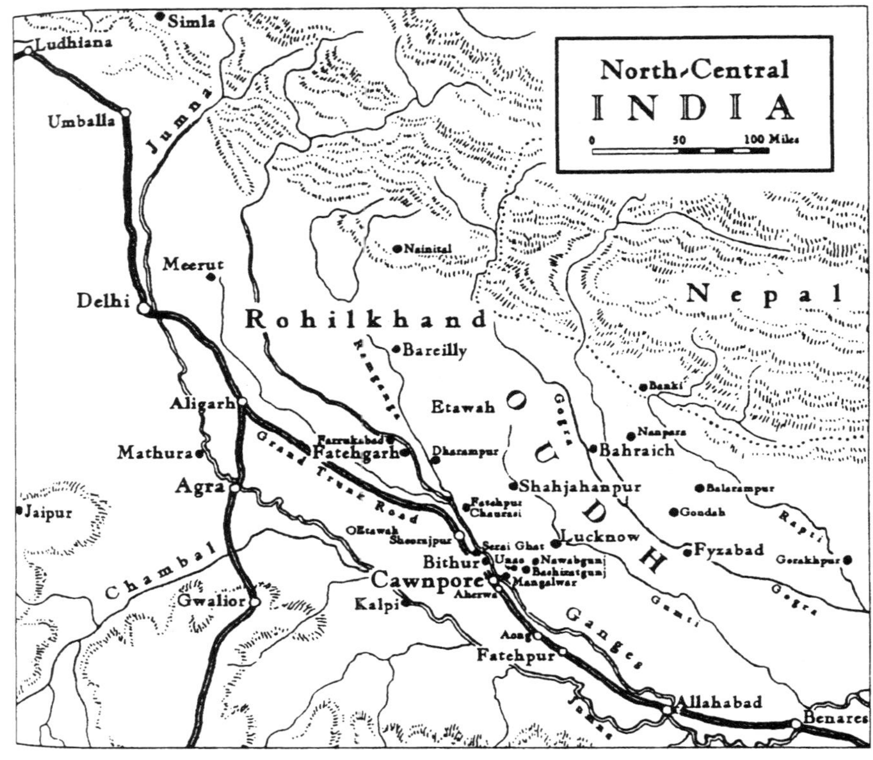

2. Map of north and central India

INTRODUCTION

INDIA IN 1857

As dusk fell on 2 January 1858 Lieutenant Frederick Roberts was chasing a group of mutineers near Khudaganj, a town on the bank of the Ganges, between Cawnpore and Fatehgarh. The young officer had been born in Cawnpore, and he was now part of the British force led by Sir Colin Campbell, which was busy pursuing 5,000 rebels under the nominal command of the Nawab of Farrukhabad. 'We overtook a batch of mutineers,' wrote Roberts later, 'who faced about and fired into the squadron at close quarters. I saw Younghusband [a fellow officer] fall, but I could not go to his assistance.' Lieutenant Roberts was awarded the Victoria Cross for two actions that day – saving an Indian cavalryman, who was about to be bayoneted by a rebellious *sepoy* (soldier) and capturing the mutineers' standard, which he wrenched out of the hands of the flag-bearers, while under fire.[1]

The flag measured nearly six and a half feet square, and bore the English cross of St George in red, on a white field. It had been obtained, somehow, from a British source by the mutineers who had then customised it with their own emblems. There was the crescent moon which symbolised the start and end of the holy Muslim month of Ramadan, a field gun that showed a fighting force, and the star-like *deepaks* of the Hindus, in mirror-work embroidery, all attached to the English flag. At its centre was a lion, cut from the coat-of-arms of the Honorable East India Company and stitched to the rebel flag. As an analogy for the Uprising of 1857, the flag would be hard to equal, demonstrating the symbiotic relationship of the soldiers to the East India Company. The Bengal sepoy army was indeed a product of the Company, one of the three Presidency armies established in the eighteenth century, initially to guard the 'factories' that housed goods for the India trade and to supplement the small number of European 'factors'. The East India Company was one among several European trading companies that arrived in India ready to buy and export goods not only back to Britain, but to China and the Malay archipelago. The British were preceded by the Portuguese and the Dutch, who were already well-established by the seventeenth century, and they were followed by the French Compagnie des Indes Orientales, the most serious rival to British hopes in the East. Indeed, the small numbers of sepoys recruited by the East India Company at Bombay, Madras and Calcutta, were used as much for the defence of the factories against other predatory European Companies, as for anything else. It was these little groups, only 300 men in one case, who were to develop, by 1857, into the three great Presidency armies of Madras, Bengal and Bombay.

During the eighteenth century, as wars broke out between Britain and France, the conflicts were played out in the Indian subcontinent too, and towns like Madras and Pondicherry in the south changed hands, assisted by the sepoy armies, who were being trained to fight in the European manner. Neither France nor Britain was shy of supporting local rulers who they thought could promote their interests, and there were regular defections from one army to another, depending on who seemed likely to be the victor in the battle for southern India.

A number of events in the late 1750s and 1760s, more significant in retrospect, had led to the East India Company consolidating its position in India. The battle of Plassey in 1757 led ultimately to the Company acquiring the right to collect land revenue in Bengal. Through a combination of luck and good leadership, the Company gained control in the south when the French-held city of Pondicherry fell in 1761. The battle of Buxar three years later resulted in the defeat by the Company of a coalition of Indian princes. These British victories were made possible by the sepoy troops, and small, miscellaneous companies of European mercenaries. Lord Robert Clive, the Commander-in-Chief in the mid-1760s, had reorganised the Indian troops into the first regular force led by a few European officers.[2] They were now armed and dressed like European soldiers, wearing the red jackets that gave them the name 'Lal Paltan', or the 'Red Battalion'.

The relationship between the sepoys and the East India Company was of mutual benefit – there was no shortage of work for well-trained fighting men in the second half of the eighteenth century, as the Mughal Empire began its slow disintegration, and vigorous new provincial rulers took the stage. For the Company, which was rapidly transforming itself from a group of merchants to a powerful administrative body, the sepoys were essential. The collection of the all-important land revenue, the key to a ruler's wealth, often had to be enforced by armed men. Sepoys accompanied the revenue collectors where money had to be extracted from feudal chieftains holed up in their fortified houses. Various groups like the Jats, the Rohillas, and the powerful Marathas, that moved into the vacuum created by the loss of central Mughal government, had to be controlled or defeated by the Company, using its Indian troops. It was a relationship that neither party could withdraw from that was so poignantly symbolised by the captured flag that Lieutenant Roberts brought back into camp that January evening. The sepoys had been fashioned into the Company's army and had eaten the Company's salt. They were, on the whole, brave, loyal and well-trained men. But they were not, in 1857, capable of suddenly transforming themselves into an independent fighting force strong enough to overthrow their employers.

The Great Uprising of 1857–58 is known by several other names – the (Indian) Mutiny is the most common, and is used both in India and Britain to describe the events that took place during those two tumultuous years. It is also called Great Rebellion, the Sepoy Mutiny, or the Uprising, and during the last fifty years or so has become known as the First War of Indian Independence. The full title of the history by Dr R. C. Majumdar, first published in the centenary year, is *The Sepoy Mutiny and the Revolt of 1857*, which acknowledges the importance of the two events that contributed to the Uprising, the military and the civilian revolt. The earliest use of the term 'Indian Mutiny' appears in the two-volume history by Charles Ball, published in 1858, *The History of the Indian Mutiny* and its sub-title is significant '*giving a detailed account of the sepoy insurrection in India; and a concise history of the great military events which have tended to consolidate [the] British Empire in Hindostan*'. Ball, about whom little is known, other than that he tapped into the British public's immediate demand for reassurance with his sensational illustrations, saw the East India Company's progress and eventual domination as inevitable. The 'Mutiny' as he called it, was only a check in that progress, but one that had been overcome, albeit at the cost of many British lives.

Both military and civilian officers writing after the autumn of 1857 referred to the events as 'the late disturbances', and there was a widespread belief among the majority of Britons, and many Indians, that the Uprising would be put down. The theatre of war was localised, although this would have been of little consolation at the time for those caught up in it. The Uprising was mainly confined to the plains of northern and central India, in what is today's Uttar Pradesh, Madhya Pradesh and western Rajasthan. Incipient revolts among the sepoys in the Punjab were brutally nipped in the bud. There were minor outbreaks elsewhere, including as far south as Hyderabad in the Deccan and as far north as Nainital but, significantly, not in the British Presidency towns of Bombay and Madras, nor in the administrative capital, Calcutta. Here, the magnificent Government House built half a century earlier by Lord Wellesley, to emulate the palaces of the Mughals, as he himself confessed, remained untouched. There were no howling mobs at its handsome lion-topped gates, although nervous European clerks and others formed themselves into volunteer rifle corps. The Governor General, Lord Charles Canning said he had never met 'such a set of old women' and there was much fussing about granting the volunteers time off from their offices for 'military duty'.[3] Only one of the three Presidency armies was involved, that of the Bengal Army, whose recruits came mainly from Awadh and Bihar. Although there were minor disturbances in the Bombay Army, it stood firm, and together with the Madras Army, was used to reconquer the areas which had fallen out of the control of the East India Company.

This is not to minimise the importance of the Uprising, but to point out that had it truly been a mass movement to expel the British rulers from the subcontinent, as happened in the years preceding 1947, then attacks on the British seats of power would have been more effective. By focusing on the old Mughal capital of Delhi, where the elderly Bahadur Shah Zafar held a ghostly court, the mutineers looked backwards, to feudal times, not forward to the reality of mid-nineteenth-century colonialism in the industrial age. In the military arena British troops were outnumbered more than 7 to 1 by Indian soldiers at the beginning of the Uprising.[4] We have no precise figures for the small number of civilian Europeans compared to the population of the Indian subcontinent. A census taken in 1870, more than a decade after the Uprising, gave a total of 212,483,247 'Asiatics', while Europeans and Americans amounted to only 89,585. Eurasians, that is, people of mixed European and Indian blood, accounted for 40,789.[5] Although it seems astonishing that such a small number of Europeans was able to rule nearly half the Indian subcontinent (the remainder was ruled by princes and chiefs), it was only with the complicity of the majority of its inhabitants that this could be done. Had every class risen up against the British in 1857, the princes, the *zamindars*, the merchants, the bankers, the priests, the *maulvis*, the agricultural workers, the pastoralists, the weavers, the fishermen and others, then of course the revolt would have succeeded. But this did not happen, and the realisation that it would not happen, gave the British the will to hold on during the Uprising and to fight back. Unwittingly, a group of *ryots* (peasants) in Bharuch District (in present-day Gujarat), had found an effective weapon, but they did not pursue its use. A 'few hundred miserably served ryots go about talking sedition,' reported Colonel Shakespear, the Resident at Baroda in June 1857, 'they say they won't pay any [land] revenue'. Shakespear also reported 'hundreds of men' at a seditious meeting, armed with swords, spears, bows and arrows.[6] A sustained non co-operation movement by the peasants who worked the land, coupled with an uprising by armed civilians, would ultimately have been much more damaging to British interests.

The Uprising of 1857 that started with the mutiny in the Bengal Presidency Army early that year was by no means the first in the history of the sepoy armies, but it was the only one which was taken up by some of the civilian population with such speed and enthusiasm. Not all the mutinies were by sepoys, indeed the first recorded mutiny in the East India Company's Army was by British soldiers in 1674, protesting about high prices and a cut in their salaries. (British Army regiments, that is, regiments formed solely of British or European troops, and regularly deployed by the Crown from the middle of the eighteenth century, also served in India. The disparity in pay between them, and the indigenous, sepoy troops, led by British/European officers, was a continual cause of friction between the two armies.) The first recorded mutiny in the Bengal Army took place after the battle of Plassey in

1757 when European troops demanded an extra field allowance and refused to march further without a fresh supply of boots and arrack (a locally distilled spirit). The commander of the time had thirty European soldiers tried by court-martial, and flogged after they were found guilty of mutinous behaviour. In 1764, the Lal Paltan, the red-coated sepoy battalion set up by Robert Clive, mutinied and imprisoned its European officers in a dispute about the unfair distribution of prize money. The mutineers were captured, court-martialled and twenty-four were blown from guns, a form of execution used by the Mughals and subsequently adopted by the commanders of the East India Company Army and the French Compagnie des Indes Orientales, which had its own sepoy troops.[7]

At least twenty-five mutinies occurred in the century between Plassey and the Great Uprising. Many were to do with money, like the so-called 'White Mutiny' of 1766 when European officers wrote to Robert Clive protesting against the withdrawal of their *batta*, a field allowance. (The officers were subsequently dismissed, but later pardoned and reinstated.) However, one of the first ideological mutinies, and the first where numbers of Europeans were killed, happened at Vellore in 1806 when sepoys in the Madras Army revolted. The men, who were garrisoned in Vellore Fort, suddenly attacked their fellow European soldiers at night, killing over a hundred, wounding many more, and shooting down any British officers who came to the rescue. In an ominous foretaste of the 1857 Uprising, the Vellore sepoys then began looting the fort. It was recaptured the next morning by Colonel Rollo Gillespie, who had no previous experience of India, leading a British regiment, the 19th Dragoons; about 350 of the mutinous sepoys were taken prisoner. The cause of the mutiny was investigated by a Commission of Inquiry, who found that the Madras Army Commander-in-Chief had introduced new dress regulations that required the sepoys to remove their caste-marks (painted symbols on their foreheads) and to wear a new European-style hat with a leather cockade. The objection of the sepoys to the new dress was that they feared it to be the first step in forcing them to become Christians. This was another theme that was to arise almost half a century later.

The Sepoy Mutiny of 1857 was not therefore unique in itself, but it acted as the trigger for a series of mutinies that spread rapidly through cantonments across northern and central India and inspired the civilian population to rebellion. The list of cantonments where *sowars* (cavalry troops) mutinied, or part-mutinied is extensive: Aligarh, Allahabad, Azamgarh, Bareilly, Cawnpore, Delhi, Dinapore, Faizabad, Fatehgarh, Ferozpore, Jabalpur, Jhansi, Jhelum, Jullundur, Lahore, Lucknow, Mainpuri, Meerut, Mhow, Nasirabad, Nowgong, Peshawar, Phillaur, Saugor, Shahjahanpur, Sitapur. Troops were disarmed at Agra, Ambala, Barrackpore, Hoshiarpur, Jhelum, Lahore, Peshawar and Sialkot.[8]

There were clearly pressing reasons behind mutinies on this scale; reasons that went far beyond those of poor pay, equipment and food, and unpopular postings. Much time and effort has gone into explaining the causes of the 1857 mutiny and the accompanying revolt and given the complexity of the subject, commentators have offered a number of different reasons. Thus the Marxist historian (Eric Stokes, in *The Peasant Armed, the India Revolt of 1857*) saw the Uprising as a popular peasant revolt, almost inevitable in fact as the British had destroyed the 'social organism' of Indian society by the introduction of the steam engine and free trade. The soldier historian (Subedar Sita Ram, in *From Sepoy to Subedar*) felt the whole thing rested on the unfair treatment of the sepoy, the disparity in pay between him and the British soldier, the fact that it was impossible for the Indian officer to advance other than by seniority, and the increasingly scornful attitude of the newly commissioned, non-Hindustani speaking English officers. The political historian pointed to the changing role of the East India Company, when it assumed the role of 'local agent' to the British government in 1834, and subsumed a number of Indian states by various underhand and doubtful methods in order to increase its land base, and thus its revenue. The alienation of the Muslim population as the importance of the Mughal dynasty declined was cited. The economic historian thought the changing balance of trade that saw India become an importer of British-made goods rather than an exporter of fine fabrics, indigo and other luxury goods had a lot to do with the unrest. An inbuilt resistance to change meant the inventions of the Industrial Revolution in Britain, in particular the railway and the telegraph, were not welcomed as inevitable signs of progress. The social historian was sure the reason lay in the Evangelical movement in Britain that allowed proselytising missionaries into India for the first time after the Charter Act of 1813, and made it easier for Englishwomen to enter the country too. The latter quickly turned into *memsahibs* and disapproved of the practice of Englishmen keeping *bibis* (local mistresses), which had formerly proved such a useful way of breaking down barriers between the races and had enabled the men to learn Hindustani.

In short, a number of reasons have been advanced, and among each of those listed above, there is more than a kernel of truth. But not *all* of these reasons applied to *all* the acts of mutiny and civil revolt that took place in 1857 and 1858. India's enormous land mass is both its blessing and its curse. Delightful as it is today to travel from the Himalayan ranges to the tropical landscape of the far south while remaining in the same country, the inhabitants of mid-nineteenth-century India, and before, were tied to small, localised areas. The very size of the subcontinent and the difficulties of transportation and communication until well into the twentieth century, inevitably meant there was a fragmented idea of India, with little concept of how large the whole country actually was. The term 'Hindustan', which means literally, the place of the Hindus, and from which the word 'India' is derived, referred in the eighteenth and early nineteenth centuries only to the area of northern India around the old capital of Delhi. Awadh and the adjoining areas, including the East India Company's cantonment at Cawnpore, were called the 'Upper Provinces', that is, provinces of the Mughal Empire, not the British.

Thus local grievances, like those of the weavers in the formerly prosperous Mughal provinces of Bihar and Bengal, were not of pressing interest to the sepoys from Awadh who formed the bulk of the Bengal Army. On the annexation of Awadh in 1856, the sepoys found that their jealously guarded right to petition the British Resident when land disputes arose in their villages had been removed, because there was no longer a British Resident at the Lucknow Court of the Nawab. Indeed, there was no longer a Nawab, the administration of Awadh having been taken over by the first Chief Commissioner, Sir James Outram. The withdrawal of the Awadh sepoys' privilege of direct access to the Resident would not have overly concerned the Rani of Jhansi, if she knew of it. Her own grievance against the East India Company was that she was not allowed to adopt an heir to the throne who would be recognised by the Company. This was as a result of a much criticised policy known as the 'Doctrine of Lapse', which meant that if the ruler of a native state died without an heir, his state could legitimately be taken over by the Company, because the dynasty was said to have 'lapsed'. The policy ignored the age-old tradition whereby a failing and childless ruler could adopt an heir, usually a nephew or a cousin, from his immediate family.

In turn the 'Doctrine of Lapse' was not of great importance to those agitated on behalf of the King of Delhi, Bahadur Shah Zafar. His kingdom had shrunk from the great Mughal Empire of his predecessors to no more than the confines of the Red Fort in Delhi. Even this would be lost when the old King died, because the East India Company planned to move his family and dependants out of the Fort to a less prominent location. There were plenty of heirs in this case, the King having fathered sixteen acknowledged sons, although none would inherit the throne, or the titles of his father.

By the beginning of 1857 then, the East India Company, acting on behalf of the British government, had managed to alienate a number of separate factions and a much larger number of people. Indeed, there was something in the Company's policy to annoy and alarm nearly everyone. Taken separately, these genuine local grievances might have been worked through, if the Company had been prepared to negotiate or even back down in the face of popular opposition, but it was not. A kind of blinkered arrogance drove it on, so out of touch with reality that warnings by respected officers like Sir Charles Napier, former Commander-in-Chief, and Sir Henry Lawrence, who was to be killed during the Uprising, were simply brushed aside. The Marquis of Dalhousie, Governor General between 1848 and 1856, had presided over the annexation of the Punjab, Satara, Jaitpur and Sambalpur in 1849, Jhansi and Nagpur in 1853, and Awadh in 1856. He had stayed on

3. The defence of Jhansi Fort against Sir Hugh Rose's troops in April 1858. From the Lakshmi Temple, Orchha

in India to see this last annexation through. When the Court of Directors in London, the governing body of the East India Company, gave its approval for the takeover in November 1855, Dalhousie moved swiftly and by 7 February 1856, Awadh had been added to the Company's portfolio. Within the month, Dalhousie was on board ship, bound for Britain, as his successor, Lord Charles Canning, arrived to take up his post. At a London banquet in August 1855 to mark his new appointment as Governor General, Canning gave what many people later thought was a remarkably prescient speech. It has often been quoted, but bears requoting. He said: 'We must not forget that in the sky of India, serene as it is, a cloud may arise, at first no bigger than a man's hand, but which growing bigger and bigger may at last threaten to overwhelm us with ruin.' Canning's words have been used by some commentators to show how quickly the Uprising developed that did indeed threaten the ruin of British India, but to others it showed a remarkable lack of awareness of the true situation. The 'sky of India' was anything but serene, particularly after Dalhousie's final annexation. Any appearance to the contrary was merely the calm before the storm that was to sweep the East India Company away.

If the sepoys could not themselves articulate all these different voices of complaint, they did at least provide the impetus for others to do so as mutiny rolled across the northern cantonments like monsoon thunder during the months of May, June and July. What caused that initial spark was the introduction of a drill for loading cartridges into the new Enfield rifles, imported from the British government arms factory at Enfield, in north London. Known as the Pattern 1853 rifle-musket, because it was developed in 1853, it replaced the old smooth-bore musket, which was becoming obsolete by the 1840s. By the time of Dalhousie's departure, 10,000 of these new Enfield rifles had arrived in India, and were being tried out in the Bengal Army. Only one British regiment, the 60th King's Royal Rifle Corps stationed at Meerut, was fully equipped with the new rifles, although they were being introduced to the sepoy regiments from the beginning of 1857.[9]

It was not the rifles that the sepoys objected to using, nor the cartridges supplied with them, but the screw of greased paper in which the cartridges were individually wrapped. Instead of tearing off the top of the paper pouch with the fingers, the old practice, the sepoys were now ordered to bite it off and spit it out, before ramming the charge, the cartridge, and the rest of the greased paper down the muzzle of the rifle. (The greased paper 'oiled' the bore of the rifle.) A rumour began, and quickly spread, that the grease used was made from the rendered fat of cattle and possibly pigs, forbidden substances for both Hindus and Muslims. On learning of this, the sepoys believed it was a further assault by the British on their caste and religion, and a direct attempt to turn them all into Christians. The reasoning behind this was that men who lost caste, or who ingested forbidden substances leading to the loss of caste, had no other refuge than the church – not a very flattering reason to become a Christian, but one that was widely believed. Once the sepoys had turned Christian, it was argued, the majority of people would be forced to convert too. In an Urdu proclamation issued from Cawnpore on 5 June 1857 under the name of the Nana Sahib, one of the leading figures of the Uprising, this was spelt out:

> The Sahibs at Calcutta [the Governor General and Council] issued an order to the effect that the main aim behind the distribution of the cartridges was to Christianise the Indian army [*kristian karna*], for once the soldiers convert to Christianity, it will not take long to convert the common people, and the fat of pigs and cows was rubbed on the cartridges. This became known through one of the Bengalis who was employed in the cartridge-making establishment.[10]

If the cartridges and the fear of forced conversion were the immediate causes of revolt, then the annexation of Awadh in February 1856 was the back-up reason. There was widespread disbelief, followed by shock and anger, when it was announced that the British had taken over this large and prosperous kingdom. The sudden departure of the last Nawab, Wajid Ali Shah, for Calcutta, was interpreted as exile for a man whose forebears had been on good terms with the East India Company, and who had made numerous payments into the Company's treasury. The implications of British rule in Awadh – increased taxation, unemployment, land seizures, destruction of property – were still being assimilated a year later. If Awadh could fall, then what next? Did the British plan to take over the whole of the country?

The mutiny is officially reckoned to have begun on 10 May 1857 in Meerut, and to have ended with the Proclamation of Queen Victoria on 1 November 1858, when the formal announcement of the transfer of the East India Company to the British Crown was made. There were incidents before 10 May, including the revolt of Mangal Pande, which are related in Chapter One of this book. There were also isolated captures of rebels after November 1858, but the main events occurred within these eighteen months. Because this is not primarily a military history, a detailed examination of battles and skirmishes between rebel troops and the British (aided by those sepoys who remained loyal), is not given. There are many books that serve this purpose, and for a straightforward factual diary, the late P. J. O. Taylor's book *What Really Happened during the Mutiny: A Day-by-Day Account of the Major Events of 1857–1859 in India* provides a chronological account.[11]

At the start of the Uprising in the Meerut cantonment, when thirty-one Europeans, including children, were killed, the mutinous sepoys decided to ride overnight to Delhi, forty miles away. Although two British regiments were stationed in Meerut, including the 60th, who had the new Enfield rifles, no attempt was made to follow the horsemen. Various excuses were put forward afterwards. Three English officers and an assistant surgeon had armed themselves with sticks as the Meerut cantonment burned around them. They vowed to 'stand or fall together' but took refuge in a lavatory (or 'the temple of Cloacina' as the Victorians coyly put it). After five hours they heard British troops marching past, and came out to join them.[12] The situation was confused by the large number of looters who poured in and a decision was taken to deal with them, and to try and stabilise the cantonment, rather than pursue the horsemen. A warning was sent to Delhi overnight, but was not acted upon, and when the wire of the electric telegraph was cut, speedy communication with the outside world ceased. The bodies of the Meerut dead were collected and laid out for identification in the cantonment theatre on Mall Road.

The sepoys arrived early on the morning of 11 May outside the walled city of Delhi, and they were confronted by the 54th Bengal Native Infantry, led out by its British officers. On being ordered to fire at the horsemen, the sepoys of the 54th simply abandoned their officers, who were killed, and joined the Meerut rebels. Both regiments now entered Delhi together, and a number of Britons were killed almost immediately, including Simon Fraser, the Resident and Commissioner of Delhi and the Delhi chaplain, the Reverend Midgeley Jennings. Staff at the Delhi Bank were killed, the *Delhi*

Gazette printing press was destroyed, and Delhi College was ransacked so that the streets were strewn for days afterwards with pages from English books. In the afternoon of the same day, as some of the sepoys tried to persuade the reluctant King, Bahadur Shah Zafar, to lead them, or at least to accommodate them, the Magazine was blown up by British officers. The Magazine, an enormous structure in the north-eastern quarter of the city, was the last British fall-back. When it became impossible to defend, it was fired so that its store of ammunition would not fall into rebel hands. Fragments of the building were hurled half a mile or more, and a large number of people were killed, including several European women and children who had fled there for shelter. Karim Bakhsh, the *darwan* (gatekeeper), a clever and literate man, was later hanged for sending circulars to sepoy regiments telling them that the cartridges prepared in the Magazine were coated with impure grease. Those Britons who did manage to escape assembled at Flagstaff Tower, a small circular building up on the Ridge, outside the walled city. From here small parties slowly made their way to the cantonment at Meerut. With its mutinous sepoys now in Delhi, and with two British regiments stationed there, it was considered the safest haven.

Then there was a curious pause, as though both the sepoys and the British were stunned into inaction by the violence that had taken place. No attempt was made by the now greatly increased army of rebels to leave Delhi and attack Meerut. They remained looting and plundering in the city, the sweet-shops being a particular target. It was the first time that many of the sepoys, recruited from the villages of Awadh, had been free to explore a city, much less a city like Delhi. There were restrictions on where the Company's soldiers, Indian or British, were allowed to go when they were in cantonments, which were usually located at some distance from the town. There were bazaars, brothels and grog shops within the cantonments for the soldiers' needs but other urban areas were out of bounds. Finding themselves suddenly in the sophisticated centre of Delhi, having chased out the British and seen the old King in person, all within the space of twenty-four hours, was an extraordinary enough experience for anyone and the effect on young men from simple rural backgrounds can be imagined. Attacks on the property of rich inhabitants were frequently made. In some cases householders banded together, shut the gates at either end of their street and attacked the sepoys with brickbats. Before the electric telegraph office was destroyed, a message had been sent to Ambala, to alert the Government of the Punjab; the same message was then carried by a British officer, riding through the night, to the Commissioner-in-Chief at Simla, because there was no telegraph connection with the summer capital.

Gathering strength, the flames of mutiny shot across the plains and there were daily reports of cantonments and cities having fallen – Aligarh 20 May, Nasirabad 28 May, Bareilly 31 May, Sitapur and Neemuch 3 June, Cawnpore

4 June, Jhansi 6 June, Gwalior 14 June, Nowgong and Banda 14 June, Saugor 1 July and so on. A sickeningly familiar pattern began to emerge. It was 'always the same experience, the mutineers made for the gaol, released the prisoners, plundered the Treasury, destroyed the Kutchery [law court] with all its Records, and gutted houses of the Christians'.[13] This almost mechanical destruction led some to believe that there was a pre-arranged plan of mutiny, an idea that was fostered by the appearance in villages of the mysterious chapattis which were supposed to be the signal for the next uprising. Unfortunately the meaning of the chapattis was far from clear. Some thought it meant the British would be successful and force everyone to eat the same bread as Christians. (This idea seems to have been conflated with the sacred bread used during Holy Communion, or the persistent rumour that bones were being ground up and mixed with the flour distributed to sepoys as another method of breaking their caste.) Others thought the sepoys were distributing the chapattis to show that the British would be defeated, while some good souls simply thought the government had ordered them to be passed round with the order to make more and send them to adjoining villages.

July 1857 marked the worst month for the British. The situation at Delhi seemed one of stalemate. The rebels made sorties out through the city gates and up toward the Ridge, where the British were grimly holding on. There were fierce battles, and as many as a thousand rebels were reported to have died in one encounter. Guns were captured and recaptured, but the British were not strong enough at this point to mount an assault on the city. However, the rebels had failed to cut off the British line of supply from Karnal, and this proved to be a fatal mistake. It was along this route that supplies of food, alcohol, ammunition and ultimately, reinforcements, were to come. The Commander-in-Chief, General George Anson, had ordered two brigades from Ambala and a brigade from Meerut to rendezvous at Karnal and then move south to Delhi. Unfortunately Anson was struck down fatally with cholera on 26 May and he died at Karnal. He was succeeded, briefly, by Major General Sir Henry Barnard, who also died from cholera on 5 July on reaching the camp at Delhi. The post was now taken over by General Reed, who became so ill that he had to retire sick on 17 July, only twelve days after taking over. In turn Reed was succeeded by Brigadier General Archdale Wilson, described as 'a soldier of moderate capacity',[14] who publicly voiced his doubts that Delhi could be captured by the British forces.

In Lucknow the British Residency was firmly under siege, surrounded by rebels who launched sporadic but deadly attacks with cannon. It was impossible for the British to break out, and they could only wait for rescue behind their makeshift barricades of earth, reinforced with doors, furniture and the contents of what had been a fine library.[15] The horrible massacres at Cawnpore had been discovered and nothing could be done except to chase the Nana Sahib from his palace at Bithur. General Havelock, having reached

Cawnpore too late to prevent the killings, now did not have sufficient troops to push on to Lucknow to relieve the Residency. In Bareilly, a large city in Rohilkhand some 150 miles east of Delhi, Khan Bahadur Khan, grandson of the last independent Rohilla chief, had proclaimed himself Viceroy of Hindustan, under the King of Delhi. Worryingly, the conflict was moving east to Arrah, where the elderly rebel leader, Raja Kanwar Singh, and his men were besieging a billiard hall, hastily reinforced by a few European civilians and fifty Sikh policemen. Had the 'Little House at Arrah' (as it became known), fallen then the way would have been clear through Bihar and down the Grand Trunk Road to Calcutta and the seat of British government. The only bright spot in a month of despair was the departure from Britain of General Sir Colin Campbell, the newly appointed Commander-in-Chief, on his way to India.

By August there had been a slight improvement in the British fortunes. Arrah had been relieved, places along the Grand Trunk Road secured, and the telegraph line partially repaired. The arrival of Brigadier General John Nicholson from the Punjab, an efficient but cruel man, had boosted morale up on the Delhi Ridge. Nicholson was heading the Moveable Column, which as its name implies, was a fast response team, made up mainly of irregular soldiers. There was a feeling, expressed by young Lieutenant Frederick Roberts (who later became Field Marshal Earl Roberts), that if Delhi was not soon taken, then a rising in the Punjab was inevitable.[16] Near the North-West Frontier, 700 men from the disarmed 51st Bengal Native Infantry mutinied at Peshawar, and some were pursued up the Khyber Pass. August was the month when everything was in the balance. The whole of Awadh was still in rebel hands, General Havelock not having succeeded in a march from Cawnpore to the relief of the Lucknow Residency. Raja Kanwar Singh, defeated at Arrah, had doubled back and was heading to Awadh to give his support.

The recapture of Delhi began on 14 September, in spite of the doubts of the man leading the assault, Brigadier General Archdale Wilson. By 20 September the city was in British hands, although with the loss of nearly a thousand soldiers, including John Nicholson. This was a hugely significant victory, both symbolically and strategically, and Lord Canning was quick to announce it in a formal *kharita* (letter) to rulers and chiefs. The fall of Delhi did, however, also release a considerable number of sepoys who could not be pursued because the British troops were too busy looting and partying in Delhi. Five days later, on 25 September, General Havelock and General Sir James Outram fought their way into the besieged British Residency at Lucknow. Although their forces were not strong enough to fight their way out again through the city, this was also a strong psychological boost, and the capture of palaces along the south bank of the river Gomti was to pave the way for the eventual evacuation of the Residency in November 1857.

In central India, Raja Kanwar Singh had reached Banda, and had joined the forces of Nana Sahib, which were led by Tantia Tope, a former gunner. This combined force was later to join up with the Gwalior Contingent and to harass the British during the early part of 1858. Help was now reaching the British. HMS *Shannon*, en route to Hong Kong, brought 400 trained artillerymen, well armed with cannon, who were landed at Calcutta, and ready to move up country. Sir Colin Campbell was installed as Commander-in-Chief and Jang Bahadur, the virtual ruler of Nepal, had offered the assistance of his Gurkha troops. The situation was still confused, and pockets of mutiny sprung up in areas which had been quiet during the frantic months of June and July. In Rajputana, which had remained generally calm under its maharajas and maharana, there was an outbreak at Kotah, in which the Political Agent, Major Charles Burton and two of his sons were killed after a desperate, solitary, defence of the Residency.

By the end of the year Awadh was still entirely in rebel hands, apart from a single outpost at Alambagh, a country house or small palace, to the south of Lucknow, where Sir James Outram was holding out during the winter. Again, in spite of a number of spirited sorties against the Alambagh, which was only defended by a high brick wall around a garden, the rebels failed to dislodge Outram, and, more seriously, failed to cut off his lines of supplies which were coming in intermittently along the road from Cawnpore. Cawnpore itself had fallen into rebel hands for the second time, captured by the Gwalior Contingent, a force of 7,000 well trained and armed men. Their numbers were increased by sepoys who had attached themselves to the troops of Nana Sahib, Raja Kanwar Singh, the Rani of Jhansi and some minor chiefs. Sir Colin Campbell defeated this considerable force, estimated at 25,000 men in two battles early in December, and with it possibly the best chance of the Uprising's success.[17] Thousands of sepoys were killed, and their guns and ammunition were captured by Campbell's troops.

While the trial of Bahadur Shah Zafar, the last Mughal ruler, was taking place in his own palace at Delhi, British forces were gathering for the recapture of Lucknow. The city was taken in March 1858, after two weeks of street fighting. The massive earthen walls built around it during the winter, and the leadership of Begam Hazrat Mahal, a wife of the deposed Nawab of Awadh, were not sufficient to save it. The road between Agra and Bombay had been reopened and General Hugh Rose's troops arrived at Jhansi, as Kotah was captured by the Rajputana Field Force under Major General H. G. Roberts. With the capture of Jhansi, the death of Raja Kanwar Singh, and the final defeat of the Awadh rebels at Nawabganj, the Great Uprising seemed to have come to an end. There was, however, a final, defiant stand at Gwalior, where the rebel leaders under the Rao Sahib (the nephew of Nana Sahib), Tantia Tope and the Rani of Jhansi had taken the fort and palace. On 17 June the Rani was killed at the battle of Kotah-ki-serai, near Gwalior and the city itself fell to the British on 19 June, its fort being captured the next day. There were plenty of minor battles still to be fought between the British and the groups of rebels who were not prepared to surrender. Much time was taken in chasing prominent leaders of the Uprising including Tantia Tope, who was captured, and Begam Hazrat Mahal, who was not.

The defeat of the sepoys led inevitably to the defeat of the civilians who had either supported them, or who had taken advantage of the disturbed conditions. A description of Saharanpur District in Rohilkhand, where the 5th BNI mutinied on 2 June 1857, is applicable to many other areas:

> The District soon broke out into irregular rebellion; but the turbulent spirit showed itself rather in the form of internecine quarrels among the native leaders than of any settled opposition to the British government. Old feuds sprang up anew; villages returned to their ancient enmities; bankers were robbed, and money-lenders pillaged; yet the local officers continued to exercise many of their functions, and to punish the chief offenders by ordinary legal process.[18]

As British troops moved in to pacify recaptured areas, sometimes in the most brutal manner, they were followed by the administrators, the collectors of land revenue, the judges, the *tahsildars*, the *kotwal*, the treasury officers, the jail *daroga* and the police. Most of these posts had been filled by Indians, who had fled on the arrival of the mutineers. Their own lives had been in danger because they were closely identified with the British government. Some indeed had been killed in office, trying to save the government's money or land records. Others had gone over to the mutineers, opening the jails to release the prisoners, and the treasuries to release money to fund the rebellion.

So why did the Great Uprising fail? In the summer of 1857 it had seemed unstoppable, a huge outpouring of popular feeling, in which nearly every element of Indian society, military, religious, aristocratic and rural seemed to have a part. It may be in the very nature of this heterogeneous group that its downfall lay. There were so many different grievances – not all of them directly the fault of the British, nor ones that could be put right by the British – that the inchoate fury which arose could find no single, useful expression. Once the British officers had been shot, their families killed, their bungalows burnt, their treasuries ransacked, their prisoners freed, what then? There was both a lack of leadership and too many leaders. The King of Delhi became the immediate icon of the rebel sepoys, but he was too old, and too much of an aesthete to provide any real authority. The Nawab of Awadh, who could have become a focus for the unhappy sepoys and civilians of his kingdom, had pre-empted the struggle by moving to Calcutta, where he was later arrested and imprisoned by the British in Fort William. Begam Hazrat Mahal, the wife he left behind in Lucknow, and their son Birjis Qadr, faced the problems of divided leadership in miniature as they quarrelled with the

Faizabad Maulvi, Ahmadullah, over tactics. Nana Sahib of Bithur was an unlikely hero at the best of times. His involvement, never fully proven, in the three massacres of the Europeans at Cawnpore, made him a bugbear for the British, but did not lead to any increase in popularity among his troops. The Rani of Jhansi, Laxmi Bai, and the Nawab of Banda, Ali Bahadur, were both pushed into fighting for the rebel cause. While the Rani, an intelligent, passionate woman, is deservedly regarded as a heroine of the Uprising, the young Nawab, with his 'fatuous manner', over-fondness for absinthe and theatrical behaviour, was forced into a stand against General Whitlock, and promptly captured. 'Not being a hero, he did not exhibit heroic conduct' remarked a British magistrate, 'but I believe if he had been left to follow his own wishes, he would not have rebelled.'[19]

The lack of charismatic leadership among the aristocracy, the people to whom the sepoys turned with an almost feudal expectation, was mirrored by the lack of military initiative. It had been deliberate policy by the British not to put Indian officers into senior positions of command. Certainly there were *jemadars* (junior officers) and *subedars* (senior officers), but in the Bengal Army, unlike the Madras and Bombay Armies, promotion was by seniority, and it could take decades to rise to the rank of subedar.[20] Even then, Indian officers were given little opportunity to manage the troops under them, and because most had no experience of commanding anything larger than a single company of 100 men, they had no idea of how to deploy bigger groups to advantage. A few officers did rise above this British-imposed handicap, notably Bakht Khan, a subedar in the rebel Bareilly Brigade, who marched to Delhi (with a British sergeant in tow) and was appointed Commander-in-Chief by the King, Bahadur Shah Zafar. He left Delhi when its fall was inevitable, regrouping his men, and eventually joining Begam Hazrat Mahal in her retreat into Nepal, long after the recapture of Lucknow. It was civilian commanders who caused the British most trouble, men like Tantia Tope, who adopted guerrilla tactics after his defeat at Cawnpore in December 1857, and the old Raja Kanwar Singh, moving swiftly across country to where he was most needed.

Lack of tactical training meant the sepoys neglected basic precautions like cutting off the lines of supply to the British troops on the Delhi Ridge and other places. Lack of strategic training meant they were unable to capitalise on their strengths and superiority in numbers at the beginning of the Uprising. The sepoy flight from Meerut to Delhi on the night of 10 May was a daring move that surprised the British and then rendered them inert for over a week. But an experienced leader would have made sure that the two British regiments stationed at Meerut, one of them consisting of raw young recruits with unbroken horses, were put out of action. Having reached Delhi, the sepoys were not inclined to leave its delights to go out again and fight. Delhi was briefly a magnet, drawing in groups of rebellious sepoys from all over northern India. *'Dilli chalo!'* 'To Delhi!' was the call that many answered, but once inside the city walls, the problem of feeding and arming the numerous troops arose. There was virtually no attempt to secure the countryside around the Mughal capital as a base from which to launch assaults against the enemy. The Gujar villagers, hereditary plunderers and cattle rustlers, controlled the villages outside Delhi, robbing the fugitive British and the King of Delhi's supporters with complete impartiality. At Lucknow, the sepoys were tied up for nearly six months in the siege of the British Residency. Of no strategic importance, it would have been better to let the Residency's inmates take their chance, and to concentrate on imposing an alternative government in Awadh, where much of the animosity against the British had arisen. At the same time, groups of sepoys from Lucknow had gone to Delhi to offer their services, only to swell the number of hungry men inside the capital.

The sepoys could not hope to match the British in arms, ammunition or communications. Some weapons had been taken from the looted cantonments, but these did not include the Enfield rifles, which were superior both in range and in accuracy. There was a constant shortage of ammunition, particularly during the sieges at Lucknow and Delhi. Some of the Mutiny Papers, the correspondence found by the British when they re-entered Delhi in September 1857, are about increasing the output of gunpowder from the factories at Daryaganj and Chiripara.[21] The rebel Commander-in-Chief, Prince Muhammmad Azam, who had succeeded Bakht Khan when the latter fell out of favour, spent much time during the siege in getting supplies of sulphur and saltpetre, both used in the manufacture of gunpowder. He also requested the ingredients for making bombs, instructions on how to make cannonballs, a supply of lead, percussion caps, charcoal, wood for making musket butts, cartridges, guns, and fodder for the artillery horses, in fact all those things that the British had in abundance. By the beginning of September the lack of sulphur was holding up the manufacture of gunpowder. Finding food, shelter and provisions for the Delhi sepoys was also problematic, and the elite Bengal Sappers and Miners Corps that had deserted at Meerut had to be supplied not only with their wages, but with cooking utensils, muskets, tents and carts as well.[22] In Lucknow, where it was the sepoys who were doing the besieging, there were similar shortages, as those inside the Residency discovered when unlikely objects were fired at them. Iron-bound blocks of wood, fashioned to fit the cannons, came whizzing in, together with carriage springs, bundles of wire from the destroyed electric telegraph, and even bullock horns. Old-fashioned technology was used too, as the skilled Pasi archers fired flaming arrows into the Residency compound with great accuracy.

The use of the electric telegraph during the Uprising gave the British a vital advantage in transmitting information about the movements of the rebels and orders to the British troops. A map of working telegraph lines in 1857 does not seem to have been produced, but we do know that at the start of the outbreak, Calcutta was connected to Agra, Allahabad, Ambala, Benares, Bombay, Cawnpore, Delhi, Gwalior, Indore, Lahore, Lucknow and Meerut. The telegraph lines were both visible and vulnerable, and were inevitably cut when a cantonment was over-run. A telegraph message is said to have been received in Delhi at 6 o'clock on the morning of 11 May from Meerut, warning that the mutinous sepoys were on their way. After that 'the telegraph wire lay cut on the ground and the poles were rotting by its ends'.[23] The telegraph link from Cawnpore was lost early in June 1857 when the villagers were reported to have broken the posts, cut up the wires and taken the wood and the wires to their houses.[24] The Lucknow to Calcutta line was cut on 5 June, and those besieged in the Residency the following month had to resort to a system of semaphore messages and lights. It was possible to 'patch in' to telegraph wires that were still in place, even if the telegraph offices had been destroyed. By the beginning of 1858, as the British regained partial control, and were able to reinstate the lines, the telegraph proved of immense value in tracking down the rebels. The progress of Ahmadullah, the Faizabad Maulvi was reported, together with the rebel infantry and cavalry regiments, fleeing from Lucknow on 16 March. Tantia Tope's movements were known as he moved across central India, and the fall of Gwalior to Sir Hugh Rose's troops was telegraphed to Lord Canning on the day it happened (19 June 1858). A brief message had been sent the previous day to staff at Calcutta, Indore and Agra saying 'The Ranee of Jhansie is killed. Maharajah Scindia has arrived. Brigadier Smith took four guns in the fight yesterday.'[25] The Mutiny Telegrams, preserved today in the State Archives of Uttar Pradesh, also chart in detail the chase and capture of many minor rebels, whose names may only be preserved in these fragile documents. Without access to this level of information, the rebels were inevitably handicapped.

Almost as serious was the lack of financial support. Mutinous soldiers had sacrificed their pay and pensions, and not all of them could hope to recoup these losses through loot. How to pay the sepoys' wages is a common theme throughout the Uprising. The grand gesture against the British and for the King of Delhi was all very well, but the soldiers still had to be paid. This is why the money from the looted cantonment treasuries that was brought into Delhi was so welcome, although Bahadur Shah Zafar was soon obliged to tap the city's rich merchants for cash too. The banker Laxmi Chand was said to have saved his firm from looting by providing daily meals for the rebel sepoys. Other traders offered to provide dhal and roti, but the mutineers responded that since they had 'determined to die, how can we eat dhal roti for the few days we have to live in this world?'[26] A daily payment of four annas was ordered instead. During the siege in Lucknow, its citizens were obliged to pay for the troops, and gold and silver utensils were melted down to make coins for their wages.

The Nana Sahib, in a proclamation issued on 5 July 1857, had offered generous pensions to the female relatives of sepoys who might be killed in battle, or to the men themselves if they lived to retire. But this was an unusual gesture. Once the treasury money had been used, further supplies of cash often had to be extracted from bankers and wealthy men by threats and cajolements. The financial community suffered greatly during the Uprising, and were the least inclined to support the mutineers. There was no 'fighting fund' set up, and unless individual rulers were prepared to bank-roll the sepoys, the soldiers were left to forage for themselves. There was always the risk, when this happened, that there would be a counter-mutiny, with the men refusing to support the rebel leaders unless they were paid. The Uprising was thus severely handicapped almost from the outset by lack of funds.

The British, on the other hand, although they accumulated huge debts, were not short of cash to pay their men, and to pay for the associated costs of war like the hire of labourers, temporary barracks and transport. As for British civilians caught up in the revolt, a charitable trust was set up on 25 August 1857, after a meeting at the Mansion House in London. It was called the India Relief Fund and within four months almost £25,000 had been collected. The Lord Mayor of London sent it to India in the form of silver bullion 'for the relief of sufferers from the mutiny'. Money also came in from well-wishers in different parts of the world – from the Mayor of Port Louis, Mauritius; the Colonial Secretary at the Cape of Good Hope; the Governor of St Helena; the Consul at Batavia; the New South Wales Committee, and Tasmania. It was learnt that the Shah of Persia intended to make a contribution.[27]

Not everyone was sympathetic towards the plight of the British refugees in India, or to Britain itself. The Uprising is often seen as a discrete, contained event, of no more than local interest, but this was not the case. The news from India was avidly followed and caused widespread comment and criticism. Karl Marx published a series of articles in the *New York Daily Tribune* (for which he was the London correspondent), as reports began to come in during the autumn of 1857. Not surprisingly, Marx had plenty to say, none of which was very cheering to the British officers and men fighting in India. He forecast the retreat of the English Army, as he called it, and thought if it did attempt to take Delhi by storming the Kashmir Gate, there was the greatest risk of failure, especially during the monsoon.

> The people in the whole Presidency of Bengal, where not kept in check by a handful of Europeans, are enjoying a blessed anarchy; but there is nobody there against whom they could rise. It is a curious *quid pro quo* to expect an Indian revolt to assume the features of a European revolution.[28]

When news of the Cawnpore massacres reached London, Marx commented quite presciently, that the sepoys' infamous conduct 'is only the reflex, in a concentrated form, of England's own conduct in India'. 'Even at the present catastrophe' he continued, 'it would be an unmitigated mistake to suppose that all the cruelty is on the side of the sepoy, and all the milk of human kindness flows on the side of the English. The letters of the British officers are redolent of malignity.'[29]

At a dinner in Germany, it was reported, a toast had been drunk 'To the King of Delhi', and the French were beside themselves with *Schadenfreude.* Edouard de Warren, a French officer in the East India Company's Army, who had been born in Madras, wrote a highly critical analytical history entitled *L'Inde anglaise avant et après l'Insurrection de 1857.*[30] 'Who should we blame for the catastrophe?' he asked rhetorically. 'Everyone', was the answer, and de Warren particularly castigated the Englishmen that he dubbed 'saints'. The 'saints' he wrote, had their roots in the bourgeoisie – they were middle-class men, descended from provincial aristocrats, austere in their private lives, and who, in de Warren's eyes, carried 'the enthusiastic Puritanism of a Knox or a Cromwell' with them to India. The politicians, or policy-makers, fared no better – 'all the leading people, financial, commercial, academics, ecclesiastics, represent this other current of ideas, which have only one target – national development [in India]'.

> The Hindus are an intelligent people – they saw conversion [to Christianity] and exploitation marching together. Love, charity, Christian brotherhood were preached at them and they saw the politicians, in the name of Christianity, carry out the successive spoliation of all the Indian royalty who still remained. They were given Bibles that they didn't want to read. …

De Warren was quite clear that it was the attempts by Evangelical soldiers like General Havelock (whom he called the 'New Lights' after the American Evangelical revivalists) to convert the sepoys that had done the damage. Coupled with the annexation of Awadh, and the dignified behaviour of its deposed Nawab ('bien trop débonnaire et trop pacifique') it was not surprising that the gentle Hindu had finally risen and that the Muslim wanted to restore the Mughal Empire to its former glory.

The French playwright, Jean Richepin, went even further and made the Nana Sahib the hero of an eponymous play produced in Paris in 1883.[31] Set in the palace at Bithur, Nana Sahib makes a number of stirring speeches about liberty and the day when his sleeping subjects awake from the long infamy inflicted on them by the British. 'Ah! c'est que j'ai longtemps préparé la révolte. / Ma haine est un verger. Aujourd'hui j'y récolte.' (The paradox of French support for Indian rulers, having got rid of their own monarch, is one which continues to fascinate the historian today.) In New York, reported *The Times* in October 1857, a large meeting, 'principally of Irish men', was held to 'express opposition to British enlistments in the United States for the war in India, and sympathy with the sepoy mutiny'.[32]

The few brave souls in Britain who ventured to express an opinion that the indiscriminate killing of Indians by British soldiers should not be condoned, were howled down. An anonymous correspondent to *The Times* in October 1857 dared to suggest, that contrary to the popular view, Englishwomen had not been raped at Delhi and Cawnpore before being murdered.[33] Major Robert Bird courageously addressed a public meeting in Southampton putting the viewpoint of the deposed Nawab of Awadh, Wajid Ali Shah, who was a personal friend. He also told an audience at Manchester on 1 May 1857 that the rebellious sepoys would have fought for the Nawab if he had resisted the annexation (a view very much at odds with the Nawab's subsequent offer to fight for the British, backed up by his sepoys and retainers).

A vast literature has grown up around the Uprising, so vast that the bibliographies themselves have become a book. The late P. J. O. Taylor's *Companion to the Indian Mutiny of 1857* has the most recent comprehensive listing, with a page on vernacular publications, but this is now more than ten years old. Nearly every Briton who survived the Uprising, and who was literate, seems to have written about their experiences, so we have accounts from officers' wives trapped in the British Residency at Lucknow, women who escaped from Delhi and found shelter at Meerut, stories from the very few people who survived the Cawnpore massacres, autobiographies from serving officers and civil administrators, and posthumous letters from victims, published by their relatives. There are official British accounts too, the best known of which is the *Narrative of Events* series, published in 1881, which was a compilation of reports from every commissioner or district officer in the North-West Provinces. Indeed, there was such an outpouring, and so much raw anger and grief, that by 1861, William Ireland, an army officer who published anonymously his account of the siege of Delhi, was moved to write: 'Englishmen ... are always drawn in chalk, if personal friends of the author, with a halo round their heads; Hindostanis in charcoal.'[34]

Apart from the Mutiny Papers, already referred to, the lack of Indian narratives written during 1857 and 1858 has long been a source of regret. Very few such accounts have been published either in vernacular languages or in English. *Travels of a Hindu* by Bolanauth Chunder, published in London in 1869, includes a short but perceptive account from a civilian eye-witness, and Sita Ram's translated history *From Sepoy to Subedar* is a useful book in spite of doubts about its authenticity. The poet Mirza Ghalib's account *Dastanbuy* was written after the recapture of Delhi in September 1857, and was, as his biographer Pavan Varma has said, an attempt by the poet to flatter the British and to re-establish his credentials in a changed world.[35] Long narratives by two high-ranking officials, Mubarak Shah, the *kotwal* of Delhi, and Hakim Ahsanullah Khan, the King's physician, were written in Urdu, and give a vivid picture of daily life under siege. There are also shorter narratives, some anonymous, like that of the opium *gomashtah* (dealer), who was in Cawnpore

PUNCH, OR THE LONDON CHARIVARI.—August 15, 1857.

EXECUTION OF "JOHN COMPANY;"

Or, The Blowing up (there ought to be) in Leadenhall Street.

4. 'Execution of "John Company;" Or, The Blowing up (there ought to be) in Leadenhall Street.' *Punch*, 15 August 1857.

for twelve days at the beginning of June 1857.[36] Criticisms have been made of these accounts, in particular that the people who wrote them or dictated them said what they thought the British wanted to hear. The same criticism can be applied to many accounts by British writers, who were writing for a wider public who knew exactly what they wanted to hear too.

Stirring events often trigger a poetic or artistic response and the Uprising was no exception. Fifty years later, a retired member of the Indian Civil Service, William Crooke, recorded a number of Indian folk songs or narrative verses that non-literate people are fond of. These commemorated the outbreak of the Mutiny at Meerut, when 'the goddess Kali wished to destroy England', the bravery of the Rani of Jhansi, and a surprisingly sympathetic view of the British besieged in the Lucknow Residency, who although 'dying of hunger, did not run away'.[37] Some truly bad English verse was composed by, among others, Lord Alfred Tennyson and Christina Rossetti. The weekly magazine *Punch*, in its original radical incarnation, had been a long-time stern critic of the East India Company. It published a striking cartoon on 15 August 1857 (before the news of the Cawnpore massacres was widely known), showing the Company and its Leadenhall headquarters being blown from the mouth of a cannon (as some rebellious sepoys had been). Instead of flying arms and legs there are rolls of paper labelled nepotism, supineness, misgovernment and other apt epithets. *Punch* was later to publish its own, rather bad, verse on the British reprisals against the mutineers, one stanza concluding 'Thy foot shall be dipped in the blood of thy foe, / And the tongue of thy dogs shall be red through the same.'

Sheet music was produced so the Victorian pianist could play exciting ballads like '"Jessie's Dream" or the Relief of Lucknow (A Descriptive Fantasia)' 'composed and arranged for the piano forte by John Blockley'. This was based on the apocryphal story of Jessie Brown, the wife of a corporal, who had been among those besieged in the Residency. Jessie's sharp ears had caught the sound of the bagpipes of the Highlanders marching to the relief in September 1857 and she alerted her companions to the long-hoped-for rescue. The music is indeed descriptive, with *allegro fortissimo* notes for the rebels, ('bombs and rockets'), *dolente* and *dolce* for the besieged, and *crescendo fortissimo* for the arrival of General Havelock, ending with a rousing chorus of 'God Save the Queen'.

One of the most controversial paintings shown at the Royal Academy in London, in 1858, was by Sir Joseph Paton, and was titled 'In Memoriam'. It depicted a group of 'maddened sepoys, hot after blood', bursting through into an underground chamber, where a group of Englishwomen and children are awaiting their fate, as Christian martyrs. Paton's picture aroused such strong feelings that he subsequently painted out the murderous sepoys, and replaced them with maddened Highlanders, bursting in to rescue the women.[38] Other less contentious paintings showed the retreat of the British from the Lucknow

5. '"Jessie's Dream," Or the Relief of Lucknow. A Descriptive Fantasia, introducing The Siege, The Dream, The Rescue. Composed and arranged for the pianoforte, by John Blockley.'

Residency, and the meeting of the three generals, Havelock, Outram and Campbell, at the first relief in September 1857. A large variety of prints were also produced showing (imaginary) battle scenes, or places where fighting had taken place.

By contrast, no visual material from this period has been found in India and no authentic portraits of Nana Sahib, the Rani of Jhansi or Begam Hazrat Mahal exist. However, a recent study by the art-historian Rahaab Allana has described a series of remarkable murals in the Lakshmi Temple at Orchha, near Jhansi, in central India. These are in the form of a narrative, and show lively scenes of the siege of Jhansi that took place in the spring of 1858, including pictures of the British in camp, drinking wine.[39] No date has been assigned to these paintings, but stylistic evidence would place them shortly after the events pictured had taken place, and while they were still fresh in the minds of the local artists.

We can consider a few images from pre-Mutiny India too. It was, to the Western gaze, a country of extreme contrasts – a place where the Jains, a Hindu sect, were so punctilious about the sanctity of life that they refused to employ Europe-made paper for their accounts, because animal size was used in its manufacture. At the same time human beings could be found dying, impaled on bamboo stakes, as punishment for some crime. The heads of defeated enemies were set up on poles in prominent places. Prejudice and fear of pollution went hand in hand with scholarship, poetry and the arts. Provincial courts exhibited the same mixture of splendour and squalor that had been noted centuries earlier. Popular shrines became places of pilgrimage for both Hindus and Muslims and there was generally a mutual respect for people of a different faith from one's own.

Yet it was possible to identify almost precisely where a person came from by the colour of their skin, their facial features, their name, their language, their occupation and their dress and headgear. Costumes were highly individualised according to one's religion or religious sect, or one's tribe. Muslims buttoned their jackets on the left breast, Hindus on the right. A recurring theme in the accounts of people escaping from the mutineers is the adoption of a disguise and another identity. Gerish Chander Bannerjee, a Brahmin of Bengali origin, who was working as a clerk in the Deputy Commissioner's office in Sitapur, had to flee for his life on 5 June 1857 'disguising myself in the habit of a fukeer' (*faqir*, a poorly-dressed, or semi-naked religious beggar). Joshua Francis, an Anglo-Indian Christian 'made my escape from the place in disguise of a Mohamedan' and walked to the railhead at Raniganj, a staggering distance of nearly 500 miles. Dr Batson, who escaped from Delhi on 11 May 1857, volunteered to disguise himself as a faqir (this was clearly the easiest character to impersonate) and go towards Meerut to see if it was safe for other Europeans to proceed there. European and Anglo-Indian women fared less well. The concealing *burqa* is not mentioned in contemporary accounts, for the reason that well-bred Muslim women did not walk out of their houses. They went out in covered carriages or palanquins. There are accounts of white women abandoning their crinolines and disguising themselves as *ayahs* (childrens' nurses), but they were caught and killed, recognised no doubt from their non-Indian walk and their inability to speak Hindustani. Few who fled by themselves lived to tell their part of the story of the Great Uprising.

One

REBELS AND RENEGADES

WHO WERE the men and women who joined the Great Uprising against the East India Company? Many will remain nameless for ever. In the aftermath of fighting, the bodies of the dead were thrown unceremoniously into defensive ditches or the nearest river. Scavenging vultures and dogs made short work of those who died in the fields, shot down in random encounters, or in flight. Others were hanged from trees or gallows. John Walker Sherer, the Magistrate and Collector at Fatehpur, who fled across country to the safety of Allahabad, saw nine *coolies* (labourers) hanging on a gallows. He commented dryly 'Something was said about "making examples" by stringing people for slight offences. The nine coolies by themselves seemed to answer that notion.'[1] Rebels who could be identified were often captured and executed on the spot, their severed heads packed in baskets of grass and taken to the nearest *kotwal*, or police superintendent so the captor could claim his reward. British officials offered handsome money for rebels they particularly wanted and the more prominent literally had a price on their heads, payable whether they were brought in dead or alive.

Such a veil of mythology has been drawn over the best known leaders of the Uprising, Nana Sahib, the Rani of Jhansi, Begam Hazrat Mahal of Awadh and others, that it is difficult to see them today as men and women thrust into prominence by extraordinary circumstances. Demonised by the British in the nineteenth century and eulogised by Indians today, these people are villains or heroes, rebels or freedom fighters, depending on which side you take. Like other iconic figures from the past, they have been fashioned into what people want them to be, or what they need them to be. Nana Sahib, the Raja of Bithur, whose proper name was Dhondu Pant, appeared on the 50 paise Indian postage stamp issued on 10 May 1984, as one of the heroes of the First War of Independence. But in Britain the Nana was seen as the devil incarnate. He was blamed for the worst loss of British life in 1857 when over 200 women and children were killed in one massacre alone at Cawnpore. He was painted in the worst possible light, and a large canvas daub at an

English fairground show in 1860 pictured him as 'a terrific embodiment of matted hair, rolling eyes and cruel teeth'. His waxwork figure remained for many years in the Chamber of Horrors at Madame Tussaud's in London. In fact, although no authentic portraits of Nana Sahib are known, he was described by the English doctor John Tressider, who treated him professionally, as 'an ordinary-looking person, of middle height, stolid features and increasing stoutness'.

It is easy to see how quickly stereotypes arise and why it seems so difficult to resurrect the men and a few women who were labelled, not only by the British, but by many of their fellow countrymen too, as rebels. But these were real people, many of whom had only the brief notoriety of a few weeks or months – men whose regiments mutinied in May and June of 1857 and who were dead by August of the same year. There are photographs of a few of them – the seventy-year-old Raja Kanwar Singh seated in a wooden carrying chair, and suffering severely from 'neuralgia' when he rebelled against the East India Company, who put a price on his head of Rs 25,000. There is also the handsome, defiant Jwala Prasad, promoted from the ranks by Nana Sahib to become a *risaldar* (a cavalry commander), who was photographed in chains, before being hanged from a tree at Cawnpore. There are even touches of unconscious humour in some of the stories of the lesser known participants who were sympathetic towards the Great Uprising. Tooraub Ali, another seventy-year-old man, had been a *khansama*, a domestic steward, in the Officers' Mess of the 60th Bengal Native Infantry, stationed north of Delhi, at Roorkee for thirty-one years. On learning that the soldiers of the regiment had mutinied, Tooraub Ali 'broke all the Mess crockery, glass and shared the plate and silver with other khitmugars' (table servants). He then took Colonel Drought's buggy and drove to Delhi to congratulate Bahadur Shah Zafar, saying 'Mobarak bandghee' ('congratulations from your slave') for having regained the Empire of India. The khansama's British employers found it difficult to understand the old man's personal rebellion. He had been shown every possible kindness by the Europeans at Roorkee, they said, and was 'thus far petted and beloved by his Employers, that on calling to enquire the health of an officer, he was offered a chair!'[2]

The divergent views on the Indian personalities of the Uprising, and whether they were freedom fighters or rebels, lead to the interesting question of how we view the people who carried out, or instigated, acts of violence during the two years when it did indeed seem that 'a wind of madness' blew across northern India. We will consider the different reasons behind the rebellion later in this chapter, but pose the provocative question here of whether *everyone* who carried out an act of violence or unlawful deed during those years should be classed as a hero or a villain. There are few unambiguous statements from those involved about what they were fighting for. The majority of the rebels, including many of the sepoys, were illiterate. (This is why professional letter-writers were attached to the regiments.) Where we have written statements from captured rebels, only a few were prepared to make defiant declarations of intent, like the Rohilla leader Khan Bahadur Khan whose last reported words were: 'It is true that I killed the Europeans; for this purpose I was born ... I have killed hundreds of English dogs, it was a noble act, and I triumph in having done it.' Probably the nearest thing we have to a mission statement is the ringing declaration by Begam Hazrat Mahal, issued in December 1858 in response to Queen Victoria's proclamation the previous month: 'If the Queen has assumed the Government [of India] why does Her Majesty not restore our Country to us, when our people wish it?'[3] But with few prepared to say what they were fighting for, or fighting against, we can only judge by their actions.

There were many who fought for far less principled reasons than the Khan and the Begam. The Gujar tribes are a case in point, and although many 'mutiny' histories ignore them completely, they seemed to cause almost as much misery as the avenging British. The Gujars, who gave their name to Gujrat and Gujranwala (both now in Pakistan) and Gujarat, came into India at some far distant point from the north-west, and were initially wandering tribesmen with cattle. By the middle of the nineteenth century large numbers of them had settled in villages around Delhi, and Meerut and even larger numbers in the old North-West Provinces. From cattle-herders they had become cattle-rustlers and petty thieves. They were quite impartial about who they robbed while 'yelling in the most horrible manner after the fashion peculiar to Goojurs'. The King of Delhi's emissaries, sent from the besieged city to ask for help from sympathetic local rajas, were stopped by Gujars on the high road and robbed of money, clothes and horses, and the King's letters were torn up. Europeans escaping from Delhi at the start of the siege were robbed by Gujars who took 'every article we possessed, even to the buttons from our clothes ... of the latter, just enough was left to cover us'. Their shoes were seized too. More serious than barefoot Europeans though were the towns plundered by Gujars, like Sikandrabad in Bulandshahr District where there was 'no force to send against them, so they plundered in perfect security', and where it was reported the 'native women suffered the utmost wickedness of savages in this respect.'[4] At Meerut, immediately after the departure of the mutinous sepoys for Delhi on 10 May 1857, the Gujars were in the town by 10 o'clock the same night, ready for an orgy of violence and plunder.

Eric Stokes, the left-wing historian, has put up a spirited defence of the Gujars, who had lost their traditional way of life and were regarded as 'natural scapegoats' by the British, but he also admitted they were 'national carriers of violence to the countryside, and that between 10 May to 20 May 1857 Gujar violence appeared as the most serious threat to British control of the countryside'.[5] There were exceptions, as in all groups. Laxman Singh Gujar of Khera occupied Fatehabad after British government officials had fled, preserved the all-important land revenue records, re-established the frightened Indian staff in their posts and generally protected the town. And the Gujars were not the only marauding tribe, but were joined at times by Ahirs, Banjaras, Pathans, Kanjars, Meos (Mewatis) and Jats. We might argue that in the face of a common enemy, the British in this case, such acts of violence are legitimate, and that any blow struck against an occupying power is justified, even if fellow Indians were the main sufferers. But it is hard to see the Gujars and their companions as freedom fighters.

There is general agreement, however, that Mangal Pande was the first hero (or villain) of the Uprising. It was this high caste Brahmin who unknowingly gave his name to the derogatory British expression for rebel sepoys – pandies. The story starts in February 1857 at Berhampore, a military station, or cantonment, some 120 miles north of Calcutta. It had been established nearly a hundred years earlier, in 1763, overlooking the Bhagirathi river, and it was a well-equipped station with its parade ground, tank, library, a fives court and skittles court (for the British officers), a sergeants' mess, chapel, cemetery and the sepoy lines. Here the 19th Bengal Native Infantry were quartered and it was here that the first mutinous act of the year took place, when the men refused to use the cartridges wrapped in greased paper for the new Enfield rifles. The fear of being unwittingly, or forcibly, converted to Christianity, was a very real fear, exacerbated by the efforts of British missionaries over the last forty years. This may sound as far-fetched today, as it did 150 years ago, were it not for the fact that a devious conversion to Christianity *had* taken place in India many years earlier. Indian historians have recorded that during the late sixteenth century, Portuguese priests had polluted Hindu wells with slaughtered cows. The villagers had unwittingly lost caste and were baptised as Catholics, taking the surname of the priest or bishop. After the Vellore mutiny of 1806, when similar fears of conversion were raised, the administrator and officer Sir Thomas Munro commented that 'However strange it may appear to Europeans, I know that the general opinion of the most intelligent natives in this part of the country is that it was intended to make the sepoys Christian'.[6]

On their refusal of the cartridges, the frightened men of the 19th Bengal Native Infantry were threatened with service overseas, in China or Burma, it was reported. This led to even more panic, for to cross the *kala pani*, or black water, and leave India was but another way to lose their caste. The men broke open the storeroom where the weapons were kept and loaded their muskets, refusing initially to surrender them. The situation was defused by their Indian officers, but the men's short-lived revolt was undoubtedly, in military terms, a mutiny. The Governor General, Lord Canning determined to make an example of the 19th and to have it disbanded. The men from the 19th were ordered to march down to Barrackpore, the Calcutta cantonment which lies about fifteen miles from the centre of the then administrative capital of British India.

Disbanding a regiment was usually only carried out when soldiers had mutinied. The days when sepoy armies were habitually disbanded at the end of a campaign, because it was considered too expensive to keep a standing army in cantonments, had gone. To be a sepoy in the Company's army in the middle of the nineteenth century was to have a job for life, if one was lucky enough not to be killed or invalided out. It meant a small, but fairly regular salary (less, of course, than European soldiers received), a tiny pension on retirement, and provision for one's widow in case of death in action. It also meant a chance to earn a share of prize money (half that of the European soldier's share), after a successful campaign, when towns or whole districts could be looted or fined to meet the cost of a local war. When a sepoy fell sick or was injured there were medical officers on hand to provide rudimentary comfort. Furthermore, a son could follow his father into the same regiment, as the sons of British officers did. Despite numerous hardships, the restrictions on rank, and the crass behaviour of young officers fresh out from cadet school at Addiscombe towards senior jemadars old enough to be their fathers, a position in the East India Company's army continued to attract men from rural backgrounds. In the quiet poverty of village life, subject to famine, drought and floods, soldiering was seen as a long-term profession, that was likely to provide the basics of life and companionship.

This is why disbandment was such a drastic, and irreversible step. At a stroke, the sepoy lost his livelihood, his pension, his medical care, his hope for the future, and even his uniform, which belonged to the government and was 'state property'. As painful to bear as all this was, what was worse was the loss of honour, and the sense of shame in returning to one's village, stripped of everything. With a particular lack of insight, or perhaps even downright ignorance on the part of British officers, the 19th Bengal Native Infantry was to be disbanded at the cantonment which had been the scene of a dreadful incident in 1824 – the Barrackpore Mutiny. Various military grievances about transport costs and equipment had led to a showdown on the parade ground. The then Commander-in-Chief refused to listen to the men's complaints, unless they laid down their muskets. When they refused to do so, they were mown down by the European artillery, with the loss of at least sixty lives. It was subsequently found that the muskets they had refused to surrender were unloaded. Barrackpore thus had a particularly nasty reputation among the sepoys, and the knowledge that a European regiment was being summoned from Burma to attend the disbanding of the 19th frightened the men into submission. Their shame was added to by the presence of the 34th Bengal Native Infantry, stationed at Barrackpore, who watched their fellow sepoys file past for their final pay and hand in their uniforms on the last day of March.

There had been unrest at Barrackpore since the beginning of the year, even before the men of the 19th had marched down and been sent home. Two bungalows had been set on fire when Santhal tribesmens' arrows with a lighted match tied to them were fired into the dry thatch. A sergeant's bungalow had been burnt down, and significantly, also the bungalow in which the electric telegraph machine was housed. Major General J. B. Hearsey, a redoubtable straight-talking officer of the old school (and who had the great advantage of Anglo-Indian ancestry, which meant he was bilingual), had reported to Calcutta in January that the soldiers were fearful of a rumour that they were to be forcibly converted to Christianity. The 34th was paraded to ask if they had any grievances, and their Commandant, Colonel Wheler, assured them that 'the rumour so industriously circulated was false, and the native officers and men said they were satisfied it was so'. General Hearsey reiterated this to the men of the 34th on 17 March. Speaking in Hindustani, he reassured them saying

> No person is permitted to force you to become Christian, nay I now tell you, if any officer or other person dare in this cantonment to annoy you by preaching to you on these subjects, to come and complain to me, your General and I will punish him if he is an officer. [7]

This message was delivered to the sepoys but it was also aimed at the men's Commandant, Colonel Stephen Glynne Wheler, and he would quickly have learnt what Hearsey had said. Colonel Wheler was an evangelical Christian and in direct contradiction of what he had told his men, he had been actively preaching Christianity to them. An item in the *Illustrated London News* of 15 August 1857 reported that prior to the subsequent Court of Inquiry that was held, Wheler wrote to the Assistant Adjutant General making his beliefs quite clear:

> As to the question whether I have endeavoured to convert sepoys and others to Christianity, I would humbly reply that this has been my object, and I conceive is the aim and end of every Christian who speaks the word of God to another.

On Sunday 29 March, the day before the disgraced 19th BNI were due to arrive at Barrackpore, the European officers, including Colonel Wheler, and his men had attended morning service at the cantonment church. About 4 p.m. a sepoy called Mangal Pande was seen on the parade ground

> straggling backwards and forward in front of the quarter-guard, armed with a musket and a sword; he had on his red jacket and regimental cap, endeavouring to incite the men of the regiment to mutiny, saying that the guns and Europeans had arrived for the purpose of slaughtering them.

Sergeant Major James Hewson came out on foot to see what was going on, and according to Havildar Shaikh Pultoo, who was an eyewitness to the whole incident, Pande fired his musket at Hewson, but missed him.[8]

The Adjutant, Lieutenant Bempde Baugh was told what had happened, and he arrived on horseback to find Pande reloading his musket. Pande fired at Baugh, missing him too, but wounding his horse, and unseating the officer. Baugh, armed with a pistol, and now on foot like the other two participants, fired at Pande and missed. Pande struck out at both the Adjutant and the Sergeant Major with his sword, wounding the two men severely. Shaikh Pultoo, the only Indian officer to come to the rescue, stretched out his arms in a conciliatory gesture towards Pande, telling him not to strike, but the havildar only managed to deflect a blow that was meant for Baugh. 'I then seized him round the waist with my left arm,' Pultoo said, which enabled the Adjutant and the Sergeant to get away, but not before they were beaten about their heads with musket butts wielded by several men from the quarter guard. Maimed and bleeding, Baugh walked past the soldiers and reproached them for allowing their officer to be cut down before their eyes without offering to assist. It was reported at the subsequent court-martial that 'They made no reply, but turned their backs and moved sullenly away.' This was potentially the most serious point of crisis. A solitary armed sepoy who appeared to have run amok could be contained, but when other armed sepoys began beating their officers then mutiny was very near. Pultoo, although now wounded himself, was still restraining Pande, and he called out to Jemadar Ishwari Pande to send four men to take Mangal Pande prisoner. The jemadar, who had initially tried to persuade Mangal Pande to give up his weapons, now turned on Pultoo, swore at him, and said if he didn't let his prisoner go, he, the jemadar, would shoot Pultoo, the havildar. 'Being wounded, I was obliged to let him go', Pultoo said later.

Colonel Wheler, as the next highest senior officer, was now called to the parade ground to resolve the situation. He ordered the guard to load their muskets and told Jemadar Ishwari Pande to take the guard and arrest Mangal Pande who was now in full flow

> calling out to the men of the Brigade to join him and die for their religion and their caste (he alluded to a small party of fifty of HM's 53rd Foot now at Flagstaff ghaut that had been sent by Lt. Sanders, Deputy Quarter Master General of the Army, and who were landing from the steamer that had arrived there for Calcutta). He called aloud to [the men of his Brigade] 'you have excited me to this, and now you b*** c****s will not join me'.

The jemadar initially refused to obey Wheler's orders, and the guard refused to advance. Wheler was then told by someone, whom he didn't name, that Mangal Pande was a Brahmin and that no one was prepared to hurt him. On hearing this Wheler simply turned around and left.

More than one British observer has noted that European officers commanding Indian soldiers adopted the 'prejudices of their sepoys' and their notion of higher and lower castes. If Pande had not been a Brahmin, but of a lower caste, the outcome might well have been very different. As it was, Wheler lamely reported what had happened to Major General Hearsey, and the General, taking command of the situation, rode on to the parade ground accompanied by his two sons, Captain John Hearsey and Lieutenant Andrew Hearsey. Forcing the reluctant jemadar at gun-point to take the guard with him and arrest Mangal Pande, the group of armed men advanced on foot and horseback. Pande then held his musket to his own chest, fired the trigger with his toe, and fell wounded on the parade ground. 'His regimental jacket and clothes were on fire and smoking,' reported the General. 'I bid the jemadar and the sepoy to put the fire out, which they did.' Pande, convulsed and shivering, was taken to the cantonment hospital, where his wound was discovered to be superficial.

General Hearsey, like Lieutenant Baugh, rebuked the men for standing by. He told them

> they had not done their duty in allowing their fellow soldier, Mangal Pandey to behave in the murderous manner he had done. They answered in one voice 'He is mad, he has taken bhang to excess.' They were afraid to secure him because he had a loaded musket. 'What!' I replied 'Are you afraid of a loaded musket?' They were silent and being told to go to their quarters, they obeyed.

Mangal Pande was tried by court-martial on 6 April.[9] All fourteen members of the court-martial were Indian officers, consisting of eleven subedars and three jemadars. The President was Subedar Major Jawahar Lal Tewari. Only the Judge Advocate and the Prosecutor, Colonel Wheler, were British. The court-martial was held in the Regimental Mess of the 34th but in order to hear evidence from the wounded men, Lieutenant Baugh and Sergeant Major Hewson, who were still incapacitated, proceedings were moved to the quarters of the two men. At the conclusion of the court-martial, its fourteen members voted unanimously in favour of a guilty verdict on the charges of inciting the sepoys to mutiny and of striking the two officers. A majority of eleven voted for the death penalty. Mangal Pande was hanged early in the morning on the parade ground where he had attempted to incite his fellow soldiers, who had been assembled to see the death penalty carried out. At his execution, an eyewitness said 'the man appeared to be quite exhausted and made no attempt to address the troops around. He has previously stated that he bore no ill-will against either of the parties who he had injured, but revealed nothing to implicate any of his comrades.'

Jemadar Ishwari Pande, who was also found guilty by court-martial for refusing to obey Wheler's initial order to arrest Mangal Pande, was hanged on the same parade ground two weeks later. The fate of both men was announced to other Indian regiments as a warning to the mutinous. In a dreadful piece of timing, the news was reported in Delhi early on the morning of 11 May, a few hours before the city was seized by the rebel soldiers from Meerut. Much later in the year, an officer, Captain Robert Tytler was asked if there had been any significant signs that disaster was so near. He remembered how the Brigade Parade was called to hear the sentence of court-martial passed on Ishwari Pande at Barrackpore, and how, on hearing the news, there was 'a murmur of disapprobation throughout the whole Regiment. Though it lasted but a few seconds, it struck me forcibly as something extraordinary, never having witnessed anything like it before.'[10]

Mangal Pande's motives and his subsequent fate have formed the starting point of several histories of the Great Uprising. He has been shown in film, song and books as a hero, the first hero, of 1857. What inspired him to act as he did has been largely forgotten, in celebrating, or denigrating, what he actually did. Charles Canning, the Governor General, who called for a report on the whole affair and wrote his own Minute on it 'desired to note' that Mangal Pande had

> called upon his comrades to come to his support, for the reason that their religion was in danger, and that they were about to be compelled to use cartridges, the use of which would do injury to their caste; and from the words in which he addressed the sepoys, it is to be inferred that many of them shared this opinion with him

although it had been explained to the Regiment that fears for their religion were groundless. Canning described Pande as 'a fanatical sepoy, most dangerous of approach', and he praised 'the determination and courage shown by Lieutenant Baugh and Sergeant Major Hewson' in tackling him. However, Canning did not want Baugh or Hewson to receive any particular recognition for their bravery because he thought that 'would give a notoriety and importance to his [Pande's] crime which it will be much better to avoid'. Canning wanted to play down the element of 'religious frenzy' that characterised Pande's condition.

> However probable it may be, judging from the words which the mutineer is reported to have used during his excitement, that religious feelings influenced him, I should have preferred if this feature of the case had been left unnoticed in the [divisional] order.[11]

Less thoughtful commentators than Canning were willing to attribute Mangal Pande's behaviour more to his use of *bhang*, a product of the cannabis plant, than religious fervour, because that somehow made his actions more explicable. It stopped, for a while at least, an analysis of why the sepoys in northern India, and not just at Berhampore and Barrackpore, were becoming increasingly discontented. The first mention of bhang had come not from

6. 'Disarming the 11th Irregular Cavalry at Berhampore [*sic*]' (the disarming actually took place at Barrackpore). 'I then ordered all the belts to be taken off, and this was not approved of, some broke their swords, others threw away their pouches but still the order was obeyed. The horses were removed and the men then pulled off their long jack boots and spurs and threw them away.'

the British officers who witnessed Pande's revolt, but from his fellow sepoys, in excusing themselves to General Hearsey, for their failure to act. Pande himself admitted to taking bhang and opium, neither of which usually produce violent behaviour, in fact quite the reverse, leading to introspection and a feeling of calm. Bhang was often taken in milk drinks in India (and still is today), and its use was particularly associated with the spring festival of Holi, which had been celebrated a few days earlier. There was nothing unusual about an off-duty sepoy taking bhang, and its use certainly did not lead to anything approaching the alcohol-fuelled rampages that the British soldiers embarked on later that year. However, the explanation that Pande's rage was drug-fuelled, whether true or not, was eagerly seized upon, without further examination.

Whatever the immediate cause of Mangal Pande's behaviour, there is no doubt that two factors were playing on his mind, as on the minds of his comrades. Their commandant, Colonel Wheler had deliberately lied to his men when he told them that the rumour about converting the sepoys to Christianity was false. By his own admission Wheler himself was actively proselytising his faith, and moreover considered it his Christian duty to do so.

Secondly, the arrival of fifty European soldiers from HM's 53th Regiment at Barrackpore, in anticipation of the disbandment of the 19th Bengal Native Infantry the next day, could only have fed the sepoys' fears that another parade ground massacre was due to take place, like the one in 1824. Mangal Pande was no young raw recruit in March 1857, but a seasoned soldier aged twenty-six, who had joined the army seven years earlier and whose previous general character was described as good.

Pande's Regiment, the 34th, was disbanded on 6 May, following an announcement by the Governor General, Canning. This was the only possible punishment. If the decision to disband the 19th for refusing orders was considered harsh, then disbanding the 34th for actually striking British officers, withholding aid from these wounded officers and refusing orders, was seen as rather too lenient by many. But the Governor General held firm, and the men were dismissed. To General Hearsey's surprise, as the men walked off the parade ground, he was suddenly surrounded by shopkeepers from the cantonment bazaar, shouting out about the debts owed by the former sepoys – 'Dohaee General Sahib, dohaee Kumpanee' ('Injustice, General! Injustice, Company!'). 'I'm an army General, not a general clerk' retorted Hearsey in Hindustani ('Paltan ka genril, katab ka genril nahin'), but he conceded that creditors who could produce a written voucher would get paid, which was 'much to the dissatisfaction of the disbanded sepoys' who had hoped they could walk away from their financial obligations.[12] As for Colonel Wheler, a Court of Inquiry at the end of May found him unfit for command. He was sent on furlough (a prolonged leave) and took early retirement on 8 October the following year.

Those who believe in the conspiracy theory behind the Great Uprising generally agree that Sunday 31 May 1857 was the date on which the Bengal Army was to rebel.[13] If this was true, then Mangal Pande had anticipated the event by a couple of months, alerting the British and ruining the element of surprise. But it is more accurate to see him as the first man to articulate the fears of the sepoys in a chain of events that led inexorably towards mutiny in the army. Military unrest was quickly exploited by unruly civilian elements, including those whom the British were later to designate as 'criminal tribes' but this was followed by the emergence of a number of genuine patriots and many more people with their own agendas for revenge and opportunism.

We are dependent almost exclusively on British records for the names of those rebels that we do know. At the end of October 1857, when Delhi had been recaptured and a shaky order restored, a request was sent out from Calcutta to the lieutenant governors of the North-West Provinces and the Central Provinces asking for 'descriptive rolls of the leading persons concerned in the present rebellion whose apprehension may be desirable … indicating at the same time, the parentage of the parties'. Lord Canning issued a formal request for the names of rebel leaders in November, and by 5 March of the following year a manuscript list of 400 names had been compiled. This was printed and distributed on 17 April 1858, with some minor amendments.[14] The rebels were numbered and listed by district, with brief descriptions of their offences, their caste, their profession or title and other relevant information. In some cases they had already been executed. Occasionally names are not given, like the entry against number 192, which states:

> The zamindars of Chowrah, styled a refractory band of Rajpoots [who] plundered and fired a factory and the auction purchaser's chownee in the Village of Chowrah and committed other acts of outrage [often a euphemism for rape] against the inoffensive inhabitants of the surrounding villages.

Often the detail is impressive, like the entry for Harkishen Singh, the *tehsildar* (district officer) of Raja Kanwar Singh. Described as about thirty years old, the tehsildar 'who took a prominent part in the rebellious proceedings in [Arrah] District [was] middle-sized, very fair, whiskers and mustaches joined, more thin, brushed backwards like an up-country sowar'. Another man, named as 'Singhboom, the son of Uchoot Singh', aged twenty-seven or twenty-eight years old, was the Raja of Porahant, and residing in the village of Chakradharpur. in Bihar. He was described as a man 'of about 5 feet, 6 or 7 inches, stout, fair complexion, flat nose, broad forehead, disjoined eyebrows, mark of smallpox on the face, right arm inoculated in one place – caste Rathore Rajpoot'. Although not all descriptions have this level of detail one can see why the list took four months to compile. Eyewitnesses had to be found and interviewed during a period when, if the worst was over, as everyone hoped, there were still local pockets of severe unrest and many more deaths to come. At this point, Lucknow had not yet been recaptured, the Rani of Jhansi was still free, and Nana Sahib had disappeared but was not dead.

Information was gathered from letters and documents found in captured forts and palaces. There was not always time to burn incriminating papers, and they were seized on by the British troops. At Saugor 'the officer commanding the detachment found and made over to the Brigadier [Sage] a quantity of Hindee letters, copies of official documents on stamp paper, etc.' The Brigadier was reluctant to part with the papers, claiming it 'a most imperative duty to possess myself of the contents of all papers captured by the troops under my command … to counteract the design of the Traitors and Rebels who surrounded us'.[15] The Governor General was forced to order such officers, who assumed a proprietorial attitude to captured items, to hand over the papers 'when done with for military purposes' to the civil authorities. Indian translators were then employed to go through such papers searching for evidence of conspiracies and the names of rebels.

It was unusual for villagers to travel very far from home, because they had neither the means nor the necessity to do so. East India Company surveyors, mapping out their rapidly increasing territories, had remarked how very limited was the villagers' geographical knowledge, often no further than the distance a man or woman could walk within a single day. The difficulties of identifying gangs of men on horseback plundering a wide swathe of countryside, as the Gujars and others did, was immense, and many of course went unnamed and unpunished. Where the villagers did have an advantage was in local knowledge. In a largely illiterate society, the power of memory and oral history was heightened. Old men would visit the villages and recite the genealogy of their inhabitants, chanting the old names for hours, in return for food and shelter. Within a small circle everyone's antecedents were known, as well as their affiliations and family relationships. If Company officials, working through their Indian clerks, spies and assistants, could tap into this localised knowledge, then one can see how the 'rebel lists' were compiled. In a semi-feudal society the landowners were powerful figures, often figures of hate and fear, and a high proportion of zamindars were named as rebels, in some cases certainly unjustly. In urban areas it was often men with status and authority who were named, especially the people connected, ironically, with keeping the peace. Again, an element of revenge in the naming of these men should not be discounted.

In some of the cases we know the status, or profession, of the men listed and we can broadly divide them into the following groups:

(i) royalty, noble and old-established families
(ii) military men
(iii) rural, including landowners, landholders, sub-divisional officers (tehsildars), villagers and peasants (ryots)
(iv) urban, including tradesmen
(v) religious/educational leaders and others

Among these categories, but not tied to any particular group, were charismatic leaders, who often attracted followers from outside their own areas (Feroze Shah at Mandsaur); indigenous leaders seeking higher status within their own districts (Khan Bahadur Khan); army officers who assumed the leadership of regiments that had mutinied; dispossessed landholders; tribal groups; servants/local employees of the British; individuals with personal grudges against the British or against other Indians, and lastly those against any kind of authority, the full-time scoundrels.

At the top of the first group are the princely families followed by the rajas, rao sahibs and nawabs. The King of Delhi (number 166 on the list) was already under trial when the rolls were printed. The surviving Delhi princes were grouped together at number 167 and it was asserted that: 'These princes residing at Benares were reported to be plotting and attempting to get the city to rise. The son of Mirza Bolaki was often seen with the Native sepoys and sowars at Benares and that just before the Mutiny took place.'

7. British troops and the British camp before Jhansi Fort, 1858. From the Lakshmi Temple, Orchha.

Two nobles living near Delhi, the Hindu Raja of Ballabgarh (number 176) and the Muslim Nawab of Jhajjar, (number 180) had already been executed. A few names are familiar to us, in particular that of 'Sreemunt Dhoondoo Punt, Nana Sahib of Bhittoor' (number 141), who carried a reward of Rs 100,000 on his head, equivalent at the time to £10,000, and the Rani of Jhansi (number 270), whose citation reads 'through whose treachery a general massacre of all Europeans of every age and sex took place' in the Fortress. Only one other woman is named in the list, the Rani Digamber Kaur (number 231) in Gorakhpur District who was 'in open rebellion against the State'. We know nothing more of her other than that she was a Sikh princess. Another woman, Begam Hazrat Mahal, a wife of the deposed Nawab of Awadh, is not listed, because her role in defending Lucknow against its recapture by the British was still some days away. But her son, Birjis Qadr, then about fourteen years old, is number 313 and described as 'Birjee Kuder – natural son of the ex-King of Oude – the puppet King of Oude'.

Although the Uprising had begun as a military revolt, few Indian officers were still being sought by March 1858. Of those who had remained with the regiments that mutinied, many had been killed in the Delhi siege and in encounters with the British. Others had returned to their villages, some laden with loot, and they kept their heads down. Not surprisingly, rebellious officers and sepoys were hunted down and dispatched with particular rigour. The Governor General had authorised payment for the apprehension of any 'sepoy mutineer or deserter', or anyone caught trying to 'seduce' the native troops. The reward was Rs 50 if the man was caught with his weapons, or Rs 30 if he was caught without them. Two jemadars, Beni Prasad and Dewa Das of Allahabad District were hanged, and Jooah Singh, who was convicted of carrying a seditious letter from the 2nd Cavalry to the zamindars of Chail and of inciting other people to rise 'has suffered death'. Mir Aman Ali (number 258), a former subedar major of the 1st Gwalior Contingent Infantry was described as 'one of the leaders of the mutineers at Gwalior', who had written to the Raja of Dholpur threatening to attack him if he gave the British any assistance.

The regiments that had mutinied and killed their British officers now needed new leaders. These were chosen by the sepoys themselves, from among their own officers. In Awadh, for example, Duleep Singh (number 322), who had been a subedar in the 22nd Bengal Native Infantry, was put in command of his regiment by the mutineers. He was described by a British officer as 'the prime leader' of the uprising at Faizabad and went on to take part in the battle of Chinhat and the siege of the Lucknow Residency. Madhu Singh (number 92), a sepoy in the Light Company, 17th Native Infantry, fired the first shot in the rebellion at Azamgarh, killing Lieutenant Hutchinson and wounding others. A reward of Rs 2,000 was put on his head. Among officers whose names we know from other sources, was subedar Baghirati Misra, of the 15th Bengal Native Infantry, who was elected colonel of the regiment after it mutinied at Neemuch in May 1857 and who was promoted to brigadier the following month. Another subedar, Sheikh Ramzan, who was stationed at Saugor, was elected 'Commander of the Mutineers' on 1 July 1857. He was killed in action at Bithur in August 1857.[16]

One category of fighting men among the rebels was not listed – the mercenaries who formed an important part of any army in the subcontinent. The East India Company Army, in its early days, had relied heavily on mercenaries, particularly from Europe. Indian rulers also employed these 'soldiers of fortune' as they were known, some of whom were extremely gifted and influential, like the Frenchman General Benoit de Boigne, who worked for the Maratha leader Mahadji Scindia. Unfortunately almost nothing is known of the mercenaries fighting against the British in 1857. Although the days were gone when local rulers could employ Europeans to train their armies, the Uprising was not entirely a domestic conflict. Feroze Shah, also known as Prince Humayan, from the Delhi royal family, was lately returned from a pilgrimage to Mecca, when he came to Mandsaur in Gwalior State during August 1857. He is believed to be the author of the Azamgarh Proclamation, which was a long list of complaints against the British, including the high assessment they placed on land, the high cost of fees in the law courts, the monopoly on lucrative trade, the importing of goods which put the Indian craftsman out of business, and the impossibility of Indians being able to progress in the Company's various departments. The Proclamation called on all to join the fight against the British. The Prince's travels outside India had undoubtedly enabled him to see more clearly the extent of British penetration in his own country. He arrived home with a small following of twenty Afghans and 'Mekranies', that is, men from Makran, on the coast of Baluchistan, who were supposedly of Arab descent. Within a few days he was joined by the Gwalior State garrison of 500 men, the majority of whom were Afghan mercenaries.

At Hyderabad, in Mysore State, where a determined mercenary-led assault on the British Residency was repulsed, the Resident reported that 'There are large bodies of Arab and Rohilla mercenaries always ripe for mischief and actuated by intense hatred to the British as foreigners and as being the dominant race in India ... from our power in controlling their lawless proceedings.'[17] Three men from Medina, in Arabia, managed to get into Delhi during the siege, having come 'to fight the English'. Some of the fiercest resistance against the British in Lucknow was from African men and women, who had been employed by the last Nawab in his bodyguard, and who remained behind when their master left for Calcutta.

Among the civil officers who were named by the British as rebels in the 'Descriptive Rolls' were senior and junior judges, a head police chief, a law court pleader, law court aides, lawyers, stewards, jail darogas, and a draughtsman in the Government Survey department at Jhansi who 'with his subordinates in office joined the mutineers and opened the Fort Gate where the Christians had taken refuge'. Some of these men were authoritative figures in their community, concerned with interpreting and upholding the law, and their anti-British stand in 1857/58 emphasised the widespread nature of the Uprising. Such men also understood the administrative structure that held their towns together under British rule, and were thus well placed to subvert it or, as happened in several cases, supplant it. Kullub Hossein (number 278) of Jaunpur was described as a former *kotwal* (an office somewhere between mayor and police superintendent), who had been suspended by the British, but who was reappointed by the townspeople when the British fled.

There were humbler people among those who joined the Uprising in the towns – tradesmen and their families for whom civil unrest could hardly have been welcome, including a fruiterer called Mandal, a goldsmith's sons, and a limevendor's sons in Bareilly. In Patna two Muslim booksellers, Pir Ali Khan and Aasaf Hosein, had, together with the zamindar Ghulam Abbas, led the disturbance there on the night of 3 July in which a British doctor, Dr Lyall, was killed. The three men had already been executed. Pir Ali Khan was subsequently found to have been corresponding about rebellion with a fellow bookseller, Musi-ul-Yuman from Lucknow, ever since the annexation of Awadh, sixteen months earlier. He had also been liaising with Wahhabi leaders in Patna, whom he tried, unsuccessfully, to persuade to join the revolt.[18] In a speech before his execution Pir Ali Khan told the Commissioner of Patna, William Tayler 'You may hang me, or such as me, every day, but thousands will rise in my place, and your object will never be gained.'

But it was the landowners, the zamindars, whose names appear most frequently in the 'Descriptive Rolls', indicating how the Uprising had rapidly moved on from a military mutiny to civil unrest and had then quickly spread to rural revolt. Because the 'rolls' do not record the status or profession of all the 406 people listed, only a rough estimate can be made, but of the men counted among the 'Persons who took a leading part in the rebellion of 1858', twenty-five were rajas, eighty were zamindars, twelve were taluqdars and eleven were military men. A list was provided of zamindars who were 'principals in plundering certain villages' in the Azamgarh district. Of these some were hanged, but others released (presumably from prison) by a certain Rajib Ali 'whom Mr Venables could not catch'. A modest sum of Rs 100 (£10) was put on Rajib Ali's head. At Fatehpur the zamindar Daryao Singh collected a number of men 'in open rebellion and killed some of the railway people'. In Gorakhpur, up on the northern border of Awadh with Nepal, it was reported that the Nagar raja 'and all the western rajas with Bali Singh at their head … took up the cause of the rebel Mahomed Hossein and seized the Government Tehsildarees'. Tehsils were administrative sub-divisions of Districts, where money from land revenue was collected and held before being remitted to the Company's treasuries in the cantonments. Seizing a tehsildari was at once a political gesture, taking a piece of actual land away from the control of the British government, and assuming responsibility for collecting and disbursing the income from it. Zamindars banded together to support local leaders, an obligation made easier by the many connections of marriage and relationships between landowning families.

Perhaps surprisingly, given that the fear of being forcibly converted to Christianity was a major factor in the Uprising, few religious leaders are listed in the 'Descriptive Rolls', neither pandits, nor maulvis, although charismatic Muslim preachers were involved in rallying supporters. In Delhi the Maulvi Mahomed Sayad raised the green flag at the Jama Masjid 'as a declaration of an obligatory war of extermination against the British' – a *jihad* in fact. He was rebuked by the King of Delhi the following day who pointed out that since all the British in Delhi were now dead, there was no necessity for a jihad. Mahomed Sayad then said the flag 'had been set up against the Hindus' but the King said he regarded his subjects, Hindus and Muslims, alike and was not going to agree to a religious war against the Hindus.[19] In Chail, Allahabad District, an unnamed maulvi was accused of 'raising his standard in this Pergunnah [*pargana* – district] and induced every Musulman there to join him'.

Understandably, the breakdown of order attracted lawless elements, although only two are named in the rolls: Ratan Singh 'a dacoit', with his followers aided Tejpal Singh, the taluqdar (landholder) of Dya, in Allahabad District and 'attempted to establish his own authority'. Hanuman (number 76), an escaped convict, who was 'aided by some villagers and a few zamindars, is reported to be committing great excesses in Pergunnah Kurra'. Others are described simply as 'badmashes' that useful catch-all word for miscreants and rogues, or as Santhals and Gonds, two of the largest *adivasi* (tribal) groups in India.

There were valid causes behind the revolt, though we must be careful about back-projecting too much sophisticated reasoning into the actions of those who rose up in 1857. It is unlikely that the groups of men who looted the cantonment treasuries were much concerned at that moment with expelling the British, although they were, in their own way, ensuring a temporary radical redistribution of funds. In a largely inarticulate rebellion, we need to look both at the few statements that survive, and at the actual acts of rebellion themselves. Bahadur Shah Zafar, the unwilling figurehead of the Uprising, issued a proclamation during the siege of Delhi, listing the reasons for the revolt and urging Hindus and Muslims to unite against the common enemy of the British. The King's own behaviour, and that of his wife, Begam Zeenat Mahal, during the siege of Delhi was somewhat ambiguous, but it is fair to assume that here he was voicing popular public opinion. His letter to the princes and people of India was printed in the King's name, at the Bahaduri Press in Bareilly, which remained under Indian control until May 1858.

The translation is stilted. 'The English are the people who overthrow all religions, have been circulating books through priests and have brought out a number of preachers to spread their own tenets. Their systematic contrivances … to destroy our religions' included legal sanctions against sati (the self-immolation of widows), and the right of widows to remarry. According to the King, the British had told the Indian people that they wished them to become Christians. To facilitate this conversion the British had chosen to provide unclean fat for the sepoys' cartridges and, more curiously, to grind down animal bones, mix them with flour and sell the result in the bazaar. 'It is now my firm conviction' wrote the old man, 'that if these English continue in Hindustan, they will kill everyone in the country, and will utterly overthrow our religions.' He admitted that 'some of my countrymen have joined the English' and he asked these renegades to reflect on their own religions. The slaughter of the English was 'extremely expedient, for by this alone will the lives and faith of both [Hindu and Muslim] be saved. You should come together and slay them.' 'You will never have such an opportunity again.' And he promised that if the Hindus *did* come and kill the enemy, then he would order the Muslims to stop killing cows, which was a frequent source of provocation. If the Hindus refused to fight the British, the King told them, they would be considered as guilty in the eyes of God as if they had killed and eaten the cows themselves. 'The solemn promises and professions of the English are always deceitful and interested ... deception has ever been habitual with them.'[20]

These were clear statements and they were acted upon by the rebels. The fear of losing their religion and then being 'Christianised' was overarching. Being Christian was intrinsically bound up with being British, in mid-nineteenth-century India, perhaps even more so than at home. Soldiers were marched to church twice on Sundays, for morning service and evensong. Many of the Company officials and military officers were practising Christians, or behaved as if they were. And it wasn't just the priests and the missionaries and the unclean cartridges – it was a kind of creeping Christianity that manifested itself in physical structures as well as in ideas, floating into obscure places like the so-called miasma that brought malaria every year, and just as deadly. Robert Tucker, the judge at Fatehpur, who was described as 'a tall, large-boned man, eccentric in some of his views' had got the words 'Thou God seest me' painted on the courtroom wall behind his chair, and at the entry to the town 'he had got permission to erect pillars by the wayside, on which he had had inscribed, in the Vernacular, the Ten Commandments, and sundry religious precepts'. The judge refused to leave Fatehpur with his fellow Britons when they fled before the unrest. He was warned that the town jail would be opened on 10 June and the prisoners let out by the rebels. The release of prisoners, whatever their crimes was a particular feature of the Uprising, and it happened wherever the British lost control. On the morning of 10 June, it was reported that 'the roads were pretty full of rough characters' making their way home or to their old haunts. Ignoring warnings, Tucker rode into town, used his rifle several times, and returned to his home in the cantonments, where he took refuge on the flat roof of his bungalow. He was attacked by a group of Muslims from the town, holding banners and 'symbols'. An open copy of the Qu'ran was carried before them, some said by Hikmat-ullah Khan, the Deputy Collector, and they were heard chanting verses from the sacred book. Tucker was shot and killed.

Hikmat-ullah Khan (number 185 in the rolls), with a price of Rs 5,000 on his head, is an interesting case, and we have a vivid description of him from John Sherer, the Magistrate and Collector of Fatehpur. Before his appointment, Sherer had been recommended by the Government Secretary in Agra to lean on Hikmat-ullah Khan 'as a man of complete acquaintance with that part of the country, intelligent, tried and entirely to be trusted'. He was, Sherer later wrote, 'tall, but with rather a stooping, invalid figure, of pale, olive complexion, and with reticent eyes. Somehow, he reminded me of the Italian Secretaries one sees in a picture gallery, with their black velvet doublets and delicate lace collars, and their calm mask-like faces.'[21] When the revolt broke out at Fatehpur on 7 June, Sherer and other Britons, watching events from the roof of a bungalow, saw a great number of people approaching, incuding Hikmat-ullah Khan 'my Italian Secretary friend with a sword, and an assumed warlike look scarcely suiting him'. Sherer and the other Britons were warned to leave Fatehpur, which they did, leaving Tucker behind to his fate. The Deputy Collector was captured hiding in disguise in Fatehpur on 16 July 1857, and was convicted and hanged two days later.

Churches and chapels were an obvious target in the Uprising. Skinner's Church (properly known as St James's Church) in Delhi was looted by badmashes, who tore the monumental slabs from the walls, destroyed the handsome chancel tomb of William Fraser, an earlier Resident at Delhi, who had been murdered in 1835, stole the plate and went into the bell tower. Here they rang the bells, then loosened them and let them fall into the church below. Church plate was an especially attractive prize for looters, because it was both intrinsically valuable and sacred to the Nazranis, (or Nazarenes) as Christians were colloquially known. At Ferozepur, some 260 miles north of Delhi, both the Anglican church and the Roman Catholic chapel were burnt. In Mainpuri (Aligarh District), the mutineers from Jhansi sacked the mission school and the mission house. The Roman Catholic chapel in Lucknow was completely sacked, with its bells torn from the belfry, ornaments and embroidered vestments stolen and the priest's house and two adjoining mission houses wrecked.[22] These buildings belonged to the Agra Catholic Mission, a long-established organisation, and now, in the mid-nineteenth century, one of several competing missions, including the Church Missionary Society (CMS), the Society for the Propagation of Christian Knowledge (SPCK) and several American Methodist missions.

Agra held a particular position in the history of Christianity in India. Although there were ancient communities of native Christians in south India, centred around Madras, where the disciple Saint Thomas had arrived in the first century to preach and convert, it was to Agra that the Jesuits had come from Goa at the beginning of the seventeenth century, at the invitation of the Emperor Akbar. (The capital of Mughal India had been moved from Delhi to Agra in the 1570s, with the construction of Fatehpur Sikri, and it remained there until the 1630s, when it was moved back to Delhi.) A plot of land at Agra had been given to the Christian community by the Emperor which was named Padretola, or 'the Padre's Ward'. Here a church and a mission were built and an area marked out for the cemetery in which some of the earliest European travellers are buried. From this accident of history, Agra became known as a centre of Christianity in northern India, certainly up to 1803 when Father Francis Xavier Wendell, the last member of the 'Mughal Mission', as it became known, was buried there.

Until 1813 British missionaries could not travel to India or work there under the East India Company's auspices. A few circumvented this by establishing themselves in pockets of European-held territory embedded in the Company's possessions, like the small Danish settlement at Serampore. Missionaries could also work in independent states with the ruler's permission, as the Reverend Christian Schwartz did at Tanjore, under Raja Serfoji II. But when the Company's Charter came up for renewal by Parliament in 1813, there was strong lobbying to allow missionaries to go to India and work there. The lobbying was led by Charles Grant, Chairman of the Court of Directors of the East India Company, and a committed Christian. As part of the Charter renewal, the House of Commons had republished a pamphlet by Grant, which he had written many years earlier, entitled 'On the State of Society among the *Asiatic* Subjects of *Great Britain*, particularly with respect to Morals; and on the means of improving it'. Grant's title indicated the increasingly popular view of many in Britain towards Indian society. The early days of mutual respect, inter-marriage and the adoption of Indian customs by Europeans, which lasted from about 1770 to 1800, had gone. Company officials were now able to express their Christian faith in public, without censure by their employer, or ridicule by their contemporaries.

The Church Missionary Society, founded in 1799, had established a footing in Agra during the famine years of 1837/38 when it fed starving people, and opened an orphanage at Sikandra five miles north of the city. Here a 'Christian village' was set up and flourished. By 1857 there were almost a thousand 'native Christians', that is, Hindu or Muslim converts. In order to provide work for the children in the orphanage as they grew up, they were taught how to print and bind books, and the Secundra Orphan Press was established. Contracts for printing government publications followed and a number of rather dull-sounding reports on land revenue and indigenous education were produced. However, these brought in enough money to fund other missionary ventures in Agra, including St John's College, which was opened in 1852 to provide a higher English education on Christian lines to Indian boys. Thomas Valpy French, who later became Bishop of Lahore, was the College Principal. By 1857 several branch schools had been opened, run on similar lines. James Thomason, the son of a missionary and the former Lieutenant Governor of the North-West Provinces, established a teachers' training college (known then as a Normal School) at Agra, in order to feed St John's with staff.

When news of the Uprising at Meerut on 10 May was received at Agra the following day by electric telegraph, the Company officials there, under the Lieutenant Governor, John Colvin, seemed mesmerised, as indeed was much of British India. No steps for defence were taken until the end of June. The telegraph wire was promptly cut by the rebels out in the countryside so news had to be brought in by hand. William Muir, who was in charge of the

Intelligence Department in Agra, wrote of that curious hiatus when he and two other officers, Harington and Reade, were nominated

> in a sort of informal way by Mr Colvin, to keep the wheels of Government in motion. Judicial, Financial and Revenue respectively, but as tract after tract fell out of our hand, the administration collapsed and the labour of conducting it shrank to nothing; there was in fact no Government to conduct. This was especially the case with my Department [revenue].[23]

The advance of rebellious sepoys from the Neemuch and Nasirabad cantonments, heading towards Delhi, to support the King, finally jolted the British into action. Because Agra housed the central jail for the North-West Provinces it contained 'a vast collection of the worst prisoners in the land', nearly 4,000 in fact, and was referred to as 'our monster Jail'. The jail *najibs*, the armed guards, had deserted and gone off in a body at the end of May, so a company of European soldiers, about a hundred men, had taken over as jailers. But now every armed man was needed to fight and the European guards had to rejoin their regiment. To forestall the release of the prisoners by the rebels, the jail superintendent, Dr James Walker, ordered that the short-term prisoners should be let out and led across the river, and that the Sikh prisoners, who numbered between sixty and eighty men, were to be pardoned and formed into an armed guard to defend the jail. The majority of the British officers and their families, abandoning the Christian village at Sikandra and, for a time, their Christian converts as well, fled into Agra Fort.

The Normal School was the first to go. It was set on fire and 'wild sowars' (cavalry troops), were reported to have been seen galloping savagely round it. The whole of the cantonment and government offices were plundered by the villagers and 'the city rabble'. Not every European had gone into the Fort, and Professor Hubbard of St John's College was murdered with the connivance of the city police, aided by 'Mewatis of Wazirpur and low-caste Muslims'. The city police then deserted their posts, and their Superintendent, Murad Ali, proclaimed the rule of the Delhi King. A week later, when the British timidly ventured out, they found the rebels had moved on to Delhi, and that British rule could be re-established. William Muir rode out to the orphanage and Christian village at Sikandra. It was a sickening sight.

> Of all that noble establishment, reared by the labour of nearly twenty years, not a single Press remains, the place is strewed with bits of broken printing presses, leaves and masses of black rubbish – the unrecognizable remains of thousands of volumes. Alas for education! Alas for the regeneration of India!

There were similar incidents at Allahabad, where the American-led Board of Foreign Missions had established an orphanage and printing press, both of which were completely destroyed.

Printing presses had been brought to India as early as the seventeenth century by the Jesuits and they were particularly associated with missionaries who needed them to print the Bible and Christian tracts in the vernacular languages as well as in English. By the early nineteenth century printing presses were enormous, solid, wooden objects, and not easily damaged. To destroy them, as Muir reported the Sikandra rebels had done, must have taken hours of concentrated hate. Even where presses were used for secular purposes, like printing newspapers, they were still seen as alien (and British) to illiterate men, and the *Delhi Gazette* press was destroyed in the first day of that city's capture on 11 May 1857. What the rebels did not realise was that the printing press is an impartial object. It will print what it is told. Proclamations issued by the King, by Nana Sahib, Begam Hazrat Mahal and other leaders were printed and circulated, but there were almost no revolutionary newspapers of the kind that appeared fourteen years later during the Paris Commune in 1871. Although vernacular-language newspapers were being published, as well as English-language papers, the only one traced so far which can properly be called a 'rebel manifesto' is the short-lived *Payam-i-Azadi* (Message of Freedom), published from Lucknow in April and May 1857.[24] The potential of a captured printing press to carry a revolutionary message was not appreciated. Between the disdain of the illiterate man for the printed word and the close association of the presses with Christian propaganda, they were bound to be an easy target for destruction, but not for use.

Another mission station had been set up at Farrukhabad after the famine of 1837/38, by the American Presbyterian, the Reverend John Freeman and his wife. Here the orphans had been taught tent-making and had established a thriving tent factory. There was also a school, a workshop and a 'Christian village', called Rakha. When the 10th Bengal Native Infantry mutinied at Fatehgarh, a number of sepoys went on to neighbouring Farrukhabad, causing mayhem and panic on the way. The mission station was 'destroyed and desecrated' and eight missionaries were killed when they fled downriver to Cawnpore, unaware that the British cantonment had fallen to Nana Sahib. A native teacher in the mission school described what happened:

> About 10.00am hundreds of villagers from the surrounding country began to pour in, and plunder the mission compound and the Christian village. Ready-made tents, timbers, tables, sofas, chairs, book shelves, brass and copper vessels belonging to native Christians … in short, all that could be carried off, was taken away in a few hours, and by the evening of that day, nothing was left but beams that were in the roofs of the houses.

The mission itself was later burnt by cavalrymen.[25]

Another target was the railway line which was being extended from Howrah, then a village near Calcutta, towards Delhi. By May 1857 there were three railway lines operating in India: the Great Indian Peninsular Railway from Bombay to Poona via Thana; the East Indian Railway, a 120-mile track from Howrah to Raniganj and its coal-fields, and the Madras Railway, experimentally running to Arcot.[26] Lord Dalhousie, the Governor General between 1847 and 1856, was an enthusiastic supporter of the Indian railway companies, and as former Vice-President of the Board of Trade he had been responsible for encouraging the railway boom in Britain. The ultimate aim was to have a network of railways linking the three Presidency ports, Calcutta, Bombay and Madras, to the manufacturing and consumer centres of India, as well as transporting troops and ammunition quickly to trouble spots. It was the logical response to the Company's policy of spreading out from its consolidated coastal bases in search of trade and land revenue.

The three lines had proved remarkably popular, and the fears which had been raised that Indians would not travel by rail because of caste or religious contamination had not materialised. The introduction of first, second, third and fourth class, and the corresponding ticket prices, had satisfied the travelling public with a suitable place for everyone, and the utility of getting goods moved by steam, rather than lumbering bullock-carts over uncertain roads, was immediately recognised. Striped awnings over the windows of the early passenger coaches gave a holiday air to a train journey. Calcutta merchants were already sending their wares by rail between Salka and Burdwan. With the extension of the west-coast line to Poona, Company officials from as far away as Nagpur now timed their *dak* (mail) to reach the railhead for the 7 a.m. or 7 p.m. train to Bombay.[27]

But the acceptance of the railway among the urban and merchant classes did not mean that it was universally welcomed. Out in the countryside, despite careful negotiations, and the purchase of land by the railway companies for a fair price, there had been resistance. In 1856 there was a clash between British engineers of the East Indian Railway and Santhal tribesmen, the latter armed with bows and arrows, and rather more modern *pangas* (choppers). Several engineers were seriously wounded. Railways were undoubtedly an intrusion, radically altering the landscape with bridges and raised embankments. Areas on the outskirts of towns were being rapidly developed to service the railways too, not just the station buildings with their wooden platforms, but the engine and carriage sheds, the bungalows of the railway employees, and the offices of the surveyors who were marking out the proposed routes. There had been protests by people in Britain thirty years earlier when surveyors and navigators began changing the face of the countryside, but here at least, the objectors could blame their own government. In India it was the British government which was changing the Indian landscape.

The East Indian Railway company planned to extend the line from Howrah to Delhi, via Raniganj and Allahabad and by the beginning of 1857 surveying and construction were well advanced, passing through Agra,

Aligarh and Cawnpore. Trains were running over about forty miles of track in Allahabad District. The first attack was at Allahabad in June, when all the new station works were destroyed, including the locomotive and carriage shops. This attack was launched by supporters of the Maulvi, Liaquat Ali, who had proclaimed a jihad against the 'accursed Christians' and who was, for a week, the Governor of Allahabad, ruling in the King of Delhi's name. Twenty-three miles away, at Barwari, railway staff and their families had to take refuge in an overhead water tank, constructed to supply the locomotives. The tank was dry, and the refugees had to defend themselves for thirty hours or so, firing down into the crowd of rebels, as they watched their bungalows being looted and burnt. They were rescued by a party sent out from Allahabad, although not without casualties.

The most dramatic incident was at Arrah, through which the new railway line passed. Richard Vicars Boyle, the engineer in charge, had had the foresight to fortify a small but sturdy building, used as a billiard hall. It was to become known as 'The Little House at Arrah'. He furnished it with arms, ammunition and provisions, and he got a detachment of fifty Sikh police posted there. When the sepoys mutinied in the Dinapore cantonment, some twenty-six miles away, and marched on Arrah, Boyle, with fifteen other railwaymen and the Sikh police, defended their makeshift fortress for over a week. They were rescued by a group of fusiliers led by Major Vincent Eyre, and twelve men from the East Indian Railway Volunteer Force. At Bhadaoli in Mirzapur District, a group of a thousand Rajputs under Adwan Singh occupied the village and began destroying the railway.[28]

As the first railway lines were being laid in India, the electric telegraph wires were being strung up on wooden posts beside the tracks and along the major highways. The railways and the telegraph had expanded together in England in the 1830s, the one driven by the other. Warnings had to be given in advance of the locomotives' approach, particularly to avoid collisions in tunnels, and to show if the line was clear or blocked. The wider potential of the telegraph was recognised when the British Admiralty paid for a telegraph line to link its London office to Portsmouth. By 1845 the British police were using the telegraph to apprehend criminals, and its commercial advantages were quickly realised too. The first experimental electric telegraph line in India was set up between Calcutta and Diamond Harbour in 1850, a distance of thirty miles. Three years later construction had started on an ambitious network of 4,000 miles of telegraph lines connecting Calcutta to Peshawar, via Agra as well as links to Bombay, Madras, Ootacamund and Bangalore. The East India Company was prepared to spend very substantial sums of money to get lines set up, like the Rs 25,056 (£2,500) advance made in August 1857 for the construction and working of the telegraph at Hyderabad and Nagpur (which was paid for from the Hyderabad Treasury).[29]

Telegraph lines strung out along the roads between north Indian towns were an easy target for destruction during the Uprising. To the villagers and the sepoys they were another sign of the Company's intrusion into rural life, and a dangerous one too. As if by magic, the British could now talk to each other over vast areas of land, and who knew what they might be saying and plotting? The telegraph was not only vital to the Military Department for deploying troops where they were most needed, but it carried messages of death through the air too. On 21 August the Magistrate at Satara, Mr J. N. Rose, reported to the Judicial Secretary at Bombay that 'Man Singh bin Narain Singh convicted of treason [was] sentenced to death, and hanged this morning under the authority conveyed in the Electric Telegraph messages received from you'.[30] Judgements and decisions which had in the past taken days to arrive now took only a couple of hours. Sir Robert Montgomery, one-time Judicial Commissioner of the Punjab, claimed that 'The Electric Telegraph saved India' during the Uprising, but this was only partially true. It had failed where it was most needed, at Cawnpore and Lucknow, being simply hacked down. Destroying the telegraph lines was not only to strike a direct blow against the British by disrupting their communications, but it also resulted in a haul of valuable materials that could be put to use against the enemy. A British officer at Meerut sketched a piece of 'extempore ordnance' he found there, a small cannon ingeniously made from the iron sheaths that protected the telegraph posts and using 'double copper wire and electric telegraph wire in small pieces well mixed up' as ammunition. The wooden telegraph posts, chopped down, were also useful as barricades, and when ammunition ran short they could be cut into pieces, trimmed and fired from more conventional cannon. There was no question of the rebels being able to use the telegraph for its intended purpose, either to communicate with each other or to intercept messages sent by British soldiers and civilians. The East India Company had deliberately restricted its use to British officers, and to Anglo-Indian signallers trained to operate the receiving and transmitting machines. As an added safeguard a secret cipher code was devised, which was known only to twelve senior civilian administrators. It was issued with the warning that 'it is intended, and it is necessary that contents of messages transmitted in Cipher should not be understood by the signallers'.[31]

Hatred of British rule, fear of being forced to accept their religion, suspicion of the instruments and machines they employed, were at the heart of the Uprising, and these sentiments were shared by a great number of people who took part in it. The result of their actions led to vacuums in administration and order where the British officials and their Indian deputies fled or were killed. It was inevitable that others, less high-minded, would take advantage of the brief interregnum of licence. Sooner or later, another raj would appear, perhaps that of a rejuvenated Mughal king, perhaps that of the Company again. There were even rumours that the Russians had arrived, turning their gaze east after their defeat in the Crimea the previous year. Land and property that could be seized now could become permanent possessions under a new regime. Plunder and land grabbing were often the quickest way to achieve this. The diary kept by the unnamed opium dealer who spent nearly two weeks in Cawnpore in June 1857 gives a vivid account of what was happening there:

> All the old zamindars who had been dispossessed of their estates, by sale or otherwise, during the rule of the government embraced the opportunity of turning out those who had been appointed in their room – the land-holders oppressed and plundered each other, and hundreds of Rajpoots were employed robbing the travellers on the roads. Those sepoys who were returning to their homes, taking with them what plunder they had collected, were in their turn despoiled of their ill-gotten wealth by the zamindars – if they refused to deliver up their plunder when called on to do so, they were killed – most of them had from a thousand to five hundred rupees in their girdles ... Many merchants expected that the Sepoys would spare their property, and that they would consequently be able to carry on business under the new government – the sepoys however murdered every Christian they found, and also fired at every person they saw wearing English garments.

Three days later the same man reported that 'the Sepoys plundered the shops of the cloth merchants, and those of the manufacturers of brass and copper vessels – the property they plundered was worth about a lack [lakh] of rupees'.[32]

A British officer, Captain Gowan, who had escaped from Bareilly when it was seized by rebels, reported the same scenes. Moving cautiously across country to Meerut, he learnt that many of the sepoys from Bareilly, having mutinied, were now on their way to their homes, travelling together in large bodies for safety. 'Pathans, Gujars, Banjaras, Kunjurs [Kanjars]' and others had swept into the town and 'resumed their inherent practice of robbing, burning and killing the defenceless and weak'. Those sepoys unwise enough to travel in small groups were plundered by the villagers, and some were even murdered for the sake of their stolen loot.

> Indeed [reported the captain] at this time everybody's hand appeared to be against every one else, and the most frightful and cold blooded murders were committed, sometimes in revenge for injuries received or imagined, sometimes under the foolish delusion that dead men tell no tales, and sometimes as if really for the very pleasure of shedding human blood. [Land which had been] sold by former owners or to satisfy Government demands was resumed and the greatest oppression and cruelty practiced by landowners and the Muslim generally – no-one ventured beyond the limit of their village unless others were with them ... While travelling about the country for the first week [the beginning of June] I do not remember one night during some portion of which the country was not illuminated by some village being burnt either out of revenge or for plunder.[33]

Anything that was moveable could be plundered and carried off. Money, jewels and arms were easiest for men on the march, and the sepoys who remained in the mutinous Bareilly Brigade took three hundred horses from a stud farm near Meerut and rode into Delhi to support the King. Civilian plunderers took things that could be re-used, including wooden doors and window frames from bungalows, furniture, floor coverings and kitchen utensils. Odder things went too. The Magistrate at Fatehpur, John Sherer, lost two caged birds, a canary and a red parrot, that he had given to a local raja, an old friend of his, to look after. The raja was looted in turn, and Sherer's cages passed into the hands of the looters. He also reported that a looter had been seen with a cricket bat, liberated from some British bungalow.

Immoveable property was another matter. British land reforms begun in the late eighteenth century had led to various zamindars being declared bankrupt and their estates being auctioned off to meet arrears in land revenue. As the Cawnpore diarist reported, the former owners now repossessed their hereditary estates, refusing to recognise the recent British-led land sales. In other cases zamindars had preferred to mortgage their estates to the moneylenders, rather than have them taken away by the British government, which led to similar hardship. There were reports of tehsil offices being broken into, and the land settlement records destroyed, as well as the murder of the unpopular moneylenders. At Bhojpur in Meerut District, 500 Gujar prisoners, released from Meerut jail on 10 May by the rebels, sacked the village, killing the local moneylender and his family of six.

One of the leading zamindars who rebelled in 1857 was the elderly Raja Kanwar Singh, a Rajput settled at Jagdishpur in Bihar. Although later described by the historian R. C. Majumdar as 'the greatest military leader that India produced', Kanwar Singh had no military background, and was no enemy of the British for most of his long life. He had fallen into debt and had been unable to obtain a loan to meet the demands of the Bengal Revenue Board. His plight was described presciently by a British official in July 1857:

> He [Kanwar Singh] is nominally the owner of vast estates, whilst in reality he is a ruined man, and can hardly find money to pay the interest of his debts. As long, therefore, as law and order exist, his position cannot improve: take them away, and he well knows that he would become supreme in his district. I do not think he will ever openly oppose the Government as long as he thinks that Government will stand, but I think that, should these districts be ever the scene of a serious outbreak, he may take it into his head that it is time to strike a blow for his own interest, and his feudal influence is such as to render him exceedingly dangerous in such an event.[34]

In fact this is exactly what did happen, and Kanwar Singh and his loyal relatives and followers became a serious threat to the British, attacking the railwaymen at Arrah in July, then moving south to join the forces of Nana Sahib at Banda. He fought at Cawnpore, chased a British troop into an entrenchment at Azamgarh and kept them pinned down there for three weeks. He was eventually fought off, but he was not captured, and he died from wounds at his Jagdishpur estate, with a price of Rs 25,000 on his head. Kanwar Singh's case was an extreme one of a zamindar who felt he had nothing to lose and possibly a lot to gain by fighting the British. He is regarded by Indians as one of the heroes of the Uprising, a man whose personal misfortune coincided with a general revolt.

Several men rose briefly to important positions when they stepped in to fill posts emptied by British and Indian officials. Whether this was opportunism or initiative is not always clear. There was a vacuum to be filled, and men stepped forward, supported by their followers, to fill it. Such a person was the Rohilla chief Khan Bahadur Khan, who was recognised as the King of Delhi's Viceroy on 15 June 1857 at Bareilly. The Rohillas were a migrant tribe, originally from Afghanistan, who settled around Bareilly, making it their capital. The Khan was a grandson of Hafiz Rahmat Khan, the last independent Rohilla leader who had died at the hands of the British in 1774 during the first Rohilla war. Hafiz Rahmat Khan was buried in Bareilly, in a large, handsome Mughal-style tomb, thus demonstrating the respect in which he was held. Khan Bahadur Khan, described by the British as 'an aged miscreant' (he was in his seventies), was now head of the ruling family at Bareilly, on a monthly stipend of Rs 100 from the British government who were inclined to treat generously the descendants of fallen rulers. The Khan also got a pension in his own right, when he retired from the East India Company's judicial court, where he had been the *sadr amin* (principal judge) for many years. He was a solid citizen, friendly to the British Commissioner of Bareilly, but something of a reactionary. Although a Muslim, he apparently supported the Hindu practice of burning widows on their husbands' funeral pyres (*sati*) which had been prohibited in the Bengal Presidency by the Governor General Lord William Bentinck in 1829.

Bentinck had been urged to the prohibition by the great Bengali reformer Ram Mohun Roy, who had seen his sister-in-law burnt to death as a sati. Previous attempts to abolish sati had been made in the past by Indian rulers, including the Mughal emperors, so Bentinck's prohibition was not a new piece of legislation, but it gave some people another grudge against British interference in traditional customs. Khan Bahadur Khan complained that 'the self-immolation of wives on the funeral pyres of their deceased husbands was an ancient religious custom: the English had it discontinued, and enacted their own regulations prohibiting it'.[35] He also complained that a new system of feeding prisoners in jail, known as 'common messing', where the inmates ate communally, was a British ploy to convert them to Christianity by forcing them to eat bread together (a central part of the Christian communion service). Despite his criticism of the British, he warned the Commissioner, Mr Alexander, that the Bareilly regiments were about to mutiny at the end of May. He shook hands with Alexander at their last meeting and said 'Apna jan bachao' (Save your own life). The Khan sent expensive gifts to Bahadur Shah Zafar, asking for his appointment as Viceroy (Nawab Nazim) to be ratified with a *firman* or proclamation. The old man began his administration by issuing a proclamation on the causes of the Uprising (including the abolition of sati, and the British policy of annexation) and he is said to have had a number of Britons executed. He set up a council of Hindus and Muslims to govern Bareilly, and in less troubled times he would have made a good ruler, but these were troubled times, and he could not contain the rebellious sepoys and the rioters in the town. Bareilly was bankrupt, so the moneylenders were harassed for loans. In-fighting broke out, with Hindus ranged against Muslims. Nevertheless Khan Bahadur Khan held out until 7 May 1858 when he was defeated by the British general, Sir Colin Campbell. He was captured two years later on the Nepalese border, tried and hanged.

Analysis of the rebels and of their fears and resentments, have shown a variety of motives, and the objects of their physical attacks have been examined in some detail, but who were their victims? Although we know almost to a man the number of European troops in India at the start of the Uprising (45,000), estimates of the white, mainly British, civilian population are much harder to come by, and consequently the numbers killed in the Uprising are difficult to establish. The memorial tablets to the victims in All Souls Church, Cawnpore, mention 'more than 1,000 Christian souls' who were killed, including the people who fled from Fatehgarh and were massacred at Cawnpore. (This figure also includes just over 200 officers and men.) This was by far the highest number of Europeans killed in one place. Seventy-seven people, including some Eurasians, were killed at Jhansi, and fifty-two Europeans in the Red Fort at Delhi, Bahadur Shah Zafar's palace, according to an eye-witness. Thirty-one were killed in Meerut on 10 May and a possible dozen more when Delhi was seized by mutinous soldiers the following day. Cecil Beadon, Secretary to the Government of India in Calcutta, signed off a list in January 1858 of Britons killed in isolated incidents the previous year. Excluding those already mentioned above, about 125 people are listed, civilians and officers, bringing the total number of deaths to about 1,270. About 167 Europeans and Anglo-Indians, both soldiers and civilians, died or were killed during the siege of the Lucknow Residency. No figures have yet been found for those killed after January 1858 in mutiny-related incidents. Because military and civilian deaths were reported together, as in Beadon's list, it is even harder to work from, but we can make a very broad guess that over 1,000 European civilians, but fewer than 1,500, were killed in total during the first year of the Uprising.

Anyone with a white face was vulnerable if they crossed the rebels' path.

Women, children and babies were all killed, mostly hacked down with swords, or shot. There was little sign of torture – the aim was to kill as many *feringees* (foreigners) as quickly as possible. Heads were sometimes cut off and stuck on poles, because there was a price on British heads too, paid by rebel leaders. There are many heartbreaking stories, related in great detail, which would easily fill a book on their own. Wives saw their husbands and children killed in front of them, before they themselves were killed. Company officials were particularly sought out and killed, in a bid to remove not just the machinery of government, but the men behind it too. Medical men seemed at a premium. The veterinary surgeon of the 10th Cavalry, Mr Neilsaw, had his throat cut and bled to death. Two doctors, the Graham brothers, were shot dead in their carriages, in front of their female relatives. The Magistrate, Mr Wedderburn, and his wife and children were shot at Hissar, in the court house. Assistant Surgeon Garner, his wife and one of his children were killed in their barricaded bungalow, which was then set on fire. Their young daughter escaped and was taken in by a sympathetic tehsildar.

If it is difficult to compute the number of Britons and Europeans killed, then it is impossible to count the Anglo-Indians, people of mixed descent, who died at the hands of the rebels. The British attitude to Anglo-Indians during the Uprising was pragmatic, born out of necessity. Anglo-Indians *had* to be trusted to support the British in this emergency, and by and large, they did though often at great cost to themselves. Company regulations did not allow Anglo-Indians to enter the army as combatants, but they could be employed as bandsmen. They were considered reliable enough to be used as signallers for the electric telegraph, as we have seen, even if they weren't trusted with the cipher codes. They have been described as the 'poor relations' of the British in India, and were often treated as such, being both patronised and ridiculed. They generally wore western clothes, or 'that curious compromise affected by native Christians, smoking cap, *chapkan* [Indian coat] and shoes with strings'.[36] 'Shoes with strings' that is, lace-up shoes were a defining feature of a westernised man. The common Indian footwear was the comfortable *mochi jooti*, the soft leather handmade shoe with a curled toe, that can be easily kicked off indoors. To abandon this for the stiff, laced, English shoe was to say something about one's affiliations, strange as this may seem to us today. Wearing hats, not turbans, was another indicator, and one so common that the word *topaz*, or *topass* (from *topi* 'hat') was used to describe a Christian of mixed descent as early as the seventeenth century. Anglo-Indians were easily identified then by their dress, their Christian religion, their accent and their occupation, if a pale skin did not give them away. Joseph Skinner, grandson of the famous Colonel James Skinner, who raised the Irregular Regiment called Skinner's Horse and who represented one of the best known Anglo-Indian families, was dragged from his grandfather's house in Delhi and killed in front of the main police *thana* (station).

Native Christians, that is, Hindus or Muslims who had been converted to Christianity, fared just as badly, the numbers killed being also unknown. Dr Chaman Lal, a convert to Christianity, was an infamous case. Although wearing Indian dress, Dr Lal was pointed out by his neighbours to the Delhi mutineers as a Christian, and he was killed in front of his dispensary. (His widow was later awarded a pension from the Company.) Hindus, Muslims and Sikhs who worked for the British were just as vulnerable, even though they had no suspicion of Christianity or mixed blood. Anyone who worked for the enemy was regarded as the enemy. Indian clerks, deputies, sub-collectors and spies, in fact anyone who served the British, was hunted down and dispatched with the same ruthlessness. Tehsildars, the local officers responsible for safeguarding the collected land revenue on behalf of the government were popular targets, with their treasuries secured in iron chests set into the floor. Bakhtawar Singh, the tehsildar at Bahadurgarh, had fled on the approach of the mutineers to Shamli, near Rohtak. Here he was joined by a Muslim tehsildar Ibrahim Khan, twenty Sikh cavalrymen and twenty-eight policemen. Surrounded by 3,000 Gujars, the men held out until their food and water was exhausted. When they surrendered, in the middle of September, they were killed. Two Hindu tehsildars, Nand Lal and Piari Lal, together with their district registrar, Kishen Singh, escaped from Hissar when it was overrun by rebels on 29 May, but they were murdered by villagers at Toham the following day, not for plunder, but because they were seen as agents of the British. Another tehsildar, Ram Baksh at Auraiya, Etah, died from wounds and injuries inflicted by the mutineers on 30 June.

Terrorism in the countryside and small towns by an alliance of rebellious sepoys, local opportunists and murderous tribes did not go completely unopposed. There were people prepared to stand firm in the face of what must have seemed like anarchy from another age. At Guggi, in Mandla, the tehsildar Devi Prasad, with a detachment of twenty police, defeated a band of rebel looters. He was forced to retreat from Mandla at the end of November 1857 when the townspeople rose against him, but he was back again at his post early in January 1858. The Rani of Basti, in the North-West Provinces gathered an army of 800 Kalhan Rajputs and fought off an attempt by the rebel leader from Gorakhpur, Mahomed Hossein, to sack the town in August 1857. She continued to harass the Gorakhpur rebels and in January of the following year killed twenty of them, captured their baggage and one gun.[37] As a reward by the British she was later given a grant of valuable land, which had been confiscated from a rebellious neighbour, the Rani of Amroha. But where do people like the Rani of Basti stand in the Indian pantheon of freedom fighters? Not very high, although in her own way she was as brave as the Rani of Jhansi. She prevented the town from being plundered and the inevitable murders of her townspeople which would have taken place.

There is the even trickier question of which position to take in conflicts where direct British interests were not involved at all, other than the general one of keeping the peace. These events were more the settling of long-standing scores, but would not have happened if mutiny was not already stalking the countryside. At Bhojpur, in Farrukhabad District, there was a serious communal disturbance between nearly 2,000 men. Rajputs and Kurmis joined together under the banner of the *thakurs* (nobles) of Bhojpur and fought the Muslim Bhattis and Pathans. Most of the thakurs were killed, but the Janjua Rajputs fought on, defeating the Muslims and burning their villages.[38] In Sadabad, Muttra District, 800 Jats under Deo Karan fought and defeated 600 Rajputs under Thakur Sawant Singh on 20 May. About twenty-five men from each side were killed and the Rajputs' village at Bisand was burnt. The Jats then re-occupied Sadabad and destroyed government property there. By 6 July the Rajputs had regrouped and this time defeated the Jats.

An even nastier incident took place in the Bombay Presidency, which was generally free of trouble. At Vejalpore in the Bharuch District a 'mob of 2,000 Muslims' in the city raised the green flag on 12 May and attacked and looted the Parsi quarter, killing 100 men, women and children. The mob was eventually dispersed by the police, fifty of the rioters being killed.[39] The small Parsi community of the Bombay Presidency was one of the wealthiest on the west coast, made up of pragmatic and philanthropic people who had long worked with the British as ship-builders and merchants. They have been described as similar to the Jewish community, with a tradition of charitable works, and an astute business sense. It is not clear from the brief report whether the Muslims were targeting the Parsis because of their religion (Zoroastrianism was seen as heathen worship), or because they were known to be close to the British, or because their households contained money and valuables. Quite possibly all three factors seemed equally important, three birds with one stone, so to speak, but this particular incident does epitomise the difficulty of assigning one particular motive to one particular group of rebels. There were a number of complicated, historical reasons for revolt, some applicable to certain areas of northern India, like Awadh, some very localised, like the old grudges between different villages and people of different faiths. While it is true that the main focus of revolt was against the British, other disputes need to be considered too, not ignored. There is no doubt that against the comparatively small number of British civilians killed, many more Indians suffered from the hands of fellow Indians. 'The peasant armed' as Eric Stokes described him, was unfortunately often armed against his fellow countrymen.

The British assumed that everyone with a white face, or nearly white face, would support them during the Uprising. When an Emergency Act relating to the importation, manufacture and sale of arms and ammunition was passed late in 1857, a debate followed about who was allowed to carry guns. Was everyone to be stopped and searched, or would some people be exempted? It was decided that certain classes of 'European British subjects and the descendants of such subjects commonly known as East Indians, or Eurasian and European Foreigners' should be allowed to carry arms and would not need certificates of exemption because 'every person belonging to them must carry in his visage and outward appearance, reasonable proof of the qualifications which cause his exemption'.[40] But there were a handful of people who, although they met the criteria of trustworthiness outlined above, nevertheless took up arms against the British. While we have established the main motives that inspired the Indian rebels, how are we to deal with British and Anglo-Indian renegades?

'Mr [Felix] Rotton seems voluntarily to have remained with the Rebels until July last [1858], to be the father of rebels and to labour under the strongest presumption of disloyalty', reported the Chief Commissioner of Awadh's Secretary, Mr T. D. Forsyth, in October 1858. Felix Rotton, who had been born in Lucknow about 1795, was the son of Major Richard Rotton, an English mercenary, and an Indian woman. Richard Rotton had served in the Maratha army until its defeat by the British in 1803. His son Felix had been employed by successive nawabs of Awadh for twenty years or so, commanding part of their artillery, and reaching the rank of captain in 1856. He fathered about twenty-two children by several Indian women, and in fact Forsyth reported that 'his wives are as numerous nearly as his children'. The Rotton daughters were married to Muslims, and the boys served as native officers in the last nawab's army. Seven of the Rotton boys joined the Lucknow rebels and fought with them against the British. Three were killed during the Uprising: James, aged twenty-one; John, also twenty-one, and Joseph, seventeen years old. (For some reason all the boys' names began with the letter J – the other rebels were Jacob, thirty-two, another John, thirty, John Shakespear, twenty-eight, and Joshua, twenty-two.) The boys were 'illiterate and perfect natives in every sense of the word', reported the Secretary.

At the time of the Uprising Felix Rotton, who was believed to have become a Muslim, was about sixty-one years old, and hardly prime rebel material. He failed to join the British and Indians who barricaded themselves into the Residency at the end of June 1857 and he continued to live in the city during the siege. He claimed to have lost property valued at Rs 20,000 during this period. He did nothing to help the British, continued the indignant Secretary 'although the descendant of an European himself, all his sons capable of bearing arms were hostile to us, and he is answerable for the sons begot'. Curiously Felix Rotton is said to have joined the rebels only in April 1858, a month after Lucknow had been recaptured by the British and when Begam Hazrat Mahal and her son Birjis Qadr were fighting a rearguard action towards the Nepalese frontier. One wonders what the defiant Begam made of her latest recruit. Felix Rotton surrendered to the British in July 1858, and his case was subsequently investigated by the Chief Commissioner, S. A. Abbott. He concluded that there was no evidence of Rotton having taken an active part in fighting against the British:

> but some of his sons are supposed to be still in arms against us and Captain Rotton expresses his readiness to shoot them as they are and if he can find them. This is proof of his loyalty. In proof of his disloyalty we have his desertion of the City with the rebels on the re-occupation of the place. ... His character and conduct are much objectionable but he is an adventurer, an old man in a foreign country and in great distress.

The correspondence was forwarded to the Governor General by Forsyth with a recommendation that Felix Rotton should continue to receive a pension, but that it was to be reduced to Rs 20 (£2.00) a month.[41]

It was noted in the Secretary's report that some other 'renegade Christians who were living in Lucknow' had been seen in European costume during the siege, and supporting the rebels.[42] One had been a cavalry officer in the Nawab's army, a German called Schmidt, about twenty-five years old. Another was named as Captain Jacob Leblond, who had served the various Nawabs for forty-three years, having joined the army in 1813 under Nawab Saadat Ali Khan. Leblond was French, the longest serving European officer in the Awadh army, which was disbanded on the annexation of the state in 1856. It would not be surprising if this man, now in his sixties, who had served his Indian masters all his adult life, felt no sense of loyalty towards the new British government. A kind of arrogance by the British kept them from admitting that other European countries might not necessarily agree with their policy in India; in fact some, including France, were highly critical. To be European was not, as the Company had generously assumed, to be supportive of its actions.

Historians have combed the Company's records for details of other renegade Europeans who fought with the rebels against the British. Curiously, it was a different kind of arrogance that lent weight to some of the supposed sightings of Europeans on the 'wrong side'. Complacent Britons simply did not believe that the rebel soldiers could have fought so well and so bravely in many cases unless they were under the command of Europeans. Experience should have told them otherwise, but nevertheless, the attitude was pervasive, and not just in military matters, that anything of real value usually had a European hand behind it. The persistent rumours that Europeans were directing rebel gunfire during the siege of the Lucknow Residency, when the British were trying to get out, and the siege of Delhi, when the British were trying to get in, is largely based on this mistaken notion of racial superiority. A British officer, who was published anonymously in 1861 (and who was subsequently named as William Ireland), had served at Delhi, and he tried to counteract this idea, by stating that 'no-one who knew how much of the work in India was really done by natives, wondered at the practical skill they now showed'.[43]

Nevertheless, a small number of Europeans or Anglo-Indians have been identified who were either coerced into fighting with the rebels, or decided to join them in fighting the British. Drummer Jones is said to have persuaded ten native Christians to leave the Lucknow Residency during the siege, after possibly engaging in 'treasonable correspondence with the enemy'.[44] He and his companions were arrested near the Iron Bridge and his subsequent fate is not known. Another European in Lucknow, called John Roberts, who, like Felix Rotton, did not get into the Residency in time, claimed he had been forced into working with the rebels. Roberts had an Indian wife and a number of children, who he felt would be at risk if he did not hide himself away from them. He sought refuge with the *chakladar* (landholder) at Salone, who said he was unable to protect him unless Roberts identified himself with the chakladar's own men, who had rebelled. As proof of his support, Roberts helped to construct a gun carriage, but later claimed, when he surrendered to the British, that he did not take part in any treasonable activity.

Hearsay reports from Delhi spoke of a one-armed European called Slae who was wounded at the battle of Badli-ki-Serai north of Delhi on 19 June, and another European was said to have been cut down by British troops in the skirmish there. A further report identified the man as having belonged to the elite 60th Kings Royal Rifle Corps at Meerut. Shadowy Europeans were reportedly seen in Delhi during the siege, but the man who figures most prominently, and who is mentioned in both Indian and British reports, was Sergeant Major Robert Gordon. Gordon had been born in Scotland, the illegitimate son of an agricultural labourer. When Delhi was retaken by the British in September 1857, he was captured, dressed as a sepoy, after fleeing downriver with Bahadur Shah Zafar's party. Gordon was described as 'a tall, sturdy-looking man, with a naturally fair face, though extremely sun-burnt, and a fine, soldier-like figure'. According to his own account, which he gave while he was being held as a prisoner by the British, the Scotsman was called Abdulla Khan. Other reports have him as 'Sheikh Abdulla' or 'Abdulla Beg'. Gordon, who had arrived in India in 1840, enlisted in the Bengal Artillery and he was rapidly promoted, probably because he was literate, suggests the historian John Fraser, who has written the most extensive account of Gordon's strange story.[45] By 1852, Gordon had been appointed Sergeant Major of the 28th Bengal Native Infantry and he was stationed at Shahjahanpur when it mutinied on 31 May 1857.

Gordon claimed that he initially hid from the sepoys, but later that evening, came out of hiding and told them 'that if they wished to take my life that they might do so. I threw myself on their mercy … I had been five years in the Regiment and think the reasons of the Sepoys sparing me was that they were very fond of me.' By nightfall the town was being plundered by villagers, so the sepoys decided not only to protect Gordon, but to take him with them as they marched to Bareilly. After various adventures Gordon reached Delhi, still in the company of the sepoys, and he was then locked up in the main police station, with another Englishman John Powell, and three Anglo-Indian clerks who had somehow escaped the initial wave of killings and the subsequent massacre in the Red Fort. Gordon was not badly treated, and in fact got a small allowance of three pice a day for his food. Indian reports from Delhi, which are not consistent, speak of two European sergeants coming from Bareilly, who were employed by the rebels as 'military engineers' and who advised them on the fortifications at the Lahore and Kashmir Gates of the city. In one account Gordon was presented by the then Commander-in-Chief, General Bakht Khan, to the aged King himself. Gordon himself says nothing of this. He seemed to have no credible explanation of why he had fled with the sepoys towards Humayun's tomb, south of Delhi, where he was captured by, or surrendered himself, to Captain Hodson.

An enquiry was set up to establish whether Gordon was to be charged with allowing himself to be taken prisoner, or the capital charge of mutiny and rebellion. Unusually, at a time when men were being tried and hanged on the same day, Gordon's case dragged on for several months. Seemingly reliable evidence from three Muslim shop-keepers who said they had seen Gordon several times being escorted by armed sepoys to work on the guns during the siege was dismissed because it could not be proven. Doubts on whether Gordon was acting voluntarily or under coercion could not be resolved, and the matter was put up to the Governor General with the recommendation that the Sergeant Major should be discharged from the army as there were 'strong grounds for entertaining a decided suspicion against him although there is no actual proof that he joined the Mutineers voluntarily'. In the best tradition of British compromise, Gordon was embarked on the ship *Alfred* as a prisoner, released from arrest once the ship was under way, and discharged on his arrival in England in July 1859. He was given a small sum of 'marching money to see him on his way'. Unfortunately Gordon then marches out of history, no doubt glad to have escaped with his life, and certainly not prepared to argue his case further in writing, as a disgraced officer might have done. He has, however, reappeared recently in the Indian film *The Rising-Ballad of Mangal Pandey* (2005), where he is portrayed in a sympathetic way by the director Ketan Mehta.

As we have seen, Anglo-Indians were recruited into the Company's army as bandsmen and drummers. The Indian regiments marched to British tunes, and even after they had mutinied, the tunes were still played. When the rebellious Bareilly Brigade marched into Delhi, with Sergeant Major Gordon in tow, it was to the sound of 'Cheer, boys, cheer', played by the Christian bandsmen. The words of this rousing song were to prove all too true:

Tho' to the homes we never may return,
Ne'er press again our lov'd ones in our arms,
O'er our lone graves their faithful hearts will mourn,
Then cheer, boys, cheer! such death hath no alarms.

Unlike the conflicting and sometimes doubtful stories of European renegades, there are a number of well-attested accounts of Anglo-Indian musicians caught up in the revolt, who were subsequently tried by court-martial and sentenced to imprisonment with hard labour. These men, or boys in some cases, were the children of European fathers and Indian mothers, distinguishable by their English names and Christian religion. Their stories, as they emerged from the court-martial accounts, were pitiable. In some cases the bandsmen had been saved by the sepoys from murderous villagers and tribesmen. Remaining with the sepoys on their way to Delhi was the lesser of two evils.

Despair drove some men on. The wife and two children of drummer William Diddier of the 3rd Company of the 6th Bengal Native Infantry were murdered by Mewatis near Allahabad. Diddier escaped with his young son Edward and he was later reported to have joined the sepoys at Cawnpore in killing the Europeans. According to John Fitchett, one of a small group of drummers who converted to Islam while on the run, Diddier was told he should not have fired at the Europeans. He replied 'that his own family had been killed and he did not care'. He was last seen at Lucknow, with three other converts, fighting with the rebels.

Anglo-Indian bandsmen answered to the sergeant majors in their regiments, and about twenty bandsmen from the 28th Bengal Native Infantry had accompanied Sergeant Major Gordon on his flight from Delhi to Humayun's tomb, following the only figure in authority that remained to them. They were killed by a party of Irregular Horse, under the command of Major Hodson, who had gone down to the tomb to arrest the King of Delhi, Bahadur Shah Zafar and his family. There may have been another renegade there too, for a previously unknown letter, published in 2006 reported that 'A European sergeant of the 2nd Grenadiers has been assisting them [the rebels] in Delhi all these months, and was caught with the King's sons and hung. Too good a death for him.'[46]

At the start of the Uprising in May it was reported by Captain Henry Norman 'that a European woman was hung at Meerut, being implicated in the arrangements for the first outbreak'. She is known only by her nickname 'Mees [Missus] Dolly' and she was born of European parents in India. She had married a sergeant in the British, not the Company's Army, but had been widowed. To support herself she set up what sounds like a brothel in the Sadr Bazaar and she was arrested two weeks after the start of the Uprising on 10 May. The charge against her was assisting in the murder of two Eurasian girls but also for 'egging on the mutineers', according to the late historian P. J. O. Taylor, who unravelled her story.[47] We know nothing else about her. It was not the kind of story to be made public, with its awful combination of treachery, working-class behaviour and the hanging of a white woman by the British. But it shows that we should be wary of classifying those who took part in the great Uprising as either heroes or villains. There were many complex motives for revolt, and much heroic resistance to it, but neither the Indians, nor the British, had a monopoly on courage or violence.

Two

THE KOTAH RESIDENCY MURDERS

COMPARED TO the huge number of violent deaths during the Great Uprising, the murders of five men at the Kotah Residency was a small tragedy. They were killed on the afternoon of 15 October 1857 by rebellious soldiers of the Maharao of Kotah, Raja Shri Ram Singh II. Two of them were medical men, Mr Salder, a sub-assistant surgeon, who was killed in his sick-bed, and an Indian Christian doctor, Saviel Cantem, who worked in the city dispensary and was hacked down in front of his wife.

But it was the deaths of the three other men that led the East India Company to set up a commission to investigate and report on the conduct of the Maharao of Kotah 'in connection with the murder of Major Burton, Political Agent and members of his family by His Majesty's Troops'. There were several unusual features connected with the Burtons' deaths, not least the motive of revenge by the Maharao's agent, Lala Jai Dayal. Unlike the random, opportunistic killings of many Europeans during the Uprising, the Kotah Residency murders were premeditated and not kept as a particular secret either. There were a number of well-intentioned attempts to warn the Burton family against returning to Kotah, which were ignored. Relations between the Burton family and the Maharao seemed genuinely friendly, and the latter appeared to support the East India Company as it struggled to regain the initiative in the autumn of 1857. On hearing that Delhi had fallen to the British after a standoff of several months, the Maharao ordered a salute to be fired in celebration (although Burton may have asked him to give the order). The manner of the Burtons' deaths, in their own home, was particularly tragic. Their bodyguards in whom they placed great confidence simply stood to one side as spectators, while father and sons defended themselves for several hours in an upper room until their ammunition ran out.

The Maharao's actions, or lack of actions, are examined closely in this chapter, because he typifies the ambivalence with which many Indian rulers viewed the events of 1857 and 1858. While there were some, like Nana Sahib of Cawnpore, whose massacres of British men, women and children cannot be explained away, there were many others in authority, particularly landholders, who pondered on where their allegiance could most profitably be placed. If it was these men who had most to gain by dismantling British rule, it was these same people who had most to lose as the British regained control. Not untypically, it was the seizure of land by the East India Company to form the new, compliant state of Jhalawar, that was put forward as the reason for the Maharao's behaviour towards the Burtons in their hour of need. But a closer reading of events would seem to suggest a more personal motive, hidden for decades.

Like those of other princely states that made up the Rajputana Agency in the nineteenth century, the origins of the Kotah royal family are both ancient and intricate. The family derived from a junior branch of the ruling Hara Chauhan Rajputs of Bundi, and had strong connections with the Mughal emperors, through military service. The revenue-producing district (*jagir*) of Kotah was bestowed on a younger son of the Bundi royal family and its beginnings as a separate state from Bundi date from 1624.[1] Towards the end of the eighteenth century the royal family of Kotah appointed a nobleman, Zalim Singh Jhala, as *dewan* (chief minister), and *faujdar* (army superintendent). This astute and powerful man, described by Colonel James Tod as 'Machiavellian',[2] became the de facto ruler of the state. Certainly he was regarded as 'regent' by the East India Company. Zalim Singh Jhala negotiated financial settlements with Afghan and Maratha warlords at a time when the latter seemed on an irresistible rise to dominance in northern India. After the third and last Anglo-Maratha war of 1817, when the Maratha chief Daulat Rao Scindia agreed to end his interference in the Rajput states and the dreaded Pindaris were finally defeated, treaties were speedily drawn up between the Company and these states, including Kotah.

By the Kotah Treaty of 1817, it was agreed that the financial tribute which had formerly been paid to the Marathas would, in future, be paid to the Company. In addition, the Maharao was to provide the Company with troops, when necessary, and these troops, later to become the Kotah Contingent, were to be drilled in the European style and to wear the Company's red uniform and headgear. The Maharao was to pay for these troops at a cost of several lakhs a year. (This contingent force was separate from the state's own small army, which was called the *Raj Paltan*, the 'King's Battalion', and which was used on ceremonial occasions and for collecting land revenue.) There was nothing particularly unusual in these arrangements – the Company made it a point, in its initial treaties with rulers, that while it would protect them from outside aggressors, it was the rulers' responsibility to pay handsomely for this protection, and to supply their own trained troops to support the Company's army. Similar treaties had been agreed, for example, almost half a century earlier with the Nawabs of Awadh, who ended up paying enormous sums to keep standing battalions insisted on by the Company.

It was the Dewan and his envoys who conducted negotiations with the East India Company, not the Maharao, and although the Maharao signed the treaty in Delhi at the end of 1817, it had the Dewan's seal attached to it. In March of the following year the Dewan proposed a 'supplemental article' to the treaty by which the Company guaranteed that Zalim Singh Jhala's descendants would enjoy the same privileges and position 'in perpetuity' as the Dewan himself had done. This the Company unwisely agreed to, and having agreed, then found itself supporting the Dewan against the Maharao Kishore Singh (1819–28) when the latter tried to take back administrative control by force. 'This political ineptitude committed the British Government to the support of the nominal ruler [the Dewan] in one agreement and of the real ruler [the Maharao] in another.'[3] However obliging chief ministers were towards the Company, and they often had more flexibility to act, it was with their masters that the Company should have engaged, in a country iron-bound by protocol.

Why things had rapidly got to a state of open warfare, is partly explained by Zalim Singh Jhala's undoubted support for the Company. He had been among the first to offer help to the Marquess of Hastings and British troops, during the Company's final push against the Marathas and the Pindaris in 1817. But there was another reason too. Although the Dewan was at the apex of his political power, there were rivalries in his own family, among his sons. A jealous younger son persuaded the Maharao to make a stand against his father, the Dewan. Maharao Kishore Singh called on his subjects to join him in opposing the all-powerful Dewan and the Dewan's own army of eight battalions. Both sides called on the Company for help, for indeed, both parties were entitled to expect it. After a futile attempt at conciliation, the Company decided to support their ally, the Dewan and on 1 October 1821 the battle of Mangrol took place some forty miles north-east of the capital, Kotah.

The British Political Agent, Captain (later Colonel) James Tod, made a final appeal to the Maharao not to risk his life and those of his men, the Hara soldiers, and the Raj Paltan, but Kishore Singh refused. It was a matter of honour. Bizarrely, Tod is then said to have given the signal for battle to commence. The Maharao's state troops, the Raj Paltan, fighting bravely, might have overcome the Dewan's substantial army, if the British troops, under the command of Major Ridge, had not then advanced. The Maharao's small army retreated across a stream and halted, only to be charged by two squadrons of the Company's 4th Light Cavalry. Both officers leading the two squadrons, Lieutenant Clerk and Lieutenant Reade, were killed, and Major Ridge was seriously wounded. Inexplicably, in this curious battle, their troops had suddenly halted in their tracks and were not directly behind them at the charge. But the damage was done. The Maharao and his men fled to Nathdwara in the neighbouring state of Mewar, where they remained licking their wounds. There were really no victors in this little-known encounter. Zalim Singh Jhala's army, impressive though it seemed in numbers, might well have faced defeat without British intervention. The men of the 4th Light Cavalry, who had let their officers ride unsupported at the last moment to their deaths, were court-martialled and dismissed for cowardice, though it was said at the time that it was not cowardice that had stopped them, but their dislike for their commanding officer, Major Ridge. The Maharao had suffered a very public humiliation, not only by his own Dewan, but by the Dewan's supporter, the East India Company, as well as the death in action of his brother, Prithvi Singh. Was it here that the seeds were sown for the events of 1857 at the Kotah Residency?

By the end of 1821, matters had been patched up. The Dewan was instructed by the Company, which may have suffered a rare fit of shame, though more likely it was the commoner symptom of expediency, to issue a complete amnesty to the Maharao's troops. The Maharao himself was brought back to Kotah and welcomed into his own palace by the Dewan and Company officials. In an effort to make peace between the two factions some administrative functions were transferred from the Dewan to the Maharao, and a British representative, Major James Caulfield, was now stationed in the city as a kind of umpire. The death of the Dewan three years later, aged eighty-four, brought a temporary cease-fire in hostilities that would last for a generation.

On the death of Zalim Singh Jhala, his son Madhav Singh took over the post of Dewan, as agreed in the 'supplementary treaty' but on his death ten years later, tension between the two 'ruling families' of Kotah increased again. The Company, very anxious to avoid another pitched battle, for the days of settling disputes by force now seemed to have passed, decided to divide Kotah in two. The new state of Jhalawar, to the south, was created for the Dewan's family in 1838 out of hereditary jagirs and lands which Zalim Singh Jhala had clawed back from the Marathas. The remaining districts formed the now somewhat diminished state of Kotah, although relatively speaking, Kotah was still the 'senior' state, with 5,684 square miles of land, compared to the 810 that Jhalawar got. Maharao Ram Singh II (1828–66), who had succeeded his uncle, Kishore Singh, had agreed in a new treaty with the Company, to the creation of Jhalawar. The bitter pill had been sweetened by Company concessions. The annual tribute, paid once to the Marathas and since 1817 to the British, was reduced by Rs 80,000, and the subsidy for the Maharao's European-trained troops, the auxiliary force, was reduced from three lakhs a year to two. These troops were renamed the Kotah Contingent, and were to play an important part in the Uprising of 1857. The Maharao was allowed to keep his own state troops, the Raj Paltan.

Through the treaties of 1817, the Company had created the Rajputana Agency consisting of a number of states which for administrative purposes

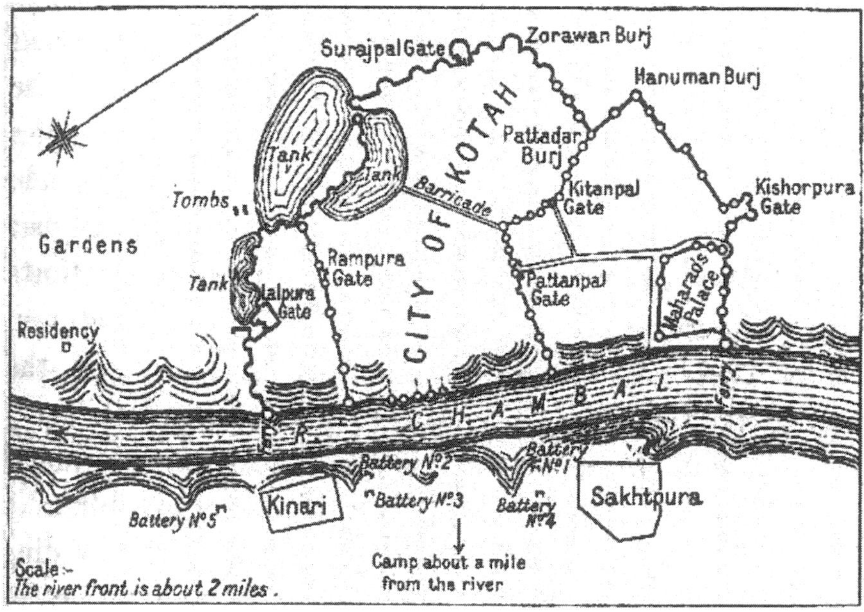

8. Old map of Kotah, showing the relative positions of the Residency, far left, the ravines, the river Chambal, the walled city and the Maharao's Palace. The smoke from the burning Residency could be seen from the Palace.

were grouped together. There were three residents – at Udaipur, Jaipur and Jodhpur – while the remaining groups, considered less important, entertained political agents. Jhalawar and Kotah states were paired together by the Company. Major James Caulfield, the Political Agent based in Kotah, reported to the Governor General's Agent stationed in the British cantonment at Mount Abu. It was during Major Caulfield's time that the British Residency (which strictly speaking should be called an Agency, since it housed the Agent), was built.

The city of Kotah lies in a plain 300 miles south-west of Delhi, on the river Chambal. It is very much Rajput country and to the west, within a hundred miles, is the hill fort of Chittorgarh, the epitome of Rajput chivalry. High stone walls surrounded the city on three sides, the Chambal forming a natural barrier on the fourth. The walls were crowned with tall bastions and there were six huge elephant-proof double gates which were closed every evening at sunset. Inside the walled city there were three distinct areas, Lalpura and Rampura, both on the river side, and the city proper, with the old palace-fort overlooking the Chambal. These three areas were divided by transverse walls, and could be sealed off from each other and held independently in a siege or attack, a feature that was to be exploited in 1857/58. The palace itself, in the south-west corner of the city, is a typical Rajput mix of stout crenellated walls topped by airy pavilions. It was frequently referred to as the fort. There is only one entrance, through the Hathipol, or elephant gate, decorated with two sculpted elephants, their raised trunks forming an arch.[4] Inside are a great number of rooms, corridors and separate chambers, decorated with glass and intricate murals. One of the largest wall paintings shows a religious festival being celebrated inside the palace itself. Crowds of men are lining up in the outer courtyard, waiting to be admitted into the Maharao's *diwan-i-khas*, the private chambers. Behind them are the royal elephants, fireworks on frames ready to be set alight, a caged tiger and sepoys of the Raj Paltan, adopting the Company's red uniform and black plumed shako, so we can date this painting from after the treaty of 1817. The men are standing to attention, their rifles over their shoulders, in case the festivities get out of hand. The mural shows the palace as an entire world, complete in itself, with gardens, small tanks and hundreds of rooms, all surrounded by high walls. Outside the walls black clouds swirl ominously about at the edge of the world, but inside the palace, all is light and movement.[5] One can read much or little into a painting like this, but the analogy of a closed society, closed first within the palace, then within the city walls, is strong.

Kotah is the old spelling of the city and the state. Today it is called Kota, but an older name is Harawati, from the Hara Chauhan Rajputs. The senior Company official stationed in the city was known both as the Political Agent for Harrowtee [Harawati] and for Kotah, just as his house is described both as a Residency and an Agency, which seems to imply a certain vagueness in British nomenclature and perhaps in British thinking about the area too. After the ill-conceived venture at Mangrol, the states that formed the Rajputana Agency were left pretty much to their own devices and resources by the East India Company. Feudal in structure, highly traditional, and ruled by long-established and generally well-respected dynasties, Rajputana saw few of the changes that the Company *raj* brought to other areas of India. A mutual tolerance arose between the Rajput states and the Company which depended on minimal interference by both parties. The Rajputana rulers, in their palace fortresses, were generally less enamoured of Europeans, European ideas and European artefacts than their contemporaries in other parts of India. Outside the cantonments a white face was still a rarity, and indeed remained so until well past the middle of the twentieth century. There were few opportunities for Europeans, whether Company men or free traders, to make money in Rajputana. Despite its striking scenery, noble forts, walled cities and *havelis* (courtyard houses), it did not attract the great Company painters of the late eighteenth century as Bengal, Awadh and the Presidency coastal cities did. There were very occasional encounters between the Rajput rulers and European mavericks, like Thomas Lonorgan, who visited Udaipur as the strong man in a travelling circus and ended up as Commander-in-Chief of the Maharana's Brigade, but in general the Europeans in Rajputana were Company officials, Company soldiers, and their wives and children.[6]

The British Residency stands outside the city wall, just over half a mile north of the nearest gate, on the bank overlooking the Chambal river. A pontoon bridge was set up for most of the year further upstream, but removed during the monsoon period when the river was in spate. A curious feature of the area is the number of ravines formed by inlets, which are deep enough to hide in during the dry season. The Residency has clearly been greatly altered since it was first built in 1830. Referred to as a bungalow in some accounts, it has always been a two-storeyed building, or at least a building with some upper rooms. Part of it was thatched, although the central portion of the roof is likely to have been flat, and the thatch may simply have provided cover over the verandahs. The handsome curved colonnade at ground floor level is very characteristic of European-style buildings of this period. The house stood in a walled compound, and there was an 'old garden' in the grounds, as well as a number of separate smaller houses belonging to members of the Residency staff, the dispenser, the office clerks and the servants. It had been the Burtons' family home for over ten years, and their seven children had grown up here. One of them, Francis Burton, referred to it almost affectionately as 'the old house'.

Charles Aeneas Burton was appointed Political Agent to the Kotah Court on 22 August 1845, shortly after his promotion to captain in the East India Company's army. He had been born at Dinapur, in Bihar, in 1812, into a military family, his father being a captain in the 8th Bengal Native Infantry. Charles was sent home to England for his education at Charterhouse, then in east London. Here he was taught, examined and passed for the Company's Military Service on 23 February 1828. He returned to India a year later, in February 1829, and was soon appointed to serve in his father's regiment as a junior officer. He may also have attended Fort William College in Calcutta to study an oriental language because he was certainly competent enough to act as an official interpreter later in his career.

Burton was granted leave, or furlough as it was called, with a sick certificate in May 1831, and he travelled back to England. Whatever complaint he was suffering from, it did not prevent him marrying in London on 1 March 1832.[7] There was an age difference of twelve years between him and his wife, Burton being just twenty years old at the time of his marriage, while his wife, Elizabeth Jane Bradley, was thirty-two. She was both a widow and his father's cousin. After Charles Burton's recovery from illness he returned to India in March 1833, with his wife, to take up a new appointment in the 40th Bengal Native Infantry. Eight children were born to the Burtons, in quick succession. The first child, born in November 1832, survived for only four months, but was followed by Charles William, born 1833; James Edmond, born 1834;

Cecil Morton and Arthur Robert, twin boys, born 1836; Francis Clarke, born 1838; Mary Elizabeth, born 1840; and Emily Jane, born 1842. All the surviving children appear to have been born in India, apart from Francis Clarke who was born in South Africa during a two-year period of leave taken by his parents. East India Company staff received half pay during their leave only if they went no further than the Cape. With a rapidly increasing family Charles Burton clearly did not want to forfeit two years pay by travelling beyond the Cape to England.

The Burtons were by no means unusual in producing a large family in a comparatively short period of time, but what is unusual is that apart from the first, unnamed, infant, they lost only one daughter during childhood. Anyone who has visited British cemeteries in the Indian subcontinent will have been moved by the rows of little graves, often recording several children from a single family who died with distressing frequency. The Burtons' eldest daughter, Mary Elizabeth, died at the age of fourteen, and she is buried in the Nayapura Cemetery, a ten-minute walk from her last home, the Kotah Residency. Her white marble tomb records simply that she was the beloved daughter of Captain and Mrs Burton, born 30 October 1840, died 25 May 1854. 'Her pious spirit passed from death into life.' Apart from this tragedy, the family prospered. Captain Burton was appointed to a number of interesting posts, including that of Assistant to the Agent and Commander of Delhi (1841–43), and Acting Interpreter and Quartermaster from 1843 to 1845 when he moved to Kotah and took up his post as Political Agent.[8] He was both a serving officer and an administrator, switching between the two roles as directed by his employer, the Company. Although the East India Company can be criticised for its hierarchical and nepotistic structure, it did show flexibility and imagination towards its employees, once they had bought their way in. As an officer, Burton saw fighting during the short Gwalior campaign of 1843, when British troops were involved in another dispute between a powerful minister and a ruler. The Gwalior forces were defeated by Company troops at Maharajpur after a fierce fight, in which six officers and fifty-four men were killed. Burton was awarded the prized Gwalior Star medal for his part in the battle, riding with the 1st Light Cavalry.[9] This was to be the last major disturbance in central India for fourteen years, until the outbreak of 1857.

Five cantonments, or military quarters, were set up throughout the Rajputana Agency by the East India Company after the treaties of 1817. They were established not only to assist the Rajput rulers in times of trouble (from internal or external sources), but to liaise with the residents and political agents, and to provide headquarters for various local military troops. Mount Abu, due west of Udaipur in the large State of Mewar, is a pleasant hill station, where, in 1857, Brigadier General George St Patrick Lawrence was stationed as Political Agent. Brigadier General Lawrence had replaced his brother, Sir Henry Lawrence, who had become Chief Commissioner of Awadh. (The third brother in this distinguished family was Sir John Lawrence, later to become Governor General.) Brigadier General Lawrence's job was to co-ordinate reports from the Rajputana residents and political agents and report direct to the Governor General in Calcutta. This was undoubtedly the best cantonment posting in Rajputana, being high enough above sea-level to escape the heat of the plains. Like other hill stations it was used as a sanatorium for invalid soldiers to recuperate from wounds and disease.

Erinpura cantonment, less favourably sited, lies some distance north, and was established in 1837 as the headquarters of the Jodhpur Legion, a corps raised by a homesick Irishman, Captain Downing, who named it after his place of birth. Nasirabad, the largest cantonment, which lies just south of Ajmer, was named after another Celt. It was established by Major General David Ochterlony, the one-time Resident of Delhi, at the end of the last Maratha war (1817–19). More popular with Indians than with his fellow countrymen, the name Nasirabad comes from his title 'Nasir-ud-daula' (Defender of the Empire) which was conferred on General Ochterlony by the Mughal Emperor, Shah Alam. Deoli cantonment is strategically placed halfway on the road from Nasirabad to Kotah, and it was here that the majority of the Kotah Contingent, about 3,000 men, were stationed in 1855. Neemuch cantonment, where the Burton family initially fled at the start of the Uprising, lies south-west of Kotah and about 150 miles south of Nasirabad. Although these five cantonments were called British cantonments, initially the majority of the soldiers stationed in them were Indian, led by British officers. It is said that there were no British soldiers in Rajputana in May 1857, apart from some invalids convalescing at Mount Abu.

When the news of the European murders at Meerut on 10 May 1857 arrived, signalling the beginning of the Great Uprising, Major Burton moved his family from the Kotah Residency to the supposed safety of the British cantonment at Neemuch, where they had a furnished house. Within a day of the revolt at Meerut, the Company had lost control of Delhi too. As a result, the Maharao's Kotah Contingent Force was ordered to Agra, to support the fearful British civilians there who had retreated into the Fort. Major Burton's immediate movements after settling his family in Neemuch are unclear, but shortly afterwards he travelled north to Deoli, the cantonment where the Kotah Contingent Force had been stationed before it was called urgently to Agra, leaving behind a small guard of 120 sepoys.

The first Uprising in the Rajputana Agency States came on 28 May when the sepoys mutinied at Nasirabad and began a spontaneous march towards Delhi in support of their King. A week later the same thing happened at Neemuch where the Burton family had taken refuge. Since the initial shock of the news from Meerut, rumours of trouble and a dread anticipation had spread through the European population as quickly as mutinous impulses had spread among the sepoys. Elizabeth Burton wrote a dramatic account of the events at the Neemuch cantonment in a letter which was somehow delivered to her brother in England. In the letter she spoke of the moment when

> reports of coming danger and mutiny among the three regiments here began to spread, fires at night took place, false alarms were constantly raised, the natives fled from the Bazaars, and a repetition of the horrors of Meerut and Delhi was hourly expected. We dared not go to bed at night, and our days were full of anticipated horrors.[10]

Major Burton, in the almost empty Deoli cantonment, was contacted both by his wife, and by the military authorities at Neemuch and asked for help. The Kotah Contingent Force was needed at Agra, and it could not be summoned back. Burton therefore put together a small army of about 1,500 men from the Bundi and Jhalawar Contingent Forces, who had not rebelled, and a number of the Raj Paltan troops, together with fifty-four men remaining from the Kotah Contingent who had been selected as his personal escort and had not accompanied their fellow soldiers to Agra. Together with a couple of guns, the officers and men set out on the ninety-odd mile march from Deoli to Neemuch, arriving there in three scorching days 'with a burning sun and hot winds blowing'.

But before Major Burton and his troops could reach the Neemuch cantonment, the sepoys rebelled. Elizabeth Burton claimed that her sons were given advance warning, and one wonders who it came from, since up to the last moment the troops had apparently remained loyal. 'We were on the point of sitting down to dinner, with merely a change of clothes in our hands,' she wrote, 'and went off to a place about ten miles distant, where our eldest son had the care of a small fort.' This was the town of Jawad, where Charles William, then aged twenty-three, was employed as the Assistant to the Superintendent of Neemuch. 'We arrived there late at night with a couple of very frightened friends, whom we protected on the way; and though we did sleep on the ground, we thought ourselves fortunate in having comparatively safe ground to lie down upon.' The group sheltered in Jawad Fort while the Burton boys took turn on guard. The next day they were joined by a large group of Britons – 'fifteen officers, six ladies and three young children' – all of whom had fled for their lives from Neemuch, where the cantonment was now being comprehensively looted. An hour later Major Burton arrived, having ridden ahead of his small army and the family were re-united. His wife continued with her story:

> Not many hours passed before the intelligence came that all the mutineers, with their guns, were on their way to attack Jawad; and as we well knew that the fort could not resist guns, we all, with our companions in misery, made a clear start to my husband's camp, sixteen miles off, which we reached jaded, terror stricken, and all very dirty.

The rebels, now growing bold, sent messengers into Major Burton's camp itself, and tried to turn his troops by offering Rs 1,000 for his head, and Rs 500 for each member of the Burton family, but his sepoys refused to be bought. Major Burton led the civilians and his soldiers back to Neemuch, which was now virtually empty because the rebellious regiments, 'the Neemuch Brigade', were on the march to Delhi, through Deoli and Agra. There were 'not more than half a dozen people left – ruin and desolation in every direction'. Both the civil station, where British families had their houses and bungalows, and the actual cantonment, with its barracks, parade ground and officers' bungalows, had been looted, then set on fire. The jail had been forced open and its prisoners released to join the rebels. The British treasury had been plundered.

> Our house, like all others [mourned Elizabeth Burton] is a ruin, a shell, without one article left us. Our beautiful books, either torn or burnt; our furniture broken up, chopped in pieces, or carried off; not a cup, plate or glass left; carpets torn up, carried away; not a single garment of any kind; our silver dishes gone; doors, windows, smashed; trinkets and curiosities, of which I had a goodly store, all taken away or destroyed – even the pictures and punkahs, and the chimney pulled down to see if anything had been hidden in it. We have nothing left. The shopkeepers have lost everything, so that we have not the means of buying common clothes. Our own servants assisted in the plunder, and they loaded four of our horses to carry away the most valuable part of our property. Luckily we had camels and horses with us on our flight, or these would also have been taken. ... We are not yet out of danger. It hangs over every white face in this portion of unhappy India.

Although the cantonment had been wrecked, Europeans here had not been marked out for murder as they had been in Meerut and Delhi.[11] Major Burton and his troops re-occupied the deserted cantonment and the rainy season of 1857 was spent in patching up the shattered buildings, as the grim news came in from Delhi and Agra.

The Kotah Contingent, sent to Agra to support the British, had mutinied there on 4 July. Like the other contingent forces in the Rajputana Agency States, its soldiers were not from Rajputana, as one might expect, but from other areas of India, and particularly from Bhojpur (in Bihar), and Awadh, where the majority of troops were recruited. If the sepoys had no particular loyalty to the desert cantonments where they were stationed, and which were geographically quite alien from their own villages, they did have a fellow feeling for other soldiers recruited from the same castes or areas. The majority of these men in Kotah were Muslims, another alienating factor in a largely Hindu state. On reaching Agra, the 700 men of the Kotah Contingent Force had been employed in collecting land revenue, burning the villages of those suspected to be on the rebels' side and hanging suspected mutineers.[12] But when the Contingent was ordered to march against the rebellious Neemuch

Brigade, who had destroyed their own cantonment and were now heading for Delhi, the loyalty of the Kotah sepoys shifted abruptly from their British officers to their fellow sepoys. A sergeant major was killed, and the sepoys fired at their officers. Only forty men from the Kotah Contingent remained aloof. The great majority joined the Neemuch Brigade, and other troops against the British at Sasia, near Agra, where they forced the British back into Agra Fort. Casualties were high on both sides. It is estimated that 500 sepoys died in the skirmish and 141 British soldiers were killed.

By the middle of July soldiers from the Neemuch Brigade had reached Delhi and the Kotah Contingent was marching north to join them. Troops from the Nasirabad cantonment were already installed in the city and were launching raids on the British who were encamped outside. Although rumours of the Uprising had been circulating as early as January 1857,[13] Bahadur Shah Zafar was taken as much by surprise as the British when the Meerut troops arrived in the Red Fort on 11 May. The suddenness of their action meant there had been no forward planning to provide food, shelter, ammunition or wages for the sepoys and there were now many more converging on Delhi. When large numbers of troops transfer their services from one ruler to another, the responsibility for feeding, clothing, housing, arming and paying them is also transferred. Although Bahadur Shah Zafar was boosted by his new supporters, men who had been trained to fight by the British, he was also short of money to pay them.

With the Kotah, Neemuch and Nasirabad Contingent forces now at Delhi, the Rajputana Agency states were left to their own resources. Luckily for the British, the states' rulers did not join in the general uprising. They maintained order in their own areas, with their own troops, and they supported Major Burton in the ransacked Neemuch cantonment until the end of July when he was relieved by Company troops from the Bombay Army, which had not mutinied.[14] With the fall of Delhi to British troops on 20 September 1857, there was a perception that the worst was over and that the tide had begun to turn. In fact this was not the case, because many of the sepoys who had fought at Delhi against the British were allowed to escape, and they now fanned out into the countryside, uncontained after months of being holed up inside the walled city.

The Kotah Maharao, in supporting the British through the revolt, had done rather well. In fact Major Burton had written to Brigadier General Lawrence, the Governor General's Agent, suggesting that, as a reward for his loyalty, part of the annual tribute from the Maharao to the Company could be written off. Burton had already presented the Maharao with a British 12-pounder gun from Neemuch as a token of appreciation for lending him part of the Kotah Contingent in June.[15] Brigadier General Lawrence approved neither of the hint on lowering the annual tribute, nor of the presentation of the gun, but he acknowledged that relations were good between the Maharao and the Political Agent, and that the former could expect 'considerable advantages' in future for his support of the latter.

News of the mutiny of the Kotah Contingent had reached Major Burton early in July while he was at Neemuch with his family. Although he had now been joined in the ransacked cantonment by officers of the Bombay Army, there was friction between the newcomers and the Political Agent. For years the Bengal Army, in which Burton served, had considered itself superior to the other two Presidency armies. Since the mutinies had broken out only among the Bengal troops, there was bound to be a certain smugness in the Bombay and Madras Armies. A spat between Burton and Captain Charles Showers, one of the newcomers, now in charge of the Neemuch station, was to have particularly unfortunate consequences. Not all the Kotah Contingent had been ordered to Agra, where they had rebelled. Some fifty-four men, as we have seen, had been kept back to act as escort to the Political Agent. These consisted of forty sepoys, two Indian officers (a jemadar and a daffadar) and twelve horsemen. Although Burton had hoped to leave Neemuch as soon as he had handed over to the Bombay officers, he now had reservations about this escort and he told Brigadier General Lawrence that 'intelligence having arrived of the mutiny of the Kotah Contingent, from which force my Escort is derived I was desirous of obtaining your instructions for the disposal of the latter previous to my return'.[16] Mutiny seemed like an underground fire, travelling rapidly along hidden channels and bursting into flame at unexpected places. The Maharao was also anxious that the escort should leave Neemuch, because he thought the men were trying to subvert his own troops, the Raj Paltan.

Both Brigadier General Lawrence and the Maharao approved of Burton's decision to send away his escort, and the men were ordered to march to Deoli cantonment. It was agreed that as replacements the same number of soldiers from the Raj Paltan would act as Burton's escort on his return to Kotah. But Captain Showers, who was described as an unpopular officer 'owing to the sternness of his character', seemed to take exception to this new arrangement, among other things, and said vehemently to Burton, 'You ought to leave Neemuch directly, and I shall send in a solemn protest against your remaining here'. Reporting the incident by letter to Brigadier General Lawrence, Burton wrote:

> considering the difference of rank, age and experience between us, and that so far from speaking in a suggestive manner, as represented to you, Captain Showers to me was dictatorial and loud, you will, I think admit I evinced forbearance and respect for the position he occupied by refraining from altercation.[17]

Something about Burton's Raj Paltan escort seemed particularly to annoy the Bombay officers – perhaps it harked back uncomfortably to the old days of men like Colonel James Tod, one of the first political agents, who some felt had grown too big for his post and was too closely identified with the Rajput rulers instead of the East India Company.[18] When, two days later, another officer, Captain Lloyd, suggested that the Raj Paltan escort should return to Kotah, Burton gave in and let them go. (In a curious little episode, Burton had wanted to distribute sweetmeats to the troops, which was the usual way of marking a particular event, but they declined to receive them.) In the same letter to Brigadier General Lawrence he reported, without comment, that 'I immediately prepared for my departure, ordering an Escort from Kotah, as the Officer Commanding declined to give me a guard'.

Burton was determined to return to Kotah as quickly as possible and he wrote that he had 'obtained after much difficulty some camels for part of the road'. He had already sent off his two sets of tents in advance, so they could be pitched for the first night's camp. In spite of incessant rain over the past eleven days, he was on the point of starting on 9 August, when a note was handed to him by the Kotah *vakeel*, Nand Kishore. In it, the Maharao told Burton he was 'most anxious to see him again after so long an absence but that he could not have entire confidence in the troops after seeing the unsettled state of the times'. This delicately-worded diplomatic letter brought an immediate and equally diplomatic response from Burton. He agreed to postpone his journey for thirty days

> and when the Kotah Durbar feels confidence enough to inform me, that I may come, I shall go there immediately. I trust the kindness of the Durbar to take care of my goods with those belonging to the Agency and office, as well as all the Agency servants, as my Kotah Contingent Escort has gone last to Deoli.

There was little that Burton could do. He knew that if he returned to Kotah and the troops were to rise against him then

> the blame would devolve upon me for disregarding the Maharao's recommendation and precipitating a Mutiny, whereas in a few days events might assume a more auspicious aspect, and the apprehension of disaffection subside. In assenting to the course so advised by His Highness he alone is responsible for the behaviour of his troops. This unforeseen circumstance is embarrassing to me; but I trust as there is no immediate necessity for my presence in Harrowtee [Kotah] the brief delay as involved will be immaterial.

Privately Burton seemed annoyed, as well as embarrassed by the continued delays. He had expected to leave Neemuch shortly after the Bombay troops had arrived on 18 July. Then he had to wait for Brigadier General Lawrence's permission to transfer his untrustworthy Kotah Contingent escort to Deoli, followed by the argument with Captain Showers, and even after he had sent his replacement Raj Paltan escort back to Kotah, and ordered a third one, it had not been sent. Finally, when he had decided to leave anyway, in spite of the monsoon rains, without an escort, gathering camels for the journey himself, he had been stopped again, on the very point of departure. There is a sense of Burton's frustration and impatience, not only in his last long letter to Brigadier General Lawrence, but in his behaviour too, when he did finally return to Kotah.

The 'few days' anticipated delay of early August stretched into five weeks. During that period, there were two further mutinous attempts at Neemuch and Nasirabad, both of which were put down. The situation in western India was confused and dangerous. There were sepoy mutinies near Mount Abu, in which some European invalid soldiers had been attacked. Then the Jodhpur Legion, quartered in the Erinpura cantonment, had mutinied, the fourth of the five Rajputana cantonments to erupt. Across the border, only twenty-four miles from Neemuch, Feroze Shah, a relative of the King of Delhi, was placed on the *masnad* (throne) at Mandsaur.

Nevertheless, in spite of these new disturbances Major Burton gave Nand Kishore, the vakeel, permission to return to Kotah to assess the situation and to find out if some of the Maharao's troops had indeed 'imbibed a mutinuous spirit' as had been reported. Nand Kishore wrote frankly to Burton that the Narayan Paltan and part of the Bhowani Paltan 'are certainly disaffected towards Europeans, but the Rajah [*sic*] is in hopes of soon being able to pacify the uncontented'. Until then he requested Major Burton to remain at Neemuch. Finally, on 15 September Nand Kishore arrived back in Neemuch with a *kharita* (a formal invitation) in which the Maharao gave the all clear: 'The [Political] Agent may now visit Kotah with impunity, for I have removed the mutinous soldiers, for here there is no fear of their causing a disturbance.'[19]

Two men in particular had been causing the Maharao trouble, and he suspected that they were tampering with his troops, and whispering thoughts of rebellion into their ears. One was Lala Jai Dayal, a man well known to Major Burton, because he had been the vakeel at the Kotah Residency until he was dismissed for 'being addicted to liquor and other debaucheries'. A vakeel's position in the mid-nineteenth century was somewhere between a lawyer and a clerk, the best description being 'an authorised representative', someone literate who could act on his own initiative, as well as carrying messages for his master. Lala Jai Dayal was employed and paid by the Maharao, to serve the Political Agent in the Residency, but as his title *lala* implies, he was also a man of substance and importance. After leaving the Residency post in disgrace, he continued to receive a token wage from the Maharao of a daily rupee, though he did no work for him. The second man, Mehrab Khan, was a *risaldar* (a company commander) in the Raj Paltan, and was described as 'a man of character and decision'. The Maharao ordered Lala Jai Dayal out of Kotah and into the 'District' by giving him a post at Shergarh, seventy miles or so to the south, far enough to be out of trouble. Mehrab Khan and ten *sowars* (cavalrymen) were sent to Etawa, some distance north-east of Kotah.[20] The mutinous troops, whom the two men were supposed to have encouraged, were also sent out of the city on duty. If Lala Jai Dayal and Mehrab Khan had followed the Maharao's orders and left Kotah, the Burtons might have been spared. But both men felt confident enough to disobey the ruler. Lala Jai Dayal 'went some seven *koss* [about fourteen miles] into the District. Mehrab Khan started also but when the troops objected to go into the District, and in the meantime, the Agent was on his way from Neemuch hither, they returned to Kotah.'[21] It seems clear from what happened later, that the Maharao knew the two men had returned, and was embarrassed that they had disobeyed his orders. Having assured the Political Agent that it was safe for him to return to Kotah, he did not now want to admit that the open defiance of the vakeel and the risaldar had made it much *less* safe.

Major Burton and his sons Arthur Robert (one of the twins), aged twenty-one, and Francis Clarke, aged nineteen, finally set out from Neemuch on 5 October. News of the fall of Delhi to the British on 20 September had reached the cantonment and there was a feeling that with the capture of the King of Delhi and the murder of his sons, the focus of the revolt had been removed. A few days before the long-delayed departure, Nand Kishore had come to Mrs Elizabeth Burton with an encouraging message:

> the Vakeel in making his salaam to me said 'the Maharao entreats you and the young lady and the young gentlemen to return for there is no danger at Kotah and the chief wishes to see you all back again for there is no danger there' and upon this my husband turned round and said 'you hear what this Vakeel says – the road is perfectly safe, so is Kotah and even if it were not, no harm would happen for the Maharao is too fond of all of us to allow anyone to injure me or mine, besides I have no enemy and what then can there be to fear?'

The *munshi* (tutor) Niaz Ali, also 'urged a return to Kotah at that time, both men saying there is no danger'.[22]

At Singoli, about thirty-five miles from Kotah, where the Burton men camped during the week-long journey, Major Burton wrote his last long letter to his wife. In it he said he was sorry that she and the remaining four children had stayed behind at Neemuch. Nand Kishore, he told her,

> the Kotah Vakeel, urges me to expedite my steps to Kotah as the Maharao is most anxious I should be present at the celebration of his Birth day, when there will be a Review of his Troops and he wants the Boys and myself to be there but our people are so tired with the double marches we have made and the heaviness of the roads, that they cannot manage it. ... The Kotah Vakeel is so sorry you did not come and is so certain that you could have done so with all safety – as there is no chance of any disturbance there, that I feel sorry we followed the advice of friends and did not all come together.[23]

The Burtons arrived in Kotah on the morning of 12 October, but not without one, last, annoying delay. Nand Kishore, having urged them to hurry on to Kotah, suddenly went into reverse and tried to prevent them entering the city. If we take the vakeel's behaviour at face value, then it is clear that he had been brought news very recently which he was not going to share with the Political Agent. Francis Burton, writing from the Residency on the afternoon of the 12 October told his mother, in his last letter, what had happened.

> Here we are you see, once more settled in the old house, but it was with the greatest difficulty we were allowed to enter Kotah for you must know that when we arrived at Khonbeepore, the Kotah Vakeel came to see Papa, and begged of him to stop at Nanta for a few days, as the Maharao wished him to stop there.[24] Papa asked him his reason for doing so, and after a great deal of talking he replied the troops could not be depended on, and if they could, he was afraid, if when any fugitive Mutineers came through, they might join them. I told Papa that it was all humbug to keep him away, and I also told him the circumstance of their doing so. Papa told the Vakeel it was great trouble for him to remain outside.
>
> Well, the Vakeel said, he would go over and consult the chief, but still advising us to go to Nanta, till he could join us. In the morning, when we arrived at Nanta, I told Papa he'd better send the things off to Kotah, and leave ourselves in the evening, he took my advice and immediately dispatched Fyze Khan to get the boats etc. ready, shortly afterwards the Vakeel came and said 'Then you're determined to go on, are you?' for he had seen our things going off. 'Yes', said Papa, 'but if you can give me any reason for not going on, I'll not go on, but go my circuit to Boondee.' This seemed to have frightened him for he spoke not again. The chief [the Maharao] comes to see us this evening, and we will pay him the compliment tomorrow. The inhabitants of Cantonments are beginning to come back now and we are beginning to turn out all notorious characters.[25]

On his arrival at the Residency, Major Burton inspected the compound, and ordered the sepoys of the Raj Paltan, who were on duty, to be relieved by the 'Bairagi Guard', and about thirty-five Sikh horsemen who had travelled from Neemuch with the family. Burton wrote a short note to his wife, reassuring her that 'all is quiet here but I use every precaution, and have about 150 select men near the house, Sikhs, Dadoopunthees [*dadupanthi*], Rajpoot, 4 sentries round the house by night and two by day, and I never stir without the revolver.' 'About 9 o'clock a salute of some 130 guns were fired in honour of Delhi.' The salute was received with anger by the townspeople, who believed that the news of the fall of Delhi was a false rumour put about by the British. Burton's choice of Residency guards to replace the dismissed Raj Paltan sepoys seems a curious one. The *bairagi* were a sect of Hindu faqirs, known for their asceticism, who roamed the country. The *dadupanthi* were followers of the sixteenth-century mystic of Rajputana, Dadu by name. Both groups had been formed into ad hoc guards who hired themselves out when soldiers were in short supply, and their main attraction for the Burtons was that they were Hindus and not Muslims. Arthur Burton makes this clear in a private letter, written the day before he was killed:

> We have got 20 sowars [cavalrymen] in that old [Residency] garden, and we also have 100 sepoys in the old lines, there is not a single Mussulman amongst them, a guard is placed at each side of the house, and at night, there is one at each corner, so you see, we are well cared for. The Maharao paid us a visit yesterday but said nothing about the Mutiny, except that he was glad to hear that Delhi had fallen.[26]

The Maharao's complimentary visit was returned on the morning of 14 October. Burton and his two sons left for the city palace riding on two elephants, with an escort of Sikhs and Bairagis. As he left the Residency compound, the munshi, Niaz Ali noted that a faqir 'was ordered into confinement by Major Burton for some conduct or other'. Only three people were present at the meeting in the palace, the Maharao, the Political Agent, and the Maharao's vakeel, Nand Kishore, who had tried unsuccessfully to persuade Burton not to enter the city. During the meeting, according to the Maharao, the problem of the mutinous Raj Paltan troops was discussed and Burton advised him to punish the ringleaders and dismiss others who were disaffected. Whether Burton suggested that the four principal officers should be hanged, as one rumour had it, is not known. What seems clear however, is that Nand Kishore went straight out after the meeting to tell Ratan Lal, the chief minister, with whom he was on 'intimate terms', and that Ratan Lal, who lived in the cantonment, told the troops.

According to a Residency chaprassi, Natoo, five minutes after the Burtons left the palace, a belated attempt was made to warn the Maharao that the Political Agent was in danger of his life. Ujjul Deen Khan,

> the adjutant of the Bhowani Paltan (who subsequently joined the rebels), said to the Maharao 'Sir, you had better not allow the Gentlemen to return to the Residency, for the Troops have thrown off all control, and may attack them on the road, or during the night.' The Maharao merely observed 'Well, the Vakeel can tell him tomorrow.'[27]

Ujjul Deen Khan also told Nand Kishore that an attack was planned by the troops as the Burtons returned to the Residency The vakeel, who had already gossiped about the morning meeting at the palace, now seemed to realise the seriousness of what was intended. He told Ujjul Deen Khan to go immediately and keep his Bhowani troops in order, because he, Nand Kishore, was responsible for the Burtons' safe keeping. It is clear that by the afternoon of 14 October at least three people knew that an attack on the Burtons was imminent – the Maharao, the vakeel Nand Kishore and the adjutant of the Bhowani Paltan. One of them told the doorkeepers at the Lalpura Gate to close the city gate early, so Lala Jai Dayal and Mehrab Khan, who had planned to kill the Burtons near the gardens outside this gate, found it shut and were unable to get through to join their comrades. The murders were postponed until the following day.

There are several eye-witness accounts of the events of 15 October 1857, which were submitted to the investigating Commission the following April. That of Mangal Singh, the *jemadar* (officer) in charge of the Kotah Agency, was written eighteen days after the murders, seemingly at the request of the remaining Burton family in Neemuch.

> On the morning of the 15th Major Burton with his two sons, went out shooting, they were in a Buggy – they got down and after going about in ravines for a short time, returned. Major Burton called over at Dr Salder's to see him, as he was laid up with Guinea worms. His sons came on to the Bungalow. He also came back a little while after and gave me orders to get ready 100 camels to be dispatched to Agra, with an Agency Peon. I accordingly went to the Baoree (about ¼ mile) where the camels were collected. About 11.00 am I heard a great noise, and observed that a large party of men were coming towards the Agency, crying 'Deen' 'Deen'. About 3 Pultans with 6 guns and a great number of Horsemen surrounded the House.
>
> I immediately ran to the Bungalow, and on reaching the compound, saw the Bungalow on fire, and guns firing. Being afraid to proceed closer, as I heard many say, that they would kill me – I concealed myself in a deep ravine near the Agency, from where I heard a constant firing going on, and it continued from 11 a.m. till 6 p.m. The rebels having murdered Major Burton, his two sons, Drs Salder and Saviel Cantem and destroying the Houses returned to their lines. No assistance whatever was rendered from Kotah, all this time. I heard that the city gates were closed from the hour the disturbance occurred, also the ghauts and all other passes were secured by the rebels.[28]

Niaz Ali, the munshi, who had told Mrs Burton at Neemuch that there was 'no danger' in returning to Kotah, was working in the Residency. At noon on 15 October he reported that:

> the troops of the Raj [Paltan], with a rabble, came running down to the Residency, the cavalry and guns approached from the eastern side, and the Infantry approached from the south side. On their arrival the Infantry fell on the outhouses, inhabited by the Office people and servants, while the Cavalry surrounded the Residency and set fire to it. They tried to kill me but I made my escape with others into a *nullah* [ditch]. I saw the firing going on at 5.00 pm the fire of the house was lit, some of the Troops went on the roof, and brought down the bodies of Major Burton and his sons, I heard from some of the mutineers that Mr Burton was alive when he was brought down from the top of the house, and that his head was cut off and tied up on a gun.

Niaz Ali identified the troops at the Residency as 'the Narayan Paltan, the Bhowani Paltan, two or three of the Goor Dun [Gordhan] Paltan, the Pargahs of Mehrab Khan, Nasir Khan and Ghulam Mahomed, with 20 or 30 swivel guns on camels, and four field guns, two drawn by horses and two by bullocks'.[29] The majority of the men who conspired to kill the Burtons were military men, including subedars and jemadars, but one civilian was identified, the portrait painter Moonavur Hossain.

A Kotah cloth merchant, Bhogi Lal, quite unaware of trouble, set out on the morning of 15 October to do business.

> I went to the Residency to sell cloth on the day Major Burton was murdered [he told the Commission]. When I saw the rebels surrounding the house I ran off to the Lall poora gate down the ravines. When I reached the gate I found it open and Mussulman guards on it. They made some demur about my entrance, but soldiers were coming out, they shortly afterwards closed the gate.

These are accounts by Indian eyewitnesses of the murders, which were presented to the Commission. There are more detailed accounts which were gathered by members of the Burton family questioning the Residency servants who had survived the attack. One of these summarises the events:

> The first intimation that trouble was afoot was brought by two Sikh horsemen of the guard … when they galloped up to the Agency Bungalow and apprised the Chobdar [the ceremonial mace-bearer] on duty that the Maharao's troops had mutinied and were advancing towards the Agency. The chobdar called to Major Burton, who appeared from a bathroom clad only in a towel: he immediately ordered the chobdar to fetch the oars for the boat that was drawn up on the river bank immediately below the Agency Bungalow. Major Burton then went to consult with his two sons who were in a neighboring room; they suggested the chobdar should bring their horses rather than the oars of the boat – and so the initial order was countermanded and their fate was sealed. Before the horses could be brought, the mutineers, led by Mehrab Khan, had over-run the stables and approached the Agency Bungalow. Major Burton and his two sons retired to the upper floor, but not before one intruder had been wounded by a gunshot from the Burtons. For some hours the siege continued and had it not been for the timidity of the mutineers would have been over within minutes. Several guns were brought to bear on the Agency Bungalow, directed by the revengeful Jeydial until at last the building was set on fire. Ladders were brought and several Sepoys ascended, and with their *tulwars* [swords] the Burtons were depatched.[30]

A slightly different account was published in a letter to *The Times* on 19 December 1857, written by Charles William Burton on 6 November. This is a more carefully edited version, for public consumption, which has lost the immediacy of the Indian witnesses' stories. According to the writer, it was the Political Agent himself who first noticed the horsemen approaching and 'believed the number of people he saw advancing merely to be some of the chief subordinates coming to pay him the usual visit of ceremony and respect'. If indeed Major Burton did think for a moment that the three armed platoons were on a friendly visit, he was quickly disabused of this idea. All the Residency servants fled, except one, a private camel-driver called Komji, who may have been summoned by Burton to discuss the proposed journey of the camels to Agra. Father and sons, accompanied by Komji, ran to a small room at the top of the house, snatching up the few weapons within easy reach. It was the younger son, Francis Clarke, who wounded one of the intruders in the thigh. The contents of the Residency were looted, and from their roof-top room, the Burtons could see their possessions disappearing through the compound gates. What they couldn't see, and looked for in vain, was any sign of a relief force coming to their rescue. Their own sentries and the Hindu guards, the dadupanthis and the bairagis, had simply melted away. The Sikh guard, mounted on horses, with matchlocks and other arms, had given no warning of the attack.

Lighted sticks were thrown up onto the thatched roofs of the verandahs, which caught fire and guns began battering the upper floor of the Agency. According to Komji's report,

> Major Burton wanted to parley with the mutineers in the hope that they would be contented if he gave himself up, and might permit his boys to escape; but his children would not allow of such a sacrifice for their sakes, and like brave men and good Christians, they all knelt down and uttered their last prayer to that God who will surely avenge their cause.[31]

A lull in the firing gave them hope that the worst was over, and the camel-driver was sent downstairs to talk to the Sikh soldiers who were supposed to be protecting the Agent 'and of whom, at the time, there were no less than 140, to beg of them to loosen the boat, that an escape might be attempted across the river. They said "We have had no orders."'

Komji's own statement, made to the Commission, added that when he asked the Sikh guards to assist the Agent, they told him 'it was madness to attempt it, and they could not give it'. Bishwa, one of the *chaprassis* (messengers) working at the Residency, also reported that the Sikhs said they thought the attack was being carried out on the Maharao's orders, otherwise they would have dispersed 'this rabble – but [we] cannot act against our Master'. Is it possible that the Sikh guard, seeing the Raj Paltan attacking the Residency and its English inhabitants, genuinely thought the Paltan had been ordered to do so by the Maharao, who had suddenly joined the rebels? A more rational explanation is that in the confusion of that autumn morning, when old loyalties were being overturned, and new masters seizing power, the Sikhs were hedging their bets. If they remained neutral, then they could not be accused of supporting either the Englishmen, or the men who had come to kill them, whichever side ultimately won.

Seeing that the guard was not going to act, a signal for the final assault was given. 'At this moment, a shot from a pistol was fired. Scaling ladders had been obtained, the murderers ascended the walls, and the father and his sons were at one fell stroke destroyed.' Nizamat Khan was named as the man who actually killed them. The Burtons had held out for five long hours, waiting for help that didn't come, and finally running out of ammunition. Had they been able to escape from the building, they would have found the city gates closed and the boats on the Chambal commandeered by the troops to prevent an escape by river and to cut off the Residency from any possible assistance.

The murder of Dr Saviel Cantem, earlier that day, was described by his widow, Louisa Cantem. About midday, she had been sitting, with her husband and children, in the house of a 'Kuranee' or Anglo-Indian clerk, in the Residency compound.

> I saw some sowars coming past the house and the Chowkedar [the watchman] said shut or pull the doors and windows, the Residency is surrounded by troops. Four Chupprassees and a 'Naga' Sepoy were in the Verandah of the Residency who immediately ran off when the sowars came. The sowars then set fire to the Residency. My husband then ran out of the 'Kurannees' house towards the Residency and was murdered on the road. Mehrab Khan Risaldar, cut him down with a sword. I saw this done myself.[32]

The news that the Raj Paltan had 'broken' was quickly brought to the Maharao in the city palace, but no one knew exactly what the Paltan was doing until the sound of gunfire was heard and smoke was seen in the distance, rising from the direction of the Residency. A number of men who were present in the palace on that afternoon later described the confusion there and the lack of leadership. The Maharao's immediate response was to go to the Residency and rescue the Political Agent. He ordered his Adjutant, Nabi Shah Khan, the orderly officer-in-waiting, to get his company ready, but the officer 'declined to do this, saying the Soldiers were no longer under his control, and that if His Highness attempted to go, there would be a disturbance'. He, the Adjutant, 'would not let him go'.

The Maharao, in his own statement, said 'all the guards in the Fort, and in personal attendance on me were Mussulmen [Muslim], and if they turned against me, it was perfectly impossible for me to proceed with a single attendant'. Instead he sent one of his men, Devi Lal, the chief military officer, accompanied by Radha Kishen 'to endeavour to parley with the Mutineers. He reported next day that all his efforts had been in vain, the army would pay no attention to him. Devi Lal was afterwards blown away, amongst others, from a gun by the rebels.'

But Mangal Singh, the jemadar, who hid himself in a ravine while the

Agency bungalow was burning and his employer fighting for his life, dismissed the Maharao's plea of helplessness.

> Why the Maharao Sahib did not proceed to the rescue of the gentlemen is to me a mystery. I have been some 24 years in the employ of Kotha [Kotah]. If the Maharao Sahib had put himself at the head of even 200 of his immediate retainers (and a considerably larger number would have followed him) and proceeded to the Agency, no doubt, but that the very fact of his so doing would at least have saved the lives of the Political Agent, and his two sons; and of this I entertain not the least doubt.

The jemadar also reported the melancholy end of the Burtons.

> The second day I heard that Major Burton's head was taken away by the rebels, which they fastened to their standard – the bodies of his two sons and others were dragged out, and left on the plain. On the night of the 16th I heard that the dead bodies of the Agent, his two sons, and the two Doctors were at first buried by order of the Maharao, but they were again taken out the same night, about 12 o'clock wrapped up in *dooshallas* [large shawls] put in boxes, and interred a second time. Jye Dial [Jai Dayal], formerly Agency vakeel, moved his family into the lines from the city and is enlisting men – about three days I remained concealed in fields and finding myself unsafe in Kotah, made my escape to … Boondee [Bundi].'

It was now clear that once again, there were two opposing forces wrestling for control of Kotah. This time it was not the Maharao Kishore Singh and his minister Zalim Singh Jhala, but the Maharao's nephew, Ram Singh II, who was fighting an even more dangerous enemy – Lala Jai Dayal, who had turned the ruler's own troops, the Raj Paltan, and was now the de facto ruler. Three days after the murder of the Burtons, Jai Dayal came to the palace asking for an increase in pay for the troops. Although it was his companion in arms, Mehrab Khan, who as risaldar had the military experience, Jai Dayal was apparently appointed Commander of the Raj Paltan by the troops themselves. The Maharao refused the request for a pay rise, although he agreed that the 'usual deductions' should not be made.[33] But Jai Dayal and his troops had the upper hand.

> They prevented my usual civil officers from attending the Durbar that day [complained the Maharao]. I reproached them for their conduct, they replied that they were ready to kill and to die. I was obliged to agree to certain terms dictated by the rebels, and to give Jeydial a paper to state [that] all that had occurred, had been done, with my consent. I had no power to resist them, as all the guns, ammunition, etc. was in their hands.

The Maharao now became a prisoner in his own palace-fort, another victim of the Uprising.

The immediate objective of the rebels, the removal of the British Agent, had been achieved. This was the initial focus of the Kotah revolt, a single, discrete target. In the early days of revolt, the murders of Europeans had been followed by sepoy marches on Delhi. But the symbolic leader of the Uprising, Bahadur Shah Zafar was now a prisoner of the British and Delhi had been retaken. With a feeling of anti-climax, and a lack of clear direction, the Kotah rebels turned on the city. Henry Chriskote, fleeing from Kotah, reported that 'the whole city is in the hands of the mutinuous soldiers', headed by Lala Jai Dayal, Mehrab Khan Risaldar and Agbudin Khan, Adjutant, and 'about 5,000 insurgents in the city, they do what they like and take what they like'. The Maharao was shut up in the city palace with 400 Rajputs and was helpless. Muslim gunners were posted at the fort by the rebel leaders. 'The Mutineers are enlisting all the recruits they can get, even boys of 12 or 14 years old. They say they intend to fight when the English come to attack them.'[34] With the fall of Delhi, and its forced evacuation by the British, an unknown number of soldiers and refugees made for Kotah, to swell the rebel forces and to bring fearful tales into the city.

Louisa Cantem, who had sheltered for a week in a nearby village after her husband's murder, returned to Kotah, and she also reported looting in the city and the disturbed conditions there. The troops, now fat with plunder, were anxious to leave, and return to their villages with their loot, which to many had seemed the main purpose of the exercise. Jai Dayal tried to persuade them to stay by lying about rebel successes against the British. He told them 'Mandesone [Mandsaur] was still in Mahratta hands, also that Agra and the whole of the country in that direction was in the hands of the King of Dehlie and that the Fort of Agra had been taken from the Firingees [the foreigners]'. 'The Lala,' said Mrs Cantem 'gets information from every direction and has his sowars patrolling about in all directions, they go in bands of fifty.' 'There were many fugitives from Delhi at Kotah, also from Indore who boast of the number of Sahibs and ladies and children they have killed. Some of the Budmashes [rogues] wished to murder me but others prevented them.' Her statement reads like that of a demented woman, which is not surprising given the shock of seeing her husband killed in front of her. When she returned to Kotah she survived 'by begging and selling the few Pots and Pans which remained in my house. Chota Lall (a Banker) was very kind to me and sent me some gram [lentils] and clothes for my children.' She also received one *ashrafi* (a coin worth about 16 rupees) from Brigadier General Lawrence, but when asked if she had anything further to support herself, answered simply 'No, nothing'.[35]

The Maharao remained a prisoner in Kotah for four months, until the end of March 1858 when Major General H. G. Roberts of the Bombay Army arrived with the 1st Brigade to release him. Roberts set up camp on the left bank of the Chambal, facing 6,000 Indian troops led by Jai Dayal.

The peculiar feature of the city, divided into three sections by internal walls, meant that during the winter, the Maharao and troops remaining loyal to him, had been able to fight their way out of the palace and occupy two-thirds of the city. He had been aided in this by Rajput troops sent from the neighbouring state of Karauli who had enabled the Maharao to hold his own until the British rescue, and by concentrating the rebels in only one part of Kotah, had made the British assault 'comparatively so easy'. General Roberts reported that he sent 200 men under Lieutenant Colonel Heatly of HM 83rd 'into the portion of the town held by the Maharao, who, since my arrival had on two successive mornings been assaulted by the rebels, and an attempt made by them to carry the place by escalade'. The fortified city was captured by storming it on 30 March. 'Instead of attacking directly the centre of the city [we] pushed along the ramparts, thus taking in reverse the whole of the barricades and guns placed in position to sweep the main approaches.'[36]

In the aftermath, Lala Jai Dayal and Mehrab Khan escaped with some of their troops, and disappeared for the next two years. The Maharao, thus unable to revenge himself on the ringleaders, told the Commission of Inquiry that 'I had no opportunity of visiting with punishment any of the rebels outside. When I got the chance, I blew away from a gun Nabi Shah Khan, the Adjutant, on orderly duty and have now in prison eighty of the same guard, who will shortly be executed.' Nand Kishore, the vakeel, whose evidence to the Commission would have been interesting, was first imprisoned by the rebels, then blown from a gun. Brigadier General Lawrence had the Political Agent and his sons disinterred for the second time to confirm the Maharao's statement that he had had them properly buried. 'I had the Burtons' coffins opened, and the bodies identified and I had too, the melancholy satisfaction of seeing the funeral service duly performed at the re-interment by the Captain of the Forces.' (There was no resident chaplain at Kotah.) They were buried in the Nayapura Cemetery, next to the grave of Mary Elizabeth, the eldest Burton daughter, who had died three years earlier.

The Commission to enquire into the murders was set up immediately after British troops captured Kotah. It consisted of Major General Roberts, overall commander of the troops, Lieutenant Colonel Holmes of the Bombay Army, Major Morrison, who had twice served as Political Agent in Kotah, before Major Burton's appointment, Captain Eden, the Political Agent at Jaipur, and Lieutenant Impey, assistant. Lawrence described the Commission members 'as competent a body to give an opinion as the importance of this case demanded, and as could probably be furnished'. The Commission's brief was to investigate four main points:

> the complicity or otherwise of the Maharao in the murder of Major Burton; if he took any steps to prevent the murder; whether if he *had* taken any steps he could have prevented the murder; and whether he was prevented by those round him from making the attempt.

'The Report on the Proceedings of the Commission' was presented to the Secretary to the Government of India by Brigadier General Lawrence on 17 April 1858. The Commission was 'unanimous and clearly satisfied of the Maharao's innocence of the Burtons' murder', but it did find him responsible for the Burtons' return to Kotah 'at a dangerous time' and 'to have been guilty of the most culpable indifference as to the fate of the British agent, and to have displayed in the hour of danger, a want of both physical and moral courage to save him'. The Maharao was found not guilty of any complicity in the murder, Brigadier General Lawrence stating that:

> No steps were taken by him to prevent it, because he was unaware of any intention to attack the Agent until too late to help him and had he tried to do so, I do not think he would have succeeded, being surrounded in the Palace by the same description of Troops as those who were attacking the Agency and who would, I feel assured, have forcibly, if necessary, prevented the Maharao going to the rescue.

The Maharao told the Commission how he had called the Raj Paltan troops together and asked them if the Burtons would be safe if they came back to Kotah. The troops gave him an assurance 'on the Koran' that they would not molest him, and on that promise the Maharao told the Burtons it was safe to return. This swearing of oaths that were later to be broken, was looked at sympathetically by the Commission.

> In trusting the oaths of the leaders that they would not injure the Agent, the Rao did no more than many British officers did, during the recent Mutinies and with the like results – the Artillery and Munitions of War were all in the hands of the Mutineers, and there were no Rajpoot chiefs or other Troops, on whom the Maharao could have called to fight for him.

He was considered 'to have been a victim of circumstances' and

> there is clear proof that the outbreak of the Troops however long meditated, was a sudden explosion, as unknown and unexpected to the inhabitants of the city as to the Maharao – had it been otherwise, the Bankers and others would as they invariably do, have got their property out of the town, and I have no doubt the Rao would have got the Agent and his sons into the Palace.

Though the Maharao was found not guilty of direct or indirect complicity in the murders, he was, however, still to be punished by the Company, presumably on the grounds that the murders had happened under his jurisdiction. It was suggested that a fine of Rs 15 lakhs (about £150,000) was appropriate 'as a sufficient lesson', with the promise to remit Rs 5 lakhs if either Lala Jai Dayal or Mehrab Khan were caught and executed by the Maharao or others. The Karauli Troops, who had enabled the Maharao to hold on in Kotah, were to receive Rs 3 lakhs from the Kotah fine. The fact that the Maharao had had the Adjutant, Nabi Shah Khan (who had stopped his master from attempting the Agent's rescue), blown from a gun was thought to be a point in his favour. And it was to be

> considered how seriously he [the Maharao] has already been punished in the loss of the Revenue for months past, the spoilation of his capital and the surrounding country, and the enormous loss of arms, cattle, and treasure taken by his mutinous Troops. Kotah has too suffered severely in dignity and prestige, by the rebel occupation of so large a quarter of the Town and surrounding villages and by the destruction of its guns by the British troops.

In future 'no Political Agent will be left, and no Force at Kotah. This too will be a matter of grief and indignity to the Maharao.' As a final punishment, the Maharao's gun salute by the Company was to be reduced from fifteen to eleven guns.

The Commission's investigation was thorough, and its findings, from the evidence assembled during a two-week period, seem justified. And yet there are still many unanswered questions. How much did the Burtons themselves contribute to their own deaths, with Major Burton's insistence on returning to Kotah against the last-minute advice of the vakeel Nand Kishore which was so arrogantly brushed aside by Francis Burton as 'humbug'? Was it this same vakeel's tip-off to the chief minister that the ringleaders from the Raj Paltan were going to be hanged, at Burton's suggestion, that sparked the attack? Did Lala Jai Dayal urge his troops to murder because he held a grudge against the Political Agent for dismissing him? Could the Burtons have been saved if they had had a proper escort made up of men lent from the Bombay Army at Neemuch? In retrospect there are many pointers to the tragedy, some unknown to the Burtons and some ignored by them, but each one, cumulatively, leading to their deaths.

Perhaps the most interesting questions are those that surround the Maharao's own role in the affair. Mrs Elizabeth Burton was in no doubt that he knew an Uprising was planned. 'I firmly believe,' she wrote in April 1858 'that all expected a mutiny, that all knew it would be, though perhaps none believed such precious lives would be lost, but no man told this to my husband.'[37] Ram Singh II had been placed in a dreadful dilemma in the summer of 1857. He wanted the Political Agent's return to the capital in order to demonstrate that the situation in Kotah was normal and that Kotah remained loyal to the East India Company during the Uprising. At the same time, he was painfully aware that two of his employees, Lala Jai Dayal and Mehrab Khan, were defying his orders and planting seditious thoughts among his own troops. The Maharao appears to have taken a gamble in persuading the Political Agent back to Kotah, a gamble which he lost within a few days of the Burtons' return.

And yet there is the Maharao's laissez-faire attitude when warned on 14 October of the impending murders – 'Well, the vakeel can tell [Burton] tomorrow'; the perception by the Sikh guard that the Maharao *might* have ordered his troops to attack the Residency; the slow-burning, bitter fuse of the humiliating defeat at Mangrol by the Company and the death of his father, Prithvi Singh on the battlefield; and lastly the loss of part of his territory to establish the state of Jhalawar. All these remembered slights may have influenced the Maharao in those desperate hours on 15 October as he watched the smoke rising from the burning Residency but decided he was helpless to act.

The Commission's last recommendation was that a price be put on the heads of Lala Jai Dayal and Mehrab Khan. The two ringleaders were eventually tracked down, mainly through the efforts of James Edmond Burton, who became a police assistant in Lucknow, and who used his native contacts in Kotah as informants.[38] They were hanged at the scene of their crimes, in the garden of the Residency in 1860, the memorial spot marked today by roses and herbaceous borders.

Mrs Elizabeth Burton erected a huge, twenty-foot high memorial over the grave of her husband and her two sons in the Nayapura cemetery. Intriguingly, however, it is not a classical Grecian or Roman-style monument, but deliberately Hindu in appearance, with a central 'altar' under a Hindu dome. There is nothing Indian about the inscription though. It reads:

> Sacred to the memory of Brevet Major Charles Aeneas Burton, 40th Regiment Bengal Native Infantry, Political Agent, Harowtee, aged 47 years and of his two sons, Arthur Robert, aged 21 years and 1 month and Francis Clarke, aged 19 years and 8 months. Three defenceless Englishmen who on the 15th October 1857, the year of the Indian Mutiny, were barbarously surrounded in the Residency by the bloodthirsty soldiers of the Maharaja of Kotah. For five hours these gallant men, a father and two sons kept the whole of the miscreants at bay, when alone and unaided they were finally overpowered and foully massacred. This tablet is erected by a broken-hearted wife and mother. 'Vengeance is mine, saith the Lord. I will repay.'[39]

The old British Residency is today the Brijraj Bhawan Palace Hotel. Before its metamorphosis into a hotel, the restored Residency was the State Guest House, where favoured guests of the Maharao were put up. In the 1930s a young Englishwoman, accompanying her government official father, was accommodated in a first floor room here. The room, like many Indian rooms, had four openings, including two leading down from the roof. Quite ignorant at the time of the story of the Burtons, nevertheless the young woman spent a terrifying night of 'cold fear', too frightened to sleep, in the room where the Englishmen had died. Hotel staff reported as late as the 1980s that 'many have heard a clipped British voice issue the disembodied command to sleepy

9. The tomb of Major Charles Burton and his two sons in the Kotah Cemetery in 1988. The inscription, which had been stolen, has now been replaced with a new plaque bearing the original wording.

guards "Don't smoke – no sleeping" and administer a smart, stinging slap across the cheek. It is widely believed that the voice belongs to the ghost of Major Burton.'[40]

The Kotah Residency murders only merit a footnote in most histories of the Uprising, because more dramatic events were taking place in Delhi, Agra, Lucknow, Cawnpore, Gwalior and Jhansi. But to examine this small tragedy in detail is to become aware of the many different strands that make up the idea of 'mutiny'. It was not a straightforward fight between the ruling East India Company and its oppressed subjects. One side was not totally right, and the other totally wrong. There were different reasons for the revolts in different parts of India, subtle undercurrents, old grievances long cherished, wounded *amour-propre*, and many others, often more complicated than we think.

Three

THE GREAT WALL OF LUCKNOW

ON 16 MARCH 1858 a young Greek photographer, Felice Beato, was issued with a permit by the East India Company 'to proceed to Lucknow and other places for eight months'.[1] Although only twenty-four years old, Beato was already a veteran war photographer, one of the first in this new field. He had travelled twice to Russia, to photograph the Crimean war and its aftermath. On hearing the news of the Uprising in India he sailed to Calcutta, and applied for permission to travel up country, accompanied by his two Maltese servants. His timing was impeccable – Lucknow had finally surrendered to the British, after two weeks of intense fighting, on 16 March 1858. It had been under rebel control since July of the previous year, when 3,000 or so British and Indians had shut themselves up in the Residency. Although those who survived the four-and-a-half month long siege had been rescued, on the final attempt, in November 1857, there were not enough British troops to hold the large city. It was left to its rebellious inhabitants until sufficient forces could be assembled and Gurkha troops under their leader Jang Bahadur had marched down from Nepal in support.

Within a week of its recapture by the British, Beato was in Lucknow, walking through a city devastated by street fighting and bombardment with heavy cannon. Bricks and debris blocked the alleys off the main street, mansions and mosques where the desperate last stands had been made stood riddled with shot. On the river Gomti, in front of an old palace, *The Sultan of Oude*, a three-masted sailing ship belonging to a former Nawab, listed at a crazy angle. On the hill, the Residency stood empty, apart from workmen who were demolishing the most dangerous structures and piling up the huge teak beams which had formed the roofs. The ad hoc cemetery around the Residency church had been comprehensively dug up in the hope of finding treasure buried with the victims of the siege. British tombs in the city's other cemeteries had been vandalised, and the three churches (two Anglican and one Catholic) thoroughly looted. Lucknow had been far more badly damaged than Delhi during its recapture, and Beato, climbing to the top of the Great

10. The Begam Kothi (middle distance) after the recapture of Lucknow in March 1858. Note the huge defensive wall to the left, with its wooden posts, and the ditch in front. This photograph by Felice Beato has not previously been correctly captioned. Beato was standing on what is today Vidhan Sabha Marg (Street), looking towards Hazratganj. The mosque to the right of the picture still exists.

Imambara and the Qaisarbagh Palace, recorded plate after glass plate of ruined buildings, torn-up gardens and tree stumps.[2] What he also recorded were extraordinary embankments of earth round the major buildings and along the river bank, some with huge wooden beams still embedded in them and standing upright. Little attention has been paid in the past to these embankments, for people have understandably been more intrigued by the battered buildings behind them. But piecing together accounts of the recapture of Lucknow with the photographic evidence, we can see how the city's inhabitants surrounded themselves with a great wall of earth against the British. How had things come to such a pass two years after the kingdom of Awadh had been annexed on the orders of Dalhousie, the Governor General? Particularly as Sir James Outram, the new Chief Commissioner had told Dalhousie that 'the city is in a state of tranquillity and that everything bids fair for the quiet introduction of our rule'.[3]

Lucknow was the capital of Awadh (Oudh) and had been since 1775, when the Nawab Asaf-ud-daula moved to it from Faizabad, some seventy miles to the east. Situated on the banks of the river Gomti, the town had developed rapidly under its cultured rulers, the Nawabs. It became a place of pilgrimage for Shi'as, with its Great Imambara, where the mourning rituals of the martyred Hasan and Hussain were commemorated every year. The Shi'a Nawabs came from Iran at the beginning of the eighteenth century, although their roots were in Mesopotamia (present-day Iraq). They established a vigorous new dynasty of rulers in Awadh, as the Mughal Empire crumbled away in the face of aggressive Maratha, and later British, attacks. It was unfortunate that the third Nawab, Shuja-ud-daula, had fought against the British at the battle of Buxar in 1764, because although he was subsequently pardoned, after paying a very large sum of money (£500,000) to the East India Company, it meant that the British had gained a toe-hold in Awadh. Shuja-ud-daula also had to agree to the stationing of Company troops in his territory for his own defence, for which he was charged a further handsome sum. The most damaging concession, however, was that the Nawab agreed to have a British Resident permanently at his court, and this led to that 'Fatal Friendship' between his descendants and the Company, which I have described in an earlier book.[4] In a successful attempt to wean the Nawabs away from the, by now, nominal authority of the King of Delhi, a crown was dangled in front of them by the East India Company, and the Nawab Ghazi-ud-din Haider became king in 1819, and Awadh became a kingdom. This was little more than a token gesture by the Company, a gesture as hollow as the gaudy tinsel crowns of which the Nawabs were so fond. (To avoid confusion we will continue to refer to them as the Nawabs.)

As British influence increased, symbolised by the expanding Residency and its adjacent buildings, the city became even more magnificent, with new palaces, imambaras, gardens, hunting parks and Palladian-style villas. Money was not a problem, for the Nawabs were immensely rich men, in spite of the huge financial demands made of them by the Company, always hard up for cash. But comparisons were drawn between the splendour of the city and the misery of many of its inhabitants, to whom wealth had certainly not trickled down. In the fertile countryside of Awadh the *ryots* (peasants) toiled under demanding and often tyrannous landowners, the *taluqdars*. Land revenue, the chief source of the Nawabs' wealth, often had to be extracted by force from the taluqdars, who had, in turn, squeezed it from the ryots.

British proposals for annexing Awadh had been made in 1831 by the Governor General, Lord William Bentinck, after a visit to Lucknow. He warned the playboy Nawab Nasir-ud-din Haider that if he 'should still neglect to apply a remedy for the existing disorder and misrule, it would then become the bounden duty of the British Government to assume direct management of the Oudh Dominions'. Bentinck left India in 1835 at the end of his governor generalship, but not before writing another finger-wagging letter to the Nawab:

> I shall fervently hope that this warning may not be without its effect and that you will in future conduct your Country in a manner better suited to the high and sacred trust conferred upon you by providence. You may rely upon it that this warning will be the last. [5]

But it wasn't. The premature death of Nasir-ud-din Haider in 1836 removed the immediate source of aggravation for the British. The next Nawab was an old, sick man at the time of his accession, and his son, Nawab Amjad Ali Shah, a rather colourless character, was not given to the public excesses of Nasir-ud-din Haider. On the accession in 1847 of the last Nawab, Wajid Ali Shah, another threatening memorandum was received from the Governor General, Lord Hardinge. In it, Hardinge hoped that by reforming his kingdom, the new ruler would 'rescue his people from their present miserable condition', otherwise he would 'incur the risk of forcing the British Government to interfere by assuming the government of Oudh'.

According to the British Resident, William Sleeman, who reported on 'a journey through the Kingdom of Oude 1849–1850' the lot of the men and women who tilled the fields was often wretched. The taluqdars grew rich at the Nawabs' expense, withholding revenue that should have gone to the central treasury in Lucknow. They 'expended the money in building forts and strongholds, casting or purchasing cannon, and maintaining large armed bands of followers ... in time, it became a point of honour to pay nothing to the sovereign without first fighting with his officers'.[6] Sleeman was not, however, despite his forty years' residence in India, and his familiarity with the local languages, an unbiased observer. His championing of the rural classes, while admirable, was at the expense of the native government. He claimed that he had never been placed in 'such a scene of intrigue, corruption, depravity and neglect of duty and abuse of authority', as when in Lucknow. He fell out with his own staff at the Residency too, accusing his assistant, Major Robert Bird of plotting against him, and the Residency surgeon, Dr Bell, of persecuting him.[7]

Sleeman's successor, and as it turned out, the last British Resident in Awadh, Sir James Outram, produced a further detailed report, which concluded that little had changed for the better. Indeed, this was not surprising, for Outram himself admitted that in the absence of prior personal knowledge of India he was dependent on the records of past Residents, and particularly Sleeman's findings. Annexation was proposed, with which Dalhousie was bound to agree, and Outram received the authority of the East India Company's Court of Directors and the Board of Control in London to implement this late in 1855. This decision was not based solely on the Residents' reports. There was, at the time, a groundswell of British public opinion that felt in taking Awadh over the Company would be conferring a blessing on its downtrodden population. There were plenty of critics of the Company at home, but very few of them were prepared to support what was depicted as a corrupt and venal native administration. A book published in May 1855 by William Knighton called *The Private Life of an Eastern King* did immense damage to the Nawabs' reputation. Although it purported to be an inside account of court life at the time of Nasir-ud-din Haider, the particular bugbear of Lord Bentinck, the inferences it drew were clearly relevant to the current debate on annexation. The book was extremely popular and quickly ran into a number of editions, two alone in the first month of publication. It was cited in Parliamentary debates on Awadh, and praised by the influential *Calcutta Review*.

British imperialism was almost at its apogee, and very few even thought to question, let alone oppose, the move towards annexation. In retrospect, the decision to take over a supposedly independent kingdom, not a state but a kingdom, created by the British, and recognised by them as such for nearly forty years, was an act of huge folly. But as we know from events in our own time, governments do make foolish decisions based on expediency, without considering the long-term consequences. It was hoped that the Nawab Wajid Ali Shah would quietly agree to let his kingdom be taken over by the British, but just in case he didn't, troops were moved from the cantonment at Cawnpore under Major General Sir Hugh Wheeler. By the time Outram returned to Lucknow from Calcutta, where he had collected his instructions from the Governor General, the troops had advanced towards the city. The Resident carried four documents with him; a letter from Dalhousie to Wajid Ali Shah, saying that the Company could no longer support his regime; a draft treaty by which the Nawab would agree 'that the sole and exclusive administration of the Civil and Military Government of the territories of Oude shall be henceforth vested for ever in the Honorable East India Company'; and two proclamations. The first, Proclamation A, was to be read if the Nawab agreed to sign the treaty. The second, Proclamation B, in case he wouldn't sign, announced that the Company was taking Awadh over anyway.[8]

Wajid Ali Shah's dignified response to the Resident's ultimatum was that since the Company appeared to have carried out a *fait accompli* in stripping him of his title, rank and honour, he was unable to sign the treaty, adding that 'Treaties are necessary between equals only'. He was given three days to change his mind, and when he declined to do so, the annexation of his kingdom was announced on 7 February 1856 at noon. There was no resistance in the city, because the Nawab had ordered his own troops, including the palace guard, to disarm, which they did. James Outram moved seamlessly from the post of Resident to that of Chief Commissioner. He met his new staff, the Judicial Commissioner Manaton Collingwood Ommaney and the Financial Commissioner Martin Gubbins, who had both arrived the previous day. Major John Sherbrooke Banks was appointed Commissioner for Lucknow and began work immediately. The Nawab's Chief Minister and other officials were summoned and told to hand over their records, and to make over the treasury to British officials. The kingdom was split into four divisions, each with a commissioner. Each division was subdivided into three districts, with deputy commissioners, making a total of sixteen major British administrators. The annexation, so long planned, went smoothly. The stunned, unbelieving response of the inhabitants of Awadh took time to grow into a groundswell of anger. The implications of British rule took time to absorb.

Within five weeks, Wajid Ali Shah had left Lucknow, with a large party, on his way to Calcutta. He was accompanied by his mother, his younger brother, and his three wives. The fourth wife, Begam Hazrat Mahal, whom the Nawab is said to have divorced about 1850, was left behind in Lucknow with her young son, Birjis Qadr. There were two Englishmen with the group – Major Robert Bird, to whom William Sleeman had taken such a dislike, and John Rose Brandon, a successful businessman, whom Sleeman liked even less. Reaching Cawnpore on the morning of 14 March, the royal party were then held up for three weeks, while Outram put various obstacles in their path. There are no accounts of a meeting between the Nana Sahib and the Nawab during the latter's enforced stay in Cawnpore, though it is likely that the Nana would have paid his respects to this distinguished visitor. While in Cawnpore the Nawab sent a letter of congratulation to the new Governor General, Charles Canning, on his appointment and added that he (the Nawab) was 'confident that through your kind assistance I may yet be restored to my territory'. It may have been Nana Sahib's secretary Azimullah, who suggested to the Nawab that if Canning refused to reverse his predecessor's takeover of Awadh, then the Nawab should go, in person, to Britain and see Queen Victoria herself.

There had been a number of Indian emissaries to Britain over the previous decade as Dalhousie's seemingly relentless policy of annexation was unrolled. The Maharaja Duleep Singh, heir to the now vanished throne of the Punjab, had gone willingly, and had become a favourite of the Queen. Azimullah himself had spent several years in Britain seeking in vain, through the law courts, to have his master's pension restored. Laxmi Bai, the Rani of Jhansi had similarly pursued her case through a British lawyer in India, John Lang, but it was a fruitless and expensive mission. In spite of these failures, Wajid Ali Shah was convinced that he had a case to put before the Queen. His predecessors had enjoyed friendly relations with the British royal family, symbolised by the exchange of costly gifts, and solicitous enquiries about the illnesses of George III. No independent state in India had a better record of loaning money (which inevitably turned into a donation) to the Company than Awadh. The initial subsidy for the Company's troops, negotiated with the Nawab Asaf-ud-daula, had risen to an *annual* payment of £760,000 by his successor. The British Resident and all his staff had received free accommodation and even furnishings for nearly eighty years. An appeal to the British Queen by the King of Awadh was surely not unthinkable. But on reaching

Calcutta, Wajid Ali Shah fell ill, possibly with a diplomatic illness, and he decided to send his mother, the Queen Mother, and his younger brother to London to put his case, one queen to another, it was reasoned. The royal party embarked on the steamship *Bengal* in June arriving at Southampton on 21 August 1856.

Once the Nawab had left Lucknow, the dismemberment of the former kingdom began. The royal menagerie and aviary were auctioned off almost at once, 7,000 animals being sold in one day, including 200 elephants. Palaces were taken over and divided up into offices for British officials. The great army of palace servants, including the menagerie and aviary attendants, the gardeners, the royal boatmen, the artists and bookbinders, newswriters, spies, dancing girls and peacock-fan bearers who had stayed behind were left jobless, and with their salaries greatly in arrears. There were over 20,000 pensioners, many of whom were the relatives of former Nawabs and who depended on the generosity of Wajid Ali Shah. Although the majority of these were to continue to receive their pensions, for the Nawab himself was eventually allocated a pension of 12 lakhs a year by the British, there was initial confusion and uncertainty about what would happen. Not all the pensioners were elderly, or without other resources – a pension from the Nawab was as much a recognition of one's status as a means of support. It was a question of *izzat*, the word that means honour, pride and one's standing in society.

The electric telegraph, which the last Nawab had wanted to set up, but which was refused him by the British, now appeared with miraculous haste, and the old banqueting hall in the Residency became the new telegraph office. The Khas Bazaar, a luxury market and trading centre between the palaces was demolished. The Queen Mother's hookah-bearer, who had been left behind, reported that her husband's shop had been cleared away. 'All the bazaar was cleared away. The English like grass better than bazaars.' On the bazaars that were spared, a new market ground rent *(teh bazaari)* was imposed. Sir Henry Lawrence, the new Chief Commissioner of Awadh, was so worried about local reaction that he wrote to Canning saying 'Much discontent has been caused by the demolition of buildings and still more by threats of further similar measures; also regarding the seizure of religious and other edifices and plots of ground as *nazul*, or government property.'[9]

The Nawab's army, consisting of fifty-two regiments with 60,349 serving officers and men, was disbanded by the British who set up their own regiments which they called the Oudh Irregular Force. But less than half the officers and men who had served in the Nawab's army could be enlisted into this, or into the new police force which was established at the same time. Soldiers in the Nawab's army had traditionally brought their own weapons with them when they entered service, so they could not be disarmed when they left. By the end of 1856 there was an estimated number of 30,000 discharged, armed officers and men, pensioned off and left to wander around the countryside, without an occupation. Not only were they armed, but they were angry and bored, men on the loose, who were to form the bulk of the forces fighting the British in a few months' time. It took months for the pensions issue to be resolved too, another cause for anger. A ruling, conveniently brought in a week before the annexation of Awadh, stated that soldiers needed to have served their full term in the Nawab's army, before they were eligible for a pension. Lists of pensioners who *were* eligible were still being batted back and forth like shuttlecocks between various government departments in November 1857, by which time the British had lost control of Awadh, and were not in a position to pay the pensions anyway. The Military Department in Calcutta claimed they could not act without authorisation from the Foreign Department, who in turn sent back the lists of pensioners telling the Auditor General to apply to the civil authorities for the rolls of eligible soldiers, and so it went on.[10] Quite apart from men who might, or might not, receive a pension, there were also an estimated 14,000 civilian contractors who had supplied the Nawab's army. They were now also without work, because the British had brought in their own contractors, and these men had no chance of compensation, even for goods already supplied, but not paid for.

There was increasing trouble in the countryside. A new land settlement, called the Summary Settlement, was put in place by the British early in 1856. It was essential that there should be no interruption in the collection of land revenue, for this was the chief source of income, apart from small amounts of customs duties. The British sought to strengthen the village communities of petty farmers against the landowners, the taluqdars. The new commissioners were urged to settle with the people actually farming the land, not those with proprietorial rights to it. There was a sudden demand that the remaining land revenue for the financial year, normally paid in monthly instalments, was to be paid in a lump sum. This severely embarrassed many taluqdars, who did not have ready reserves of capital and could not now use the strong-arm methods which had been such a feature of Nawabi Awadh, before annexation. A number of petitions were sent to the Governor General during the spring of 1857. The Raja Farzand Ali Khan complained about the 'Act of Settlement officer' who turned him off his estate in Khairabad District. Gardeen Tewaree was dispossessed of his villages, the Rao Bahadur Bakht Singh of Bundelkhand had his hereditary lands taken from him, Bahadur Jang Khan of Dadri lost his jagir; Mehrban Singh, the zamindar of Salone lost half his village through a decision of the Deputy Commissioner, and Raja Arjun Singh of Porahant employed Mr George Norton to act on his behalf in appealing against the settlement.

Some were actually imprisoned for debt, a shameful thing for the rajas and rao sahibs of what had so recently been their kingdom. Raja Hanumant Singh of Kala Kankar, taluqdar in Rampur District, who was ordered to jail, complained to Captain Barrow, Deputy Commissioner of Salone, saying

'Sahib, your countrymen came into this country and drove out our King. You sent your officers round the districts to examine the title to the estates. At one blow you took from me lands which from time immemorial had been in my family.'[11] There were similar cases, similar causes for a deep-seated resentment. Before annexation taluqdars were estimated to have owned 67 per cent of the land. After the British settlement, this was reduced to just 38 per cent. We get an indication of the warlike atmosphere already present in the countryside. Many of the taluqdars lived in small forts, supported by feudal armies, men they could call upon and arm in times of trouble. In September 1856 the Chief Commissioner ordered 574 forts in Awadh, belonging to the taluqdars and zamindars to 'surrender all warlike stores or artillery' by the first day of October but this did not happen and was in any case impossible to enforce.

There were thus at least three separate and disgruntled groups of people in Awadh by the spring of 1857 – the royal family members who had stayed behind in Lucknow, and the numerous dependants and former staff; ex-army men, still without their pensions, and former army contractors, now without jobs; and the taluqdars and zamindars out in the country, with their petitions against the Summary Land Settlement still pending. It needed little to set this dangerous mixture alight, yet the British seemed to be sleepwalking towards disaster. Difficult questions were inevitably referred to Calcutta, and even petty matters reached the Governor General, when they should have been dealt with on the spot. In reading through hundreds of manuscript documents for 1857 and 1858, the overwhelming impression is of civil officers covering their backs, in a vast bureaucracy where initiative was frowned upon, where precedents were always cited in response to a fresh query, and where few had the imagination to look up from their papers to see what was actually happening outside their offices. The separation between military officers, who could react quickly to a situation, and the civil officers, who couldn't even imagine the situation, let alone react to it, was profound.

Sir Henry Lawrence had been moved from his position in Rajputana as Agent to the Governor General, and appointed Chief Commissioner of Awadh in March 1857. It was to be his final posting. He replaced the officiating Chief Commissioner, Sir Coverley Jackson, who had managed to alienate nearly everyone in his short period of office, including his own staff, the two Financial and Judicial Commissioners, Gubbins and Ommaney. A jail outbreak early in March prompted the Governor General to send Jackson back to the Revenue Board in Agra, where he could do less harm. Lawrence was at least sensitive to what was happening in Lucknow, if not in the rest of Awadh. We have already seen his disquiet with the rapid changes in the city, the demolition of loved buildings, the requisitioning of others, including some of the palaces, and the discontent visible in the streets. Shortly after his arrival he reported ominously to Canning that 'This very morning a clod was thrown at Mr Ommaney and another struck Mr Anderson while in a buggy with myself'.[12]

On 18 April 1857 Nana Sahib arrived in Lucknow, with his secretary Azimullah Khan for what was almost a state visit. He was received by Martin Gubbins, who found him 'arrogant and presuming'. He met Captain Fletcher Hayes, the Military Secretary to the Chief Commissioner, and a man who had the delicate task of negotiating between the British and the members of the royal family who were still in Lucknow, with their many and various complaints. Nana Sahib met Sir Henry Lawrence, in a courtesy call, where nothing of any importance was discussed, and then toured the city with his entourage. A more interesting meeting took place with Mirza Bedar Bakht, a grandson of the Delhi King, who had arrived in Lucknow to meet Nana Sahib, and to discuss the printing of a pamphlet headed *Rissalah Jihad* (Officers' Jihad) which called on Muslims to arm themselves and fight. The pamphlet was printed on a French printing press, which Azimullah Khan had brought back with him from his European visit, and which was now carried to Lucknow.[13] The same press was subsequently used to print the revolutionary paper *Payam-i-Azadi* (Message of Freedom), which was financed by Nana Sahib, and edited by the King of Delhi's grandson. Henry Lawrence was so alarmed that he immediately had the press closed down, banned the paper, and threatened that anyone who was found with a copy was liable to execution. Nana Sahib by now was safely back in his palace at Bithur.

At the beginning of May, the new recruits of the 7th Oudh Irregular Infantry, stationed in the Mariaon cantonment at Lucknow, refused to accept greased cartridges for their rifles. It seems extraordinary that these were still being distributed to the sepoys after the violent reactions against them in Berhampore and Barrackpore, and their issue could only be seen by the Lucknow sepoys as a provocation. Lucknow has some claim to be the place where the Uprising began in earnest. The refusal of the cartridges took place on Friday 1 May. Two days later, a letter sent by the men of the 7th Oudh Irregular Infantry to the 48th Bengal Native Infantry, also stationed in Lucknow, was intercepted. The letter spoke of the planned murder of the British officers of the 7th and also stated: 'We are ready to join in any *tamasha* – tell us what we are to do.' A tamasha is a jolly occasion, defined as an entertainment, a sport or a spectacle, but not surprisingly, Henry Lawrence didn't find it funny. Learning that the troops were about to mutiny, he confronted them on the Mariaon cantonment parade ground that Sunday evening with all the European troops he could muster. A panic ensued, over fifty officers and men were arrested, and the remainder surrendered their arms and returned to their barracks. Twenty mutinous soldiers were subsequently convicted, sentenced, and hanged in front of the old Macchi Bhawan fort, a former palace of the first Nawabs. Had it not been for Lawrence's immediate response to the discovery of the plot, this would have marked the beginning of the Great Uprising. The mutiny at Meerut, exactly a week later, on Sunday 10 May, thus became, by default, the recognised start of the revolt.

On 12 May, as a reward for the four loyal soldiers who had intercepted the 'tamasha' letter, Lawrence ordered that a *durbar* or reception should be held on the large lawn in front of the old Residency. (Although there was no longer a Resident living there, the mansion had retained its former name.) Carpets were laid on the lawn, and chairs arranged in rows, facing the handsome building. Comfortable sofas were pulled out on to the Residency's verandahs so the assembled civil and military officers could watch the event. In what was intended to be a morale-boosting speech, Lawrence emphasised the handsome pensions that sepoys in the new Oudh Irregular Army units could hope to get for themselves and their dependants. There was no shortage of soldiers for these new units either, indeed 'only last week, in this very city' he announced, '300 men were called for, and 32,000 clamorous for service eagerly rushed forward to partake of the bounty of the Government'. The dreadful irony of his statement, that there were 31,700 men still out there desperate to find work, does not seem to have struck him. Two officers and two sepoys were each presented with Rs 300, a shawl, a sword of honour, a jacket, and embroidered cloth, Sir Henry distributing the gifts 'with his own hands'.[14] It was to be the last festive occasion at the Residency. Within a few days the lawn was being dug up to make a defensive barricade, and the houses of wealthy Indians on the perimeter of the thirty-three-acre hill top were seized and fortified. An ex-soldier reported seeing convoys of carts filled with grain and munitions heading towards the Residency at dawn. Firewood, charcoal and fodder for the cattle also arrived, in preparation for a lengthy siege.

The question of escaping from Lucknow, as an alternative to being besieged there, never seems to have been seriously considered by the British. The usual route to Calcutta started with a day's journey by mail-coach to Cawnpore, followed by a steamer down the Ganges to the Bengal Presidency. There was also the longer journey by road through Benares. With the news that the Europeans at Cawnpore had been ordered into the entrenchments surrounding the old Dragoon Hospital buildings on 21 May, escape via Cawnpore became impossible. Equally impossible was the long road journey through a now hostile countryside. There was a substantial number of British civilians in and around Lucknow, who simply could not flee, including 600 women and children, the dependants of soldiers and administrators who had been drafted in following annexation. There were also the old-established European residents including teachers, shopkeepers and pensioners. Among the Indian men and women who chose to stay with the British were clerks employed in the Company's offices, sepoys who had not mutinied and remained loyal, converts to Christianity, domestic servants including ayahs, and somewhere in between, the Anglo-Indians. All these people were as much at risk as the British.

To his credit, Henry Lawrence acted decisively and quickly once the dreadful news from Cawnpore arrived, and he realised that the only chance of saving his fearful subjects and their dependants was to stay and fight. At first he intended to gather everyone in the Macchi Bhawan fort, overlooking the river Gomti and the Stone Bridge, one of only two fixed crossing points (the other was the Iron Bridge, and there was a pontoon bridge further down-river). However, he was persuaded against this by Company engineers who believed the fort would be too easy to undermine, because of its basement galleries and sanitation outlets. The Residency complex, although covering a larger area, could not be so easily undermined, and its rising ground meant that it could be defended, even with low parapet walls. An army of coolies was employed by Lawrence, at three times the normal daily wage, to throw up earthen parapets and to dig trenches – an eerie forerunner of the great wall that would be built six months later, probably by many of the same workmen.

The anticipated mutiny came on the evening of 30 May in the Mariaon cantonment, when troops from four regiments set fire to the officers' bungalows, killing three British soldiers, including the senior officer, Brigadier Isaac Handscomb, and wounding two others. Countermeasures were taken by Lawrence, and the next day some sixty officers and sepoys were captured, many of the others fleeing northwards along the Sitapur road to Delhi. Of the 4,000 Indian troops stationed in and around Lucknow, between 600 and 700 remained loyal to the British. Disturbances now broke out in Lucknow itself, which were soon quashed by the city police, but this demonstrated to Lawrence how volatile the situation had become. He had already ordered all European women and children to the Residency complex, where they were accommodated, like the refugees they were, in cramped conditions among the elegant private houses and public offices.

Outside the Macchi Bhawan fort the public hangings continued, day by day. Twenty-two 'conspirators' were hanged in batches, as well as the sixty mutineers captured on 31 May. Lawrence ordered an 18-pounder gun to be put on top of the fort's gateway, pointing down the street to the gallows. Arrests of six men and one woman supposedly involved in an 'extensive conspiracy' were also made. The prisoners were:

> 1 and 2. Mirza Hyder Shikoh and Humayun Shah 'connections of the late royal Family of Delhi' who were 'suspected of intriguing', as many of their retainers and friends had been observed in the crowd on 31 May.
> 3. Agha Usguree, servant to the two men above, and an inhabitant of Lucknow.
> 4. Mustafa Khan 'a nominal elder brother of Wajid Ali Shah', who had laid

claim to the throne, but had been set aside by his father as being illegitimate and who had 'since lived on small means and continual hopes'.
5. Mirza Jehan Kudr, the son of Wajid Ali Shah's brother, the 'General Sahib, lately deceased in Europe'.
6 and 7. Nawab Mirza and Shureefoon Nissa [Sharif-un-nissa], either the son and daughter of General Sahib by a slave girl, or his adopted son and daughter.[15]

The Qaisarbagh palace, the last Nawab's residence, was raided and carriage loads of jewellery, treasure and weapons were removed from it and taken to the Residency. 'The crown jewels would make a pleasant addition to army prize money' wrote Captain Birch.

> They were certainly very impressive. There were some very fine pearls and emeralds, some of them being as large as eggs. There was also a bonus in the form of a large brass cannon and a quantity of arms, so many in fact that it took several days to load them on to carts and take them to the Residency.[16]

The treasure, together with 23 lakhs of rupees, was carefully buried in barrels in front of the main Residency building. All through that curious waiting period of June, as dreadful news came in and all of Awadh and beyond seemed to be in flames, preparations for the expected siege continued. The electric telegraph line between the city and Benares was cut on 4 June, and the line to Cawnpore was interrupted the following day. To the south of the city, at La Martiniere College, a large, fanciful building erected over the tomb of its founder, Major General Claude Martin, the masters and boys made their own preparations for defence. Provisions were brought in, doorways barricaded up with bricks, connecting bridgeways to adjacent wings destroyed, and the older boys put on sentry duty at the top of the building. But on 18 June came the order from Lawrence to abandon the college and the sixty-odd boys and their masters moved into the Residency, occupying one of the houses commandeered a month earlier, that of the moneylender Shah Behari Lal.

Although the city was cut off from telegraphic communication now, news continued to come in, some of it brought by British refugees, who had managed to escape from Sitapur, Secrora and Daryabad. The Lucknow bankers learnt from the Delhi bankers that Bahadur Shah Zafar had appointed Nana Sahib as Subahdar (Governor) of Cawnpore, Faizabad and Lucknow. 'He has not got it yet!' wrote Mrs Brydon defiantly on 14 June.[17] A doctor's wife, she was one of the besieged and kept a diary which was not published until the end of the twentieth century. She also noted that the city police had requested that they should not be called sepoys, as they said 'that name is blackened'. The desperate situation in Cawnpore, where Wheeler was holding out with about a thousand Europeans waiting for a relief column that came too late to save them, was followed closely. Indian spies known as *cossids* brought messages, at the risk of their lives, and the *dak* (post) was still getting through, in spite of the difficulty of unsafe roads.

The waiting game ended abruptly on 30 June, when Lawrence learnt that rebel troops were on the road from Faizabad, coming into Lucknow to attack the British. He rode out to meet them, accompanied by 600 soldiers, British and Indian, and was met at Chinhat, six miles from the city, by almost 5,000 officers and sepoys. An eye-witness said that the rebel troops were commanded 'by a Russian Officer, a fair, handsome looking man of about twenty-five years of age, with light mustachios and wearing a cavalry uniform'. He was thought, however, to have been Captain Schmidt, the German cavalry officer in Wajid Ali Shah's army. Many of Lawrence's Indian troops deserted to the rebels, and the remainder, soundly beaten, retreated in haste to the comparative safety of the Residency, closely followed by the rebel soldiers. A round shot from their cannon hit the chimney of Martin Gubbins's house, and the Residency building itself was shelled repeatedly. 'The sad engagement at Chinhat had done us infinite mischief. It will make the mutineers so bold. They have now completely surrounded us and our real siege has commenced,' Mrs Brydon reported.

Inside the Residency complex were about 3,000 people. Of these, approximately half were Europeans, soldiers, civilians, young children and schoolboys from the College. The others were Indian soldiers, the state prisoners who had been arrested on 31 May, servants, camp followers and Anglo-Indian bandsmen. The story of the siege is one of the best-known episodes of the whole Uprising, and possibly of Empire history too, up there along with Rorke's Drift, the death of General Gordon and the relief of Mafeking. The siege was to last for four and a half months, until the middle of November, during which time numbers fell to nearly 1,500 through death and desertion. Of those who survived, ten published full-length books about their experiences, and the letters and diaries of the Reverend Polehampton, who died from cholera, were published posthumously by his widow. We know more about what life was like during the Residency siege than about any other event of the Uprising, but we know it only through the eyes of the Company's military and civilian officers and their wives. Only the Swiss merchant, Ruutz Rees, presented the non-official view. There are no accounts from the other ranks, the sergeants' wives, the Indian soldiers serving the British, or the Anglo-Indian bandsmen.

Much less is known about what was going on outside the Residency, in the city of Lucknow itself, whose streets circled the Residency hill. The sound of firing was almost constant, as round shot, shell and bullets flew overhead, crashing into walls, and killing people and animals. Occasionally 'fearful cries and screams' would be heard from the city streets, the result of plundering concluded the listeners on the hill. Not all the bandsmen and drummers were inside the Residency, and groups of musicians trained by the British could be heard playing popular tunes, including 'The Girl I Left Behind Me'. It was especially taunting to hear the dismal sounds of 'God Save the Queen' played over and over again outside the barricades. There appears to be only one short, contemporary, written account of life in the city during the summer of 1857. This was a letter from a man called Gujral Brahmin, first published in a Calcutta paper and reprinted in the *Illustrated London News*.

> On Sunday July 12th about eight o'clock I left Lucknow, up to that time all was well. The Europeans were in the Residency, and the mutinous troops were attacking from the outside; great plunder was going on in the city. Outside the Residency there are many thousand men, but they are not all fighting men. Many of them are the people of the city and lookers-on. There may be about twelve regiments and a few Rissalehs. More than 100 of the mutineers are killed daily. Of those who die, they who have relations are burnt otherwise the bodies are thrown into the Goomtee river. The wounded are carried away in doolies and treated. Both in the city and in the camp there is great tumult; the mutineers do not now keep up so severe a cannonade as they did at first and it is probable that their supplies of ammunition are running short; for at night there is no firing from the guns now, though musketry firing goes on. The sepoys who have plundered the city are walking homeward with their spoil. The mutineers are searching the city for saltpetre. Provisions are plentiful and the Bunneahs have been told to keep their shops open, and sell for ready money. All the mutineers have put up in the gardens of the city people, of which they have forcibly taken possession. Raja Goor Bux Singh, the Rajah of Rumnuggur and Rajah Nawab Alee and a great number of the petty neighbouring Rajahs, have joined the fight and given their assistance; but neither Rajah Man Singh, nor his followers, are there.[18]

Raja Man Singh was an influential taluqdar, who had promised to support the British, after an appeal by Henry Lawrence and the hint of a rich reward. With the death of Lawrence on 4 July, hit by a cannonball, and an unsuccessful attempt to relieve the Residency, the Raja had changed sides when it looked as if the British were losing. The following year, shortly before the recapture of Lucknow, he was back again on the British side. His changes of heart reflected the ambivalence that many felt, although not all expressed so clearly.

Gujral Brahmin, the letter-writer quoted above, failed to mention a highly significant event which had taken place shortly before his departure. On 5 July Birjis Qadr (Mirza Mohammad Ramzan Ali), the fourteen-year-old son of Begam Hazrat Mahal, was crowned as successor to his father, Wajid Ali Shah. As a Hindu, Gujral Brahmin may have felt that the coronation of the young Muslim prince, fifteen months after the Awadh monarchy had been abolished at annexation, did not affect him. But it was to lend shape to the resistance against the British and provide a focus for the Uprising in Awadh, and beyond, especially after the fall of Delhi. The coronation took place in the Chandiwali Barahdari, a pavilion in the central garden of the last Nawab's palace of Qaisarbagh. It was attended by a large crowd of taluqdars and army officers of the new Awadh force, who watched Begam Hazrat Mahal and her son arrive in procession, as the Nawabs had done in the old days. This was no token ceremony by a group of rebels, as the British would have liked to believe, the putting of a puppet king on a non-existent throne, but a solemn occasion that brought together the leaders of groups alienated since annexation and now confirmed in their determination to regain the lost kingdom. Symbolically, the boy was crowned with a simple turban of silk and gold thread, called a *mandeel*, because the crowns and crown jewels had been taken by the British.[19] At the end of the ceremony a twenty-one-gun salute was fired, which was clearly heard on the Residency hill, and which led the besieged British to excited speculation that the relieving force had arrived to save them and a orgy of drunkenness among the men defending the battery. In fact the last Nawab, Wajid Ali Shah, had been entitled to a twenty-one-gun salute, agreed by Queen Victoria on the recommendation of the Government of India. The Nawab had stood second in precedence only to the King of Delhi, and in front of five other rajas and nizams.[20]

One man was absent from the coronation, on the plea of a leg injured in the battle of Chinhat. This was the mysterious Maulvi (preacher) of Faizabad who had first arrived in Lucknow in January 1857 – 'mysterious' because both his background and his real name were unknown. He is referred to in the records of the time as Ahmad Ali Shah, as Syed Ahmadullah, as Maulvi Ahmadullah Shah, as Sikandar Shah and as Danka Shah (from *danka*, a drum, because he was usually preceded by a drummer). The historian Rudrangshu Mukherjee has provided the most accurate account to date of the Maulvi's antecedents, based on information from an assistant surgeon in Agra, Wazir Khan.

> The Maulvi gave himself out to be a disciple of Mehrab Shah, a holy man from Gwalior, where Ahmadullah Shah said he had resided for a long time. Ahmadullah Shah preached as a fakir in Agra and in other parts of the North-West Provinces, propagating a holy war against the British. He was around forty at the time of the outbreak; a man of little learning, having a smattering of Persian and Arabic and some English. Apparently he had been to England and spoke with 'great apparent familiarity' regarding places in England.[21]

Establishing himself in the Moti Masjid in Hussainabad, a large, walled Shi'a complex, the Maulvi began holding regular meetings after prayers, preaching a jihad against the unbelievers, the *kafirs*. He called upon the Muslim faithful, 'and even the Hindus, to arise, or be ever fallen'.[22] Clearly a charismatic man, the Maulvi soon attracted a band of supporters, armed men mounted on horses and camels. From Lucknow he travelled to Faizabad, where with a certain bravado he continued to call for jihad and to avenge the death of a fellow maulvi, Amir Ali, who had died in disturbances and was buried there.

A warrant was issued by the Deputy Commissioner of Faizabad, and when the Maulvi and his followers refused to go quietly, Company troops were sent to arrest him. A pitched battle took place, with casualties on both sides.[23] The Maulvi and two of his supporters were jailed. Dr Najaf Ali, who worked at the Faizabad Cantonment Jail, became friendly with Ahmadullah, who was undoubtedly a persuasive character. It is said that the doctor provided the Maulvi with extra rations during his imprisonment, and that when the jail was broken open by rebellious sepoys of the Oudh Irregular Infantry and Cavalry on 7 June, Dr Ali got the Maulvi safely away in disguise. On returning to Lucknow he established himself and his followers in the Taron-wali Kothi, the Star House, which had been built by a British astronomer as the observatory for an earlier Nawab and was now lying empty.

The relationship between the Maulvi and the Begam was an unhappy one. Both were ostensibly working towards the same end – the removal of the British and the reinstatement of the old, pre-annexation order. Although the Maulvi preached jihad, he appeared to have no affiliation with any particular group, and mixed freely with Shi'as and Sunnis. (He has previously been mistakenly identified as a Wahhabi from Patna.[24]) From his actions during the siege of the Residency, when he co-ordinated and led several attacks, it is possible that he had had military training at some point. That there was friction between him and the Begam's supporters is clear. He was not at first invited to join the military junta which had been set up in Lucknow, the Sazman-Jawanan-e-Awadh (Organisation of Awadh Soldiers), and he was barred from living in the centre of the city. This antagonism was to escalate into open warfare within a few months:

> as rebel reverses increased and the troops grew dissatisfied with the conduct of the court party, his forceful personality, holy character and military judgement commanded increasing support from all sections of the army. Jai Lal Singh [the army commandant] and [Begam] Hazrat Mahal were forced to agree to his return to Lucknow, where he began to style himself Viceregent of God [Khalifat-ullah] and to pose a serious threat to the pre-eminence of the court faction.[25]

This is not the place for a day-by-day account of the progress of the siege of the Residency, nor the sufferings of those within it, nor the equally heavy loss of life among the besiegers. This is ground which has been well covered over the last hundred and fifty years. In strategic terms, neither side was the winner. The original intention of the rebel sepoys at the end of May was to go to Delhi to join Bahadur Shah Zafar's supporters. The King of Delhi had already issued a general *firman* (proclamation) stating that he had possession of the whole country, and requesting the Awadh troops, among others, to join his standard. Had they done so, the outcome of the Great Uprising might have been very different. It was Raja Mahmudabad, a wealthy taluqdar, and

Khan Ali Khan, an official from Salone, dismissed by William Sleeman, who persuaded the troops to besiege the Residency instead of marching to Delhi. Having forced the British into a corner, it was then hoped to frighten them into surrender, because this would have had an important symbolic impact throughout northern India. But this plan came to nothing, as the full horror of the Cawnpore massacres became known at the end of July. There the British *had* surrendered to Nana Sahib's men, on the promise of safe conduct downriver to Allahabad, and they had all been slaughtered for their pains. Surrender was the last thing that the inhabitants of the Lucknow Residency intended to do. Their stubborn resistance, in the face of daily death and lack of food, meant that thousands of fighting men were tied up outside the makeshift barricades for months, running out of ammunition, and sustaining even heavier losses than the British, but unable to leave.

Abortive attempts to reach the Residency had been made in July and August when General Sir Henry Havelock had advanced along the Cawnpore to Lucknow road. On three occasions he had been checked at the walled village of Basharatganj, thirty miles from Lucknow. Here he was faced with an estimated 30,000 men with fifty guns, not rebel sepoys this time, but armed zamindars, and not fighting for an idea, but fighting to defend their land, the most ancient incentive of all. Havelock and his thousand or so men withdrew to Cawnpore. 'Every valley is held against us' reported Colonel Tytler (the same man who had remarked on the murmuring of his troops in Delhi), 'the zamindars having risen to oppose us; all the men killed yesterday were zamindars.'[26] With Havelock's forced withdrawal over the Ganges the only Britons left in Awadh were those in the Residency.

It was not until September that a further relief was attempted. By then the Commissioner of Lucknow, Major Banks, appointed by Henry Lawrence on his deathbed, had also been killed. Ommaney, the Judicial Commissioner was dead, as was the chaplain, the Reverend Henry Polehampton, and General Sir John Inglis was now in charge. Sir James Outram, newly returned from invading Persia earlier in the year, joined Havelock and the two were able to press along the Cawnpore road to Lucknow, this time successfully. The Alambagh Palace, in a large walled enclosure south of the city, was captured, and this was to become the British headquarters for the next six months, although it was not held without a struggle during the winter of 1857/58. Early on the morning of Friday 25 September troops, including the 78th Highlanders, pushed forward from Alambagh, across fields and through *topes* (orchards) of mango trees and bamboo towards the walled garden of Charbagh, which was 'desperately defended' by two Awadh divisions under Mirza Baqar Ali and Hira Lal Hakim, both of whom were killed. The wooden Charbagh Bridge which crossed the Haider Canal was a scene of dreadful carnage, an estimated 1,600 Indian defenders being killed.[27] No attempt seems to have been made to mine the bridge. The British troops fought on, through the barricaded streets, lined with handsome European-style houses, their windows now bricked up, and every roof-top parapet a vantage point for a musketman. The Residency was reached about 4 o'clock that afternoon, to wild acclaim from those besieged inside, but the cost to the British was heavy. An estimated 600 men and 60 officers were killed and wounded. Among the dead was Colonel James Neill, whose cruelty towards captured rebels sickened even his own officers.

What Outram and Havelock quickly realised, and what those who had been inside the Residency since the end of June also realised, was that the relieving force was not strong enough to break out and fight its way back to Alambagh, let alone take with it 500 women and children, as well as the injured. Cavalry sent out from the Residency as an experiment had to retreat under fire. The longed-for relief force turned out to be a reinforcement, not a means of escape. Luckily it was discovered that there were more food supplies squirrelled away than had been thought at first, so the newcomers did not starve. In fact the food supplies had been poorly managed from the start. There was no common store of food, and while many subsisted on 'rations' of chapattis, dhal and meat, with a little tea, others, including Martin Gubbins, the Commissioner, who had prudently laid in 'private stocks', feasted on champagne, rice puddings, eggs, milk and even sugar.

Extraordinarily, no one seems to have protested, and although there were raids by the soldiers on the cellar of Monsieur Deprat, a wine merchant, food supplies were not pilfered. Those who could afford to bought tinned food, hams and jars of jam, honey and pickles at the auctions held after the frequent British deaths. Sir Henry Lawrence's larder fetched extremely high prices, a tin of soup going for £1.15*s*. Soap became a valuable item, as did clothes, even second-hand ones. There was no shortage of certain luxury goods, and Mrs Harris, the chaplain's wife, noted on 30 September that 'We bought some very pretty cups and saucers today from a soldier of the 90th. The Ferreed Bux [Farhat Bakhsh Palace] was full of china and all sorts of valuable things, and the soldiers are constantly offering articles for sale.'[28] The fact that there were fancy teacups, but little tea to put in them, added to the increasingly surreal nature of the siege. Britain's rigid class structure, exported abroad intact, meant that, even in the face of malnutrition and death, the dividing lines were still maintained. Just as there were officers and men, so there were ladies and women, the latter being the wives of the sergeants and 'other ranks'. The chaplain's wife went to meet some of the 'women', who had come in as refugees from Sitapur when the regiments there had mutinied. She gave them

> a few old dressing-gowns and things of mine which I thought would be useful, as they had lost all their own clothes. One of them is expecting to be confined immediately. They were very cheerful, and seemed quite to have got over their

troubles. It is wonderful how little that class of people seem to feel things that would almost kill a lady.[29]

The defences around the Residency hill were not as impermeable as many imagined. News came in, not only from the Indian spies who risked their lives to carry messages for the British, but from servants who were able to get out, and sometimes back. Of the 700 sepoys and servants at the beginning of the siege, 230 were said to have 'deserted' by the end, creeping out into the city. It was clear that there were also spies within the Residency, carrying messages to the rebels outside. This was empirically tested when the state prisoners were moved into an upper room of the old banqueting hall, which had become the hospital when the telegraph office ceased to function. Within a day attacks on the building by cannon had ceased. Henry Lawrence's fatal injury had been caused, people thought, because the rebels knew, from inside information, exactly where his office was. The plight of the state prisoners was anxiously followed, not least by the former ruler, Wajid Ali Shah, whose half-brother, two nephews and a niece were among them. The Nawab and some of his ministers were now state prisoners themselves, having been taken into Fort William on 15 June, following an alleged attempt to subvert sepoys in Calcutta.

The Nawab was in an unenviable position. His mother, brother and son, with a large retinue of over a hundred people had been in England for almost a year, petitioning the Court of Directors at East India House on his behalf. All the Nawab was offered was a pension of 12 lakhs a year, and the right to remain 'king' but in name only. There was no question of Awadh being restored to him, and the title would cease on his death. It was suggested by the Directors that the young princes should be 'trained and educated to become useful citizens so as to prevent them from sinking into degraded habits of life'.[30] An audience with Queen Victoria had produced nothing more than a polite but stilted conversation.

Three petitions had already been presented to the Prime Minister, Lord Palmerston, to the Board of Control, and to India House on the Nawab's behalf. A fourth, drafted for the Nawab by his legal representative, Maulvi Masih-ud-din Khan, included the radical suggestion that if Wajid Ali Shah and the heir apparent, Mirza Mohammad Hamid Ali Bahadur, were allowed to travel to Awadh, the unfortunate situation there could be resolved to the advantage of the British Government:

We have learned with great concern that a rebellion has been created in Hindustan as well as in Oudh [the petition began]. We were ready to serve the British Government to the best of our ability and power. As several accidents have now taken place in Oudh we beg to make a similar petition again to say that our exertions will at this time prove of real benefit. At the time when Oudh was taken, one lac of ryots as well as sepoys and especially zamindars made

> declarations to the effect that they were satisfied with our rule and Government and expressed their regret at the Circumstances of that territory being taken – these declarations they made of their own accord and will and for the love they have to me, without being forced or requested by anyone to do so. The paper containing declarations in question which was submitted to me some days after Oudh was annexed is now with us. We had had about 25,000 Sepoys who were all discharged. A few of them only had accepted the service of the British Government and the rest have been thrown out of employ.
>
> Moreover such servants as Burkundazes, Thanadars, Chuprassies and others, who were to the number of some thousands were dismissed and 10,000 men who are the friends and relatives both of the King and the Heir Apparent lost their appointments. It is well known to us that if the aforementioned persons and many other Ryots be placed under the Standard of the King, all the affairs will be properly arranged; for every one is anxious for the honor and prosperity of His Majesty and heartily wishes for his good. If it is settled that if the King, on account of his illness or any other cause, cannot proceed (to the North West), the Heir Apparent who is now in London may go to Hindoostan with an English Army, make all arrangements in the name of the King of Oudh, send for the people and direct them to face the rebels. We are able to make every arrangement and settle all affairs on the part of the King, as well as we shall either make a treaty for our own Kingdom with the British Government, according to the stipulation contained in the Treaties which subsisted from of old between the two States, or conclude a new one as the circumstances of the case may require. We beg to state that formerly a similar case took place when the Hon'ble Company left the Government of Cabool, they made over the rule of the country to Dost Mohammed Khan and it was fully known to all that the territory was given by the Company to the Ameer. The advantages which the British Government will reap by the adoption of the above measures are detailed in the petition and there is no doubt about the same. We are fully certain that the Hon'ble Company will take possession of the territory of Oudh and that their power is again to be established there; but if you render to the King of Oudh such justice as solicited, it will serve to spread your Glorious Name throughout the world and to afford great pleasure to the people of Hindoostan.[31]

The letter was forwarded, without comment, by John Stuart Mill, the philosopher and political commentator who was working in East India House as a political secretary. What is interesting about this diplomatically worded petition (apart from the delicate reference to the British defeat in the First Afghan War), is that it does not mention Birjis Qadr. The young man had been already crowned as heir, a fact that Wajid Ali Shah would certainly have known. Nor is there mention of Birjis Qadr's mother, Begam Hazrat Mahal, one of the Nawab's wives, whom he is said to have divorced about 1850. Had Mirza Mohammed returned to India, instead of frittering his time away in London and Paris, to his father's great despair, how would he have treated Birjis Qadr, his half-brother? And did Wajid Ali Shah really believe, in the face of all the evidence against it, that he could possibly be restored to the throne? The fact that the Begam and her son did not accompany the Nawab when he left for Calcutta in March 1856, and made no move to join him during the following year, would accord with a divorce between the couple six years earlier. The Nawab seems to have repudiated her entirely and his young son, although he left them financially secure. His overriding feelings, seen in his dignified response to the Parliamentary Blue Book on Oude (1856), his letters and his poetry, was one of regret for past glories, and puzzlement at his present unfortunate predicament. Whether he could ever have been a focus for the rebellion in Awadh is still debated in Lucknow, even today.

Sir Colin Campbell had arrived in Calcutta on 13 August 1857, summoned out of retirement by Lord Palmerston. Campbell, who later became the first Baron Clyde, had been a soldier since the age of sixteen and he had fought in major conflicts of the nineteenth century, including the Sikh Wars and the Crimean War. Although seventy-one years old when the Prime Minister called on him, Campbell did not hesitate. He was appointed Commander-in-Chief with control over the three Presidency armies, though by a curious anomaly he could not actually issue orders to the armies unless he was stationed in that particular Presidency. Thus orders for the Madras and Bombay armies, while Campbell was in the Bengal Presidency, had to come through the Governor General.

The final relief of the Residency began in November, like the previous attempts, from Cawnpore. This time it met little resistance and the British established themselves to the south of the city, near the Alambagh Palace, which had been held since the first failed rescue attempt. Campbell had about 5,000 men, including 450 from the Naval Brigade, led by Sir William Peel. The plan was to follow along the south bank of the river Gomti, in order to avoid street fighting, and to establish a safe corridor through a string of riverside buildings. Each building was surrounded by a garden, and each garden was walled, with a substantial gatehouse. Holes had to be punched in the walls before the soldiers could enter and cross the compounds. This was a technique which was to be used to good effect in the final assault on Lucknow, four months later.

Gradually the buildings along the river were penetrated in the face of fierce resistance. At the Sikanderbagh, a substantial walled enclosure with a two-storied garden pavilion, 2,000 sepoys and supporters fell to the British assault, half of them from the reconstituted Nadiri Regiment. By dusk the Shah Najaf, containing the tomb of the Nawab Ghazi-ud-din Haider, the first King of Awadh, had been captured, and British troops slept here before the final assault. On 17 November James Outram, and General Havelock rode out of the Residency to meet Colin Campbell in front of the Kurshid Manzil, the old moated palace which had been the Mess House of the 32nd. The battered survivors from the Residency were led to safety over the next two days along a screened corridor created by the relieving force, and

11. The Macchi Bhawan Fort, Lucknow, April 1858. This was heavily defended by the inhabitants of the city. The earthen wall and posts have not yet been cleared. Photograph by Felice Beato.

covered by the rifles of HM 93rd Highlanders and Peel's Naval Brigade. With them went the crown jewels, treasure and money taken from the Qaisarbagh palace, buried in the Residency during the siege and now stuffed into seventeen barrels and eight chests. Both treasure and survivors were escorted, painfully slowly, to the Alambagh Palace where General Havelock died on 24 November from dysentery, after a few days' illness. From Alambagh the refugee column moved to Cawnpore, and then by road down to Allahabad and safety. Lucknow was left, at last, to its inhabitants. Colin Campbell refused to leave a temporary garrison stationed in the city, because it was too dangerous, although he did leave James Outram and a body of troops in possession of the Alambagh.

Most histories of the Uprising ignore the period between the final relief of the Residency on 22 November 1857 and the recapture of Lucknow on 15 March 1858. There are few accounts of those four months and no administrative documents of the reconstituted court under Birjis Qadr and his mother, Begam Hazrat Mahal. The absence of the latter is easily explained. The Begam had moved into the Qaisarbagh palace and this was the headquarters of the resistance movement against the British. For this very reason, the palace was the target of uncontrolled looting by British, Indian and Nepalese troops on the recapture of the city in March, as we shall see in the next chapter. Officers were unable, or unwilling, to stop the frenzy of plunder for several days, and the opportunity to find and translate documents, as had been done at other captured forts and palaces, was lost. We have none of the domestic detail as we do from the Mutiny Papers found in the Red Fort at Delhi after Bahadur Shah Zafar's flight. Some newsletters exist because they were sent from Lucknow to supporters outside, and proclamations by Birjis Qadr and Hazrat Mahal were printed and circulated. Further information was gleaned from the depositions of prisoners tried by the British in 1859, but ironically most of our written information comes from Indians in Lucknow who were spying for the British. Their reports were collated by Major Carnegie, working in the Intelligence Department, and provide the clearest picture of what was going on.

After the British lost civil and military control over Awadh at the end of June 1857, the old pre-annexation administration of the Nawabs was re-established. It was only fifteen months since this had been dismembered and the familiar posts and titles were quickly put back in place. The naib or deputy, equivalent to the chief minister, was Sharaf-ud-daula (Ghulam Raza Khan), who had served in the same position under the Nawab Muhammad Ali Shah, twenty years earlier. The Raja Jai Lal Singh, a taluqdar in the Faizabad District, who had been a prominent courtier during the time of Wajid Ali Shah, was appointed Collector (of revenue) and he also had an important role with the Awadh Force (as the rebel army was known). He acted as the liaison between Hazrat Mahal's court in the Qaisarbagh palace and the army, whose headquarters were in the Khurshid Manzil, a short distance away. Jai Lal Singh was also in charge of the defensive works which were being put in place against the British. According to the statement by Munshi Wajid Ali, 'The making, repairing, digging entrenchments, mines, supplies, labourers, scaling-ladders were all under Jyelall Sing; he used also to go to superintend the attacks and neither court nor assault could take place without Jyelall's consent.'[32] Allied to this was his role as treasure-seeker, ordering the digging-up of various hoards of money and jewellery buried in the houses of wealthy men. The former chief minister, Ali Naki Khan, who had accompanied his master to Calcutta, was said to have lost lakhs of money which were dug up to pay the sepoys. The third powerful man in government was Mammu Khan, who was appointed 'darogah of the diwan khana', equivalent to the superintendent in charge of the Begam's political offices. These men, with about twenty others, formed the new government of Awadh, answerable to the Begam and her son. They were divided into two groups, to deal with civil administration and military strategy.

An immense task lay before them. The celebrations over the British withdrawal from the Residency were tempered by the loss of many fighting men, 2,000 alone in the Sikanderbagh, and the realisation that for all their efforts it had not been possible to prevent the British relief force from entering and leaving the city. But despite the losses sustained, there was no shortage of manpower. It was estimated that there were more than 50,000 armed men in Lucknow in the middle of November, although less than half of them were trained soldiers. The remainder were fighting under their feudal masters, the taluqdars. The wily Raja Man Singh, whose frequent changes of allegiance indicated which side had the upper hand, brought 7,000 men with him. The ending of the Residency siege freed the men who had been firing into it and undermining it, and an official proclamation that the British had abandoned the city was widely broadcast, which attracted more people into Lucknow. With the fall of Delhi at the end of September and the failure of the British to capture its fleeing defenders, sepoys who wanted to fight on flocked to Lucknow. This in turn presented its own problems, for these men had to be fed, paid and sheltered during the cold weather. At the end of 1857 there may have been as many as 100,000 armed men in and around Lucknow, carrying a variety of weapons including rifles, swords, spears and even bows and arrows.[33]

With the Mughal capital fallen to the British, hopes were pinned on Lucknow, with its boy king and its huge army of fighting men. If the city could hold out against a future attack, then the loss of Delhi might be avenged. Preparations for defence began on an unprecedented scale. Martin Gubbins, trapped in the Residency with his champagne, had noted the fortifications already erected during the siege. He saw

> screens made of wooden palisades, placed in a bank of earth and the roads and passages were everywhere intersected by their ditches and traverses – their batteries were usually formed of strong rafters of wood stuck upright and deeply embedded in the ground, and strengthened and supported by a bank of earth, a square embrasure being left in the centre for the muzzle of the cannon.[34]

Now these earthworks were to be extended round much of the city.

Unlike Delhi, the city of Lucknow was not surrounded by a sturdy wall, nor does it ever seem to have been. There were certain streets that could be closed off at each end by gates, like the old Chowk, in the heart of medieval Lucknow. In the absence of a city wall, each substantial building had its own high wall around its compound. Lucknow was a curious mixture, often remarked upon, of European-style houses, huge religious buildings and tortuous narrow alleys that led through the mohallas, the clusters of smaller and often poorer houses.

The idea of building defensive walls round the city and fortifying major complexes was suggested almost immediately after the British withdrawal. Begam Hazrat Mahal sanctioned five lakhs of rupees for construction and made a personal donation from the sale of her jewellery and valuables. A meeting of the military council divided the city into four sectors. Because the British had attacked twice from the south-east, this was where the first major defensive wall would be built. In the 1830s, the Nawab Ghazi-ud-din Haider had been persuaded by the British Resident of the time to build a canal south-east of the city that would link up with the Ganges. The project, under a British engineer, was begun, but became bogged down in disputes, recriminations and the unwillingness of landowners to have it cut through their lands.[35] The scheme was eventually abandoned, but not before a sizeable stretch had been built, fed by the Gomti. Flowing east to west, the canal passed immediately north of the Charbagh Gardens, before petering out several miles further on. Although a narrow canal, no more than five feet across, it presented an obstacle to would-be invaders, because of its steep sides and its few wooden bridges, that could easily be disabled.

This was to be the first line of defence, a 'wet ditch' as it was called, and immediately behind it, as one approached the city, a huge earthen embankment was built, properly loopholed and with embrasures, or openings, for the rebel guns. William Russell, the Irish reporter, who covered the recapture of Lucknow for *The Times*, was staggered when he saw it. He described the high parapet of earth behind La Martiniere College, beginning at the Gomti and sweeping to the left. He noted the 'enemy's trenches' and sunken 'rifle pits', which were in fact used by musket and matchlockmen. Russell described the defensive wall as 'a great railway-looking embankment'.[36] The first great wall ran from the Hosseinabad Bridge, east of the Charbagh, to the river, a distance of two and a half miles. Further west, and crossing the new Cawnpore road, which General Havelock had marched along in September, was an even longer mud wall and dry ditch, running from the fortified village of Para, through Jalalpur village to the Yellow House, which lay north of the British-held Alambagh Palace.

It was extraordinary that in spite of intense military activity, it had not been possible to dislodge James Outram and his garrison from here. The Alambagh was not a particularly large building, but it had been designed as a miniature castle, with turrets, and parapets. Like similar buildings, it stood in its own grounds, with a substantial wall around it, and a lofty two-storey gatehouse fronting the road. Nine times rebel troops had left Lucknow to attack this isolated building, which stood in the middle of fields, and nine times they had been driven back by superior British weapons. Even the presence of Begam Hazrat Mahal herself on one occasion had not been sufficient encouragement for the building to be taken. Neither had the road to Cawnpore, the only link with the British force during that winter, been successfully blocked. A deliberate policy on the part of the villagers around Alambagh to withhold food and fodder certainly inconvenienced the British, but as long as supplies continued to come in from Cawnpore, their non-co-operation was a futile gesture. It was thought that by building the earthen wall between Alambagh and the city the British base would be cut off and could not be used to launch the assault.

In case these two major defences were breached, it was decided to fortify Qaisarbagh, the administrative headquarters, as well as the Moti Mahal, another huge palace complex, and the Khurshid Manzil, the military headquarters. Stockades and parapets were erected across the main streets, and every house was loopholed. Moti Lal, a merchant who left Lucknow in January 1858 for Allahabad, reported that entrenchments had been made from the Taronwali Kothi (the Observatory), up to the Sher Darwaza, where Neill had been killed, and along to the Chattar Manzil.[37] A moat was dug around Qaisarbagh, filled by the waters of the Gomti. The Sikanderbagh, where so many men had been killed, had a parapet built up in front of its tall gateway. Embankments were thrown around outlying buildings to the south-east, beyond the line of the canal embankment, including Dilkusha Palace, a hunting lodge in an enormous park, and La Martiniere College. To the extreme north-west, the isolated Barowen Palace at Musa Bagh was fortified. The stone bridge crossing the river in front of the Macchi Bhawan fort was surrounded by embankments, and the strategic Tripolia Gateway that led to the Great Imambara had earth walls reaching to its second storey. The entrance to the Macchi Bhawan, where Henry Lawrence had hanged the mutineers, was surrounded with ditches and fortified embankments, bristling with upright teak timbers embedded in the earth. The gateway of the fort was bricked up, with a small embrasure at the top. A similar scene was photographed outside the Rumi Darwaza, which had been the processional route between two major religious complexes. It was assumed that the Gomti would form a natural northern barrier against an attack and that now the eastern, southern and western boundaries of the city were defended by walls and entrenchments, Lucknow was as impregnable as it could be. By March 1858 General Sir James Hope Grant reported that the inhabitants 'had fortified their stronghold to the utmost extent of which they were capable. The Kaiser Bagh constituted the citadel.'[38]

Outwardly, Lucknow presented a united face against the common enemy, the British. But there was serious dissension between Begam Hazrat Mahal's party and Maulvi Ahmadullah's supporters. Some of it was ideological. The Maulvi, who had refused to attend Birjis Qadr's coronation, on the plea of an injury sustained at Chinhat, announced in December 1857 that he was the Vice-Regent of God. As such, he expected Birjis Qadr and his mother to acknowledge him and carry out his orders. We are more cynical in the west today about people like the Maulvi, who make dramatic claims to be divinely inspired, but there is a long history of such charismatic preachers in India, who appealed to both Muslims and Hindus. The Maulvi's effect on the people of Lucknow and the sepoys who had come from Delhi should not be underestimated. He was an inspirational character, although he cannot have been an easy person to work with, let alone to co-opt on to a council of war planning a coherent military response to the coming British assault.

The defenders of Lucknow split into two factions – those supporting the Begam and Birjis Qadr, formed from the Oudh Irregular Army sepoys who had mutinied, and the sepoys from Delhi, who were generally behind the Maulvi. Different rates of pay for the two forces exacerbated the problem, the local sepoys getting Rs 12 per month, while the Delhi sepoys got Rs 7 per month. The first showdown came on 18 December when, according to British reports from their Indian spies, the Begam invited the Maulvi to a meeting. Ahmadullah, who had set up his headquarters in the old Observatory, had been forced out during the fighting in November when the people besieged in the Residency were finally rescued by troops under Generals Havelock, Campbell and Outram. Ahmadullah moved west to Gaughat, on the Gomti, and starting building a bridge of boats across the river. The Begam objected to this and sent Mammu Khan to stop him.

This was the initial dispute, and Hazrat Mahal, realising how damaging it could be, invited the Maulvi to Qaisarbagh for a reconciliation. The Maulvi agreed to the meeting, but only on the condition that neither the Chief Minister, Sharaf-ud-daula, nor the Diwan-i-Khana, Mammu Khan, were present. This the Begam agreed to, and the meeting ended cordially with the Maulvi agreeing to send his troops, the Delhi sepoys, due east to stop the rumoured advance of Gurkha troops under the Nepalese leader Jang Bahadur. Accordingly the Maulvi's sepoys set out on 24 December towards Daryabad, to meet the Gurkhas, but they had not gone very far when a horseman stopped them with a letter supposedly from the Maulvi. The letter-writer said that the object of the Begam and her Chief Minister in sending the men to intercept the Gurkhas was simply a ploy to get them out of Lucknow so the city could be handed over to the British by the Begam. The letter-writer further suggested that harmony would not be restored until Sharaf-ud-daula was forcibly removed from the scene. Although the letter was almost certainly a forgery, and possibly even planted by the British to divide the defenders of Lucknow, the troops took it as a *hukumnama*, an order, and returned to the city. Here they were caught up in a brawl with the Begam's troops and a hundred men in all, from both sides, are said to have been killed outside the north-west gate of Qaisarbagh on 7 January 1858, in an intense two-hour fight that only ceased with the Begam's arrival.[39] A further move to divide the rebels came with an offer from James Outram to the Begam. A guarantee of one lakh rupees a year as pension and a treaty with Queen Victoria was offered if Hazrat Mahal would surrender. Outram's letter was tossed contemptuously aside.

At the end of January 1858 the Begam was alerted by a letter from Raja Kanwar Singh, the old zamindar from Jagdishpur in Bihar, saying that the British had reached an agreement with the Nepalese leader, Jang Bahadur. In return for providing his Gurkha troops to assist in the recapture of Lucknow, he had been offered the town of Gorakhpur, plus a substantial share of the anticipated prize money and loot. Hazrat Mahal countered this by offering him not only Gorakhpur, but the cities of Azamgarh, Arrah, and Benares as well, if he would side with her. Two men from Lucknow were sent to Jang Bahadur at Gorakhpur, to put her offer. Half spies, half ambassadors, they were disguised as faqirs of the Qalandari sect, a curious cross-over group of wandering Muslims who had adopted the ways of Hindu *sadhus* (holy men). Both were captured by the British and put to death, and 9,000 Gurkha troops began their march towards Lucknow in support of the Company's army.

Their progress was painfully slow, estimated at only six miles a day, because the troops were accompanied by their wives and camp followers. So it was not until the beginning of the hot season in March that Colin Campbell, Commander-in-Chief, was ready to move on the city. A huge army had been put together for the reconquest and it was confidently stated that once Lucknow was taken, the whole of Awadh would fall.[40] This proved not to be the case, although the retaking of Lucknow was of great symbolic importance, as had been the rescue of the people from the Residency four months earlier. On 2 March a total of nearly 58,000 men began advancing towards the city. With Colin Campbell in overall control, the armies were led by three generals – Outram, Franks and Jang Bahadur. They brought with them 11,677 horses and 132 guns. The majority of the soldiers were British, sent out from England to boost the Company's army. Against them were an estimated 36,000 men, including the Maulvi's 8,000 troops, 2,400 of the Delhi sepoys, 2,200 of Raja Mahmudabad's men, 1,800 of Khan Ali Khan's men and over 2,500 volunteers.[41] Moti Lal, the merchant, had estimated that there were nearly 50,000 armed men in Lucknow in January, including the Bole Battalion (the former 22nd Bengal Native Infantry), the Jellasore Battalion (formerly the 56th BNI) and the former 9th BNI. He noted however, that the ratio of villagers armed with muskets was 600 men to every 400 sepoys.

As anticipated by Begam Hazrat Mahal, the British took up positions to the south-east of Lucknow, facing the canal and the great embankment behind it. They had secured the country houses of Dilkusha and Bibiapur. La Martiniere College, although strongly defended by the rebels, also fell to the British. But the first attack on the city itself did not come from the south-east. In a daring move Campbell divided the army into two wings and sent Outram's troops across the Gomti on an improvised bridge of casks, and up on to the Faizabad Road, to the east of the city. From here, they advanced across the old racecourse, taking the Chakkar Kothi, the round grandstand, after a sustained bombardment. They were now directly opposite the palaces that lined the south bank of the Gomti. Placing batteries of guns at strategic angles, they began firing into the city, across the river, the one approach that had not been defended by barricades. The largest battery, of twelve guns, was directed on to the embankment behind the canal where the Awadh forces stood at their loopholes, unable to engage the enemy who were raking them with cannon from their left. The wall and the canal had seemed impregnable, but it was breached on 9 March by Campbell's troops, who seized it and then began to fight their way into the city along the road from La Martiniere College.

Some of the fiercest fighting was at the Begam Kothi palace, surrounded with earthen palisades and embedded upright teak planks. Almost 5,000 of the Awadh Forces were concentrated here, and when the barricades were eventually breached, the majority retreated, leaving some 700 men to fight to their deaths. Their bodies were rolled into the ditches in front of the barricades, and remain there today, under the pounding traffic of the Vidhan Sabha Marg, without any kind of memorial. Once the Begam Kothi had fallen to the British, it was possible to move forward towards the fortified Qaisarbagh Palace where Begam Hazrat Mahal was still holding out. Using the same tactics that had been employed in the November rescue, the British advanced by punching their way through the walls of the houses and palaces, instead of approaching directly along the main streets where they could have been picked off. After the large religious complex of the Sibtainabad Imambara had been taken, it was possible to enter the outer courtyard of the Qaisarbagh, the seat of the Awadh government, and the richest prize. Fortuitously the Gurkha troops under their leader, Jang Bahadur who had been slowly making their way towards Lucknow, arrived on 14 March just in time to join in the uncontrolled looting that now took place.

Because Campbell had not expected Qaisarbagh to be taken so quickly, having underestimated its attractions for the troops, the Iron Bridge over the Gomti had not yet been secured by the British. It therefore remained open on the night of 14 March allowing an estimated 20,000 people to flee across it and escape eastwards along the Faizabad Road, which had been left unguarded. Hazrat Mahal was persuaded to flee the following day, and she and her supporters took refuge in Barowen, the elegant country house popularly known as Musa Bagh. A final offer of surrender with honour from James Outram had been treated with the same disdain by the Begam as earlier proposals. Pursued by Outram's troops, the last major encounter took place on 19 March, when several hundred of Lucknow's last defenders were killed at Barowen. The Begam, now an exile, fled towards the Nepalese border, where she continued to fight and issue defiant proclamations. From Barowen several thousand more fugitives managed to escape the British. As had happened at Delhi, it was impossible to pursue and capture the fleeing rebels, familiar with the countryside and able to move more quickly.

The Maulvi and the Chief Minister had both fled to the Dargah Hazrat Abbas, an important shrine to the west of the city. According to British reports, Ahmadullah had taken the minister hostage, hoping to bargain his way out, or perhaps to settle an old score. Indian accounts claim that Sharaf-ud-daula was killed and his body mutilated by Brigadier Edward Lugard and

12. The interior of Sikanderbagh pavilion, photographed by Felice Beato in March/April 1858. Note the unbricked doorway to the right of the building, where corpses had been covered with earth and entombed since November 1857.

his men. Whatever the truth is, Maulvi Ahmadullah escaped, or was allowed to escape, and lived to fight another day.[42] The number of Indians killed in the recapture is unknown, but clearly it exceeded the modest British total of 127 killed and nearly 600 wounded.

The Nawab, Wajid Ali Shah, never saw Lucknow again, resigning himself to a luxurious exile in Calcutta. His mother and brother both died in Europe, on their fruitless mission to Queen Victoria. Both are buried in an unmarked grave in Père Lachaise Cemetery, in Paris. Two of the state prisoners, Mirza Hyder Shikoh and Humayun Shah, who had endured the siege of the Residency and were subsequently taken to Allahabad with the British refugees, were released at the end of 1858 without charge.[43] The Lucknow palaces were comprehensively looted, and the great walls that were supposed to defend the city were demolished, the labourers being paid by fines levied on the citizens of the city. Superior firepower, a larger army, and more imaginative tactics all contributed toward the British victory. Divisions between the rebels, lack of modern weaponry and lack of decisive military leadership had made the reconquest easier. Had the Nepalese leader been persuaded to join Hazrat Mahal and her defenders, and had the vacillating Man Singh not changed sides again, things might have been different. Certainly there was no lack of courage and ingenuity on the part of the men behind the great wall of Lucknow.

Felice Beato's best known Lucknow photograph, taken in March 1858, is that of the Sikanderbagh, the battered pavilion which was captured in November 1857 with the loss of many Indian lives. In the courtyard lie skulls, bones, still articulated skeletons and clothes, the whole scene described as 'the most eerie and perhaps the only [photograph] that gives us an honest glimpse at what our Lucknow really went through'.[44] But had the bodies really been lying there, unburied, for four months? Or did Beato have them disinterred to make his picture look more realistic, as some photographic historians have claimed?[45] In fact the bodies of the men killed on 17 November 1857 had to be speedily removed, because Sikanderbagh was on the escape route for the newly released British refugees from the Residency. Elephants were used to drag the corpses out, the dead and the dying having been burnt in a grisly funeral pyre. Some were unceremoniously tossed into a pit or pits beside the main road. Others were entombed in the entrenchment ditches dug as defences. Still others were said to have been walled up within the Sikanderbagh pavilion itself, piled into the side rooms, covered with earth and the doors roughly plastered over. The compound was cleaned and made ready for the women and children, who were received with biscuits, bread and butter and cups of tea and remained there for several hours until *doolies* (palanquins) were ready to take them on to safety.[46]

However, Sikanderbagh was stormed again on the morning of 11 March 1858, when human remains were apparently still visible. The historian John Fraser has examined the mystery of 'Beato's bones' and has traced an account by James Wise, a medical officer, who noted that on re-occupying Sikanderbagh 'The heaps of Pandys in the east room, over which we heaped earth, lie a festering mass'. It was also suggested that scavenging dogs had disinterred some of the sepoy bodies buried in the ditch or the pits. A description of Beato at work, written many years after the events, noted 'The great pile of bodies had been decently covered over before the photographer could take them, but he insisted on having them uncovered to be photographed before they were finally disposed of'.[47] Almost certainly then the bodies are those which had been walled up in the 'east room' mentioned by Wise. In fact a close examination of the photograph shows that the doorway to the right, or east, of the building is open, and that the debris in the courtyard and on the verandah is likely to have come from that doorway being recently broken open so the bodies could be removed for disposal. The three men in the centre of the photograph are likely to be the labourers who have unbricked the doorway and the horse to the left was Beato's transport to the Sikanderbagh. Whatever the story behind the image, it is a grim reminder of the true cost of the defence of Lucknow.

Four

THE PRIZE AGENTS

> The people are all coming back to the City, and the Shops are being opened, so that we shall have many things we want. There has been a great deal of plundering, or as it is called here 'looting' – but we have had too much to do and have been out of the way of such things … we hope to get some prize money but nothing has been ordered on that subject yet.[1]

JAMES GIBBON was writing to his mother on 31 March 1858 from Lucknow, where he had been part of the relieving force under Sir James Outram. As an officer he was hopeful of getting his share of the prize money distributed to soldiers after a successful action and he speculated that it might be as much as £400 or £500. The word 'loot' comes from the Hindustani *lut* meaning 'depredation, plunder, pillage, spoil or booty', and had entered the English language towards the end of the eighteenth century, after a series of Company wars against Indian rulers. Looting played a particularly important part in the Great Uprising. We have already seen that it was a powerful incentive for many of the rebels, both sepoys and civilians, who would loot indiscriminately from fellow Indians as well as Europeans caught up in the revolt.

What is perhaps surprising is that the role of the Company's Prize Agents has received so little attention in histories of the Uprising. The agents, sanctioned by the British Army in India and the Company army, were licensed looters, whose job it was to raid houses and properties after the capture of a city and seize anything of value. Their task was threefold: firstly, to punish the rebels, or those suspected of rebellion, by confiscating their possessions; secondly, to recoup some of the money expended by the Company on putting down the revolt, for war is always an expensive business; and thirdly, to reward officers and men with prize money, providing an incentive for them to recapture the rich but rebellious cities of northern India. The misery caused by the Prize Agents in the autumn of 1857, particularly after the fall of Delhi and subsequent capitulations, cannot be underestimated. It led to disputes between the military officers who began to regard property seized by their agents as belonging to the army and not the government. Civilian administrators like Sir John Lawrence complained bitterly, but without effect, to the Governor General that confidence among the Indian merchants could not be restored until the Prize Agents were reined in.

Search parties sent out on treasure-seeking expeditions were bound to cause alarm and dismay among the civilian population. The Prize Agents were not simply taking discarded arms and ammunition from captured forts, as part of the spoils of war, but searching house after house, street by street, in some of the richest and most sophisticated cities of northern India. The rewards were immense, but so were the opportunities for corruption, self-enrichment at the Company's expense, intimidation of householders and general ill-will towards a government that allowed plundering to go on for weeks until there was nothing left to take. 'The atrocities committed by the Government native Troops [the mutinous sepoys] served, no doubt, as severe punishment, but no one ever thought that the capture of Delhie by Englishmen would be attended with more cruelty to the general population, than that by a Nadir', wrote Sannat Nana from Mhow in November 1857.[2] He referred to the last sack of Delhi by the Persian ruler Nadir Shah in 1737, when the fountains in the main street, Chandni Chowk, ran red with the blood of its slaughtered inhabitants, and the troops were hardly able to carry their loot, including the Peacock Throne, home with them. By the middle of the nineteenth century the inhabitants of Delhi might have hoped for fairer treatment than their predecessors had received 120 years earlier. After all, British politicians and missionaries were frequently emphasising the benefits of 'Christian civilisation over heathen cruelty and purposes',[3] but when it came down to it, it didn't seem to make much difference whether the looters were Christian, Muslim or Hindu.

The origins of British prize money date back to medieval times, and arose at sea when captured ships and their cargoes became the property of the Crown. The monarch had three choices: the prerogative to keep the proceeds of the sale; to distribute the money to the sailors who had captured the vessels; or to keep a proportion of the proceeds and distribute the remainder. Distribution was initially made by the captain to his crew, after a successful capture, but this was formalised in 1708 when an Admiralty Prize Court was set up to evaluate competing claims and arrange for distribution to sailors in proportion to their rank. The system worked well, conflicting claims were tried in open court and 'naval prize money is usually distributed in a few months after its acquisition, whereas military prize money appears to be locked up for several years'.[4] The fact that there was no similar regulatory body for army prize money led to lengthy delays where disputes arose. In the great Deccan Prize controversy, as it became known, prize captured in 1803 when Arthur Wellesley, commanding the Madras Army, defeated the Marathas, was not distributed until 1826, by which time many of the soldiers were dead. There were involved discussions on the difference between booty captured without

13. The Prize Agents at work. Note the Sikh sepoys standing guard while a British officer threatens a terrified *baniya* (merchant) with a pistol, as the recovery of prize goes on.

resistance and booty captured in the course of a battle. Then there was the difference between 'actual capture', that is, prize captured by a specific group of soldiers, and 'constructive capture' when, for example, a fort was taken by one unit who were being supported by other troops in the area. Was everyone entitled to prize, and how many miles distant could fellow soldiers be to claim constructive capture? And whole towns, or parts of a town could be held to ransom too, the unhappy inhabitants being charged for the privilege of moving back into their own homes. Thus there were endless opportunities for litigation, and lawyers rubbed their hands over such cases, their fees diminishing the capital amount in question.

Lord Palmerston, as Prime Minister, in his second term of office (1859–65) set up a Royal Commission on the subject, a delaying tactic still used today. A Bill was passed with the purpose of extending the jurisdiction of the High Court of the Admiralty to include military as well as naval booty,[5] but this was an unsatisfactory compromise that does not seem to have been resorted to often. It is not surprising therefore that when opportunities arose in India, as they frequently did, for obtaining prize money there should be disputes and delays in paying it out. In spite of all this, when the money was finally paid out, it had often amounted to considerable sums, even for lower-ranking soldiers. After the capture of Seringapatam in 1792, the total amount of prize money was 45 lakhs of rupees, equivalent at that time to nearly half a million pounds sterling. There were very specific rules on how the money was divided up – that was the one area where there was no dispute. Once the total sum was known, then everyone could calculate what they would get. Naturally the army commanders got the largest share. Lord Lake is said to have got £38,000 after the capture of Agra in 1803, and Sir Colin Campbell, the victor at Lucknow, had 'a direct personal interest, to the amount of many thousand pounds, in the successful prosecution of the claim put forth on behalf of Sir Hugh Rose'.[6]

Basic salaries for soldiers differed according to their race and where they were serving. The sepoy in the Company's Bengal Army got Rs 7 a month (about 14 shillings) from which he had to find some of his uniform and his food. A private soldier in the Company's European Regiment got a basic salary of just over Rs 10 a month and a private soldier in Her Majesty's Army got about Rs 15 per month.[7] There were various allowances including *batta*, which was originally to cover the extra expense of serving in the field, that is, away from the cantonment, and this sum came to be regarded as a small, though welcome addition to the basic wage. Attempts to remove *batta* from soldiers in cantonments, where their expenses were less, led to furious responses, and sometimes mutinies by European and Indian soldiers. Sir Eyre Coote, leading a mixed bag of troops after the battle of Plassey in 1757 was faced with just such a situation and apart from flogging the European mutineers, he hinted that the sepoys would lose the chance of prize money if they did not return to duty.[8] Prize money won through capture was thus both an incentive and a reward, even though sepoys received only half the amount that the white soldiers got.

In the absence of a government body to pay out prize money, Prize Agents were appointed by ballot from among the officers of the regiment. They acted as members of a military tribunal whose job it was to calculate the amount that each soldier got after a successful campaign. In some cases a Prize Committee would be set up, whose function was similar. Muster rolls of soldiers who had taken part in the campaign would be drawn up, and from this the Prize Rolls would be compiled. Not every soldier on the strength of the regiment would be eligible, for some would be sick and others would be on leave. Once the Prize Rolls were approved, certificates were issued, like the one for Assistant Surgeon Charles Dodgson Madden who 'served with the 43rd Light Infantry in the suppression of the Indian Mutiny 1857–1859 and was with the regiment at the surrender of Kirwee, and as such is entitled to a share of the booty date: 20 March 1867'.[9]

Collecting prize or treasures which could be turned into money had the added justification after the Uprising that the rebels were being punished, even if they had not been apprehended. Unfortunately discrimination was not always made between the guilty, the innocent and those who had already suffered from looting by the rebels or the badmashes. It was reported in

July 1857, for example, that soldiers under General Havelock 'were allowed to plunder the town of Futtehpore [Fatehpur], in retribution for the recent rebellion of its inhabitants' and that 'the General thought it right that an example should be made of Futtehpore, and the Sikhs were left behind for the not unwelcome task of looting and burning the place'.[10] By an order of 29 January 1858, prize and treasure that was taken direct from rebels went straight to the army. This was applicable, for example, to forts where rebels had surrendered, fled or been killed. 'Indirect' prize, that is things like promissory notes for bank deposits and hidden treasure went to the Crown and was made over to the civil authorities, who attempted to realise its worth through auction sales. Lieutenant Colonel de Renzie Brett, of 3rd Madras European Regiment and President of the Prize Committee Saugor Field Force complained that perishable property captured at Banda and Kirwee was realising less than half its value, because it was being sold at Allahabad instead of a larger city. There was 'small competition' for the shawls here, he complained, 'compared to that of Calcutta where there is a considerable European population of every denomination, whom from experience we found to be the principal purchaser of this article'. Nevertheless, the Colonel added, whatever profits were made from the proceeds of the sales were being 'placed to the credit of Her Majesty'.[11] Thus Queen Victoria and her government benefited directly from the sale of goods looted by the British.

Delhi and Lucknow, the most populous, the richest and the most rebellious cities were also the most profitable in terms of prize. The fact that their populations seem so small to us today shows how much wealth was concentrated in a comparatively tight urban area. The first Delhi census, completed in 1846, gave the number of inhabitants as nearly 138,000, with a majority of Hindu households (19,257) compared to Muslim households (14,761).[12] By 1857 it had risen to 153,000. The population of Lucknow had exceeded that of Delhi for most of the nineteenth century, and surprisingly, continued to do so until the beginning of the twentieth century. A detailed census had been carried out in Lucknow in 1856, after the annexation of Awadh, giving a total of 370,000 people in the capital city, although this is thought to be an underestimation by a local historian.[13] Even allowing for a decline in Lucknow's population as the last nawab and his court moved to Calcutta, it was still more than double that of Delhi.

The final assault on Delhi by British troops began on 14 September 1857. Delhi had been in rebel hands since 11 May that year when the sepoys from Meerut had arrived to pledge their loyalty to the Delhi King, Bahadur Shah Zafar. In spite of large numbers of well-armed and well-trained soldiers in the walled city that summer, they had been unable to dislodge the British troops who clung stubbornly to the Ridge, outside the city. Now under Major General Archdale Wilson, commanding the Delhi Field Force, retribution was at hand. In the early hours of the morning the troops were lined up and the orders for the assault read out. Those wounded would be left where they fell. *If* the assault was successful, *dooli* bearers (stretcher bearers) would be sent out to collect them. If not, they were to prepare for the worst. No prisoners were to be taken, because there were no spare men to guard them. There was to be no indiscriminate plundering. Prize Agents had already been appointed to collect and sell all captured property, and all prize taken was to be put into 'a common stock for fair division after all was over'.[14] Wilson's General Order, composed on 6 September, was to be widely ignored. Even as preparations for the assault were being made, warnings were given about what would happen. The *Illustrated London News* foretold that

> The fate of Delhi must be an example to future ages; and with an army composed as ours is of fierce Affghans and half-civilised Sikhs, bearing in their hearts every legendary and present grudge, and an insatiate longing for plunder it will be hard indeed to bridle elements so various and unruly, or to put a limit to their excesses.[15]

Colonel Edward Greathed, who was to play a significant role in the storming of Delhi, complained of the plundering habits of some of the Punjab troops.

> The appointment of Prize Agents will, I hope, prevent an indiscriminate pillage. But the Punjab troops are inveterate plunderers. One of Coke's men [from the 1st Punjab Infantry, 'Coke's Rifles'] shot a 'Pandy' yesterday and a number rushed out to plunder the corpse ... there is no restraining these fellows and the sooner they go back to the frontier when the work is over, the better.[16]

There were thus plenty of warning signs about what could happen if discipline was not maintained after, as well as before, the recapture of Delhi.

After breaching the Kashmir Gate, the guns of the Delhi Field Force were dragged onto the lawns of Delhi College and fired at the remains of the Magazine, which was stormed on the morning of 16 September. Vast quantities of ordnance, ammunition and stores were found here, showing that the earlier reported shortages of supplies had been overcome and that the sepoys had been well prepared for the final assault. It was however the superior equipment of the British that proved to be the most powerful weapon, as it would again at the recapture of Lucknow, six months later.

On 18 September, Bahadur Shah Zafar, with his family, the remaining loyal soldiers and the Christian bandsmen left the Red Fort through the water gate, and fled downriver to Humayun's tomb, some six miles to the south of Delhi. By 20 September, Delhi had truly fallen, the rebels 'abandoning their camp, carriages, property and many of the wounded'. The cost in British lives had been heavy – over 1,061 officers were killed, including Brigadier General John Nicholson who commanded the main storming party at the beginning of the assault. General Wilson established his headquarters in the Diwan-i-Khas, the private apartments of the King, and Major Anson of the 9th Lancers wrote joyfully the next day 'Delhi is wholly and completely ours. Not a shot has been fired today, and the Prize Agents are busy at work.'[17] 'The townspeople have all fled leaving the greater part of the property behind them,' reported Wilson. However, this property included almost unlimited supplies of beer and brandy in the deserted shops. The warning that it would be difficult to restrain the Afghan and Sikh troops from plunder proved correct. It was, if anything, an understatement, but a useful defence in explaining why the victorious troops had not attempted to chase the rebels fleeing from Delhi who were making their way to Lucknow to carry on the fight.

In a report to the Governor General from Delhi on 21 September, General Wilson explained that:

> Your Lordship need not be informed of the disorganisation and a temporary absence of restraint and control which follow as a consequence on the assault of a large city – even with a force composed of the best disciplined troops – but when it is considered that a large portion of my force consists of new levies, raised from among Tribes who have been brought up in habits of plunder and with no ideas of discipline of any description, the improbability of organising in the moment of success a column of sufficient strength to follow in pursuit will be manifest. Order is now being rapidly restored and I am using my best endeavours to push on a column in the direction taken by insurgents down the right bank of the Jumna.

But the impetus had been lost.

> The troops here have been greatly demoralised by the severity of the duties they have so long had to perform, their heavy losses and the immense amount of plunder and liquor which fell into their hands on their obtaining possession of the city and it has been found impracticable to organise a column earlier to pursue the enemy.[18]

Those troops who were not busy plundering were drunk and incapable of action for several days. It is tempting to imagine what would have happened if the sepoys who had held Delhi for four months had been directed by an inspired leader. A determined attack on the city once the liquor shops had been emptied would have found little resistance, but the sepoys had moved on.

Within the palace of the Red Fort itself, the gates were blown open with a 250-pound charge of gunpowder, and its last ten defenders killed. There was not a great deal of treasure here, for the Delhi King had not been a wealthy man, compared to the Nawabs of Awadh. There were a few things to be had though, 'and the first comers served themselves to some nice loot in the shape of English guns and rifles and native curiosities from the zenana. There are some very rare copies of Persian books found,' reported Major Anson. 'I was in the Palace this morning' he went on chattily, 'and picked up a few playthings for the children.'[19] But outside 'the city is a perfect picture of desolation, completely abandoned. A vast amount of property was left behind, which our Native troops are possessing themselves of with great gusto.'[20] 'The ruin and desolation apparent all over the city are indescribable. Valuable property of all kinds is lying about broken and uncared for. Our brave troops will not want for prize money even if they should not get a heap of it in the palace.'[21]

Would there be anything left for the Prize Agents, one wonders? How did they go about their task, when the soldiers, Pathan, Sikh and British seemed to be doing it for them? And was there a difference between 'prize' and 'loot'? In theory, there should have been. As we have seen, the Prize Agents' work was to punish the rebels by confiscating their property, recouping some of the war costs and rewarding the soldiers. Looted goods, taken indiscriminately after the fall of Delhi from houses, public buildings, places of worship, or simply found lying in the streets, went to the people who took them, the soldiers, sepoys, officers, Company officials, their wives and even the odd missionary.

No one seemed to think there was anything wrong in looting or in buying looted goods. An argument put forward in favour of the Delhi looting by the soldiers and sepoys, quite apart from that of the hardships they had suffered during the summer of 1857, was the delay in paying out prize money. It was better to have cash, or goods that could be turned into cash, in hand straight away, it was reasoned, and this idea of immediate gratification permeated the victors' attitudes, from the highest to the lowest. The Reverend William Butler, Superintendent of the first American Missions in India, who had arrived the year before, wandered through a still deserted Delhi in December 1857 and up the steps of the Jama Masjid. Although everything of value had long since been carried off, he did manage to find something.

> I entered their treasure room, and on the ground, covered with broken boxes and rubbish, I found those marble slabs (of the existence and use of which I had previously heard), one professing to bear the impress of Mohammed's hand, and the other of his foot. I found them where they kept their most venerated things. Those who sought only precious metals and other valuables had not considered them worthy of removal, but to me they were deeply significant and, as 'looting' was the order of the day, I carried them off, to the great amusement of the Beloochee [Baluchi] soldiers, who laughed at the idea of the 'Sahib' soiling his clothes to carry away 'such useless things as those dirty stones.'

'As long as they last they will be an evidence of the debasement of Oriental

Mohammedanism, furnished by the treasure room of its greatest mosque,' he added piously.[22]

Butler, a fervent denouncer of Hinduism and Islam, whom even the saintly Sir Henry Lawrence thought was mad, evidently found no anomaly in stealing Muslim treasures, and at the same time condemning the rebellious sepoys who destroyed his little mission chapel in Bareilly.

Choice articles of loot were presented as gifts to important people, and were received by them with no scruples at all. The Commissioner of Patna, writing to the Government Secretary, Cecil Beadon, in April 1858, told him that he was transmitting

> three packages of Marble articles found in the house of the rebel Rajah of Satree when the place was taken by Colonel Rowcroft. One is a marble chair of State which Colonel Rowcroft begged might be presented to the Governor General. The others are images of Hindu deities and are forwarded for presentation to the Asiatic Society.[23]

Sir Colin Campbell was presented with two oil-paintings taken from the throne room of Qaisarbagh Palace in Lucknow, which he subsequently passed on to the Royal Engineers Officers' Mess in Chatham. Campbell also presented to Lady Canning, the wife of the Governor General, four black swans, which he said was the only booty he brought with him from Lucknow.[24] Loot could cover anything moveable, including animals, which were considered fair game. Lieutenant Colonel Malcolm, commanding the Field Force at the little town of Shorapur, in the Gulbarga District, wanted instructions 'relative to the disposal of the captured property of the Rajah, and that which appertains to the State'.[25] In particular he wrote that 'It will be very desirable to dispose of Elephants and Cattle to avoid unnecessary expense for their maintenance'.

Although the original concept of prize had been something which belonged in title to the reigning monarch of England, but which was granted at his or her discretion to the sailors or soldiers who had liberated it, the lines are blurred between what went to the Government of India (and ultimately to the British Queen), what went to the different states where prize was found, and what the army got for distribution to officers and men. That the Prize Agents themselves were confused is shown by Renzie de Brett's statement that the sale of the prize goods was benefiting Queen Victoria, when it should have gone to the army. In another anomaly the Government of India was found purchasing oriental manuscripts offered for sale by the Prize Agents and 'Oriental Books confiscated during the Mutiny'. The Governor General learnt that among the oriental treasures were about 2,000 rare and valuable manuscripts which Canning was 'anxious to purchase for the Government of India'. Some of these had certainly been looted from Bahadur Shah Zafar's library in the Red Fort, so they were 'rebel property'. But so was the prize taken from the Raja of Shorapur. Canning asked that the sale of the manuscripts be postponed until a European officer could examine them 'as the duty of selection cannot be entrusted with confidence to any native',[26] but in the end it was decided to purchase all the manuscripts.

The Delhi Prize Agents went about their work systematically, by dividing the city into sections and issuing Company officers with 'tickets for so many days' hunting'. Their work was made easier because the great majority of Delhi's inhabitants were now outside the city walls. Those who could had fled on the recapture of the city, and were to remain homeless for months, living in tents, or finding shelter with sympathetic villagers. Those who remained were too frightened to leave their homes, and stayed shut up in them for several days, suffering their own privations. The celebrated poet Mirza Muhammad Asadullah Khan, known as Ghalib, and his family had endured the siege from their *haveli* (courtyard house) near Chandni Chowk. Unable to go out for provisions, even if they could have found any, they had had to ration their water supply carefully. But they were saved by a fortunate chance. A number of *hakims* (Muslim doctors) lived in the same lane as Ghalib's family, and these hakims were associated with the Sikh Court of Patiala. After an agonising two-day period of indecision, the Maharaja of Patiala had allied himself with the British, and on the fall of Delhi he was allowed to post his own soldiers at the entrance to the lane, to protect its inhabitants. This ad hoc arrangement prevented these houses from being looted, and the inmates were able to go out for food and water from the nearest well, although they were warned not to cross Chandni Chowk at the risk of their lives.[27]

> [Because] the force left to protect the city was inadequate to the duty of providing guards for all the gates, the Palace Magazine, and for defending the sick and wounded and other garrison duties … it was considered necessary to block up all but three or four gates, and to prevent the entrance of the inhabitants except under protection papers.[28]

In theory, the so-called 'protection tickets' or protection papers were issued to honest citizens who had taken no part in the rebellion. It did not give them the right to move back into Delhi, but was merely to show that their houses were protected from the Prize Agents. The tickets or papers were to be attached to the main door of the house. In practice, General Archdale Wilson, from his Red Fort headquarters, had ordered that all tickets were to be countersigned by him personally, with the result that few people managed to obtain protection for their property.

Charles Saunders, the Delhi Commissioner, wrote at length about the situation to William Muir, who was collating intelligence reports in Agra. Even the few houses for which their owners had managed to get protection could not be saved in the anarchic conditions that prevailed inside Delhi, for

> no guards could be furnished, and before two or three days had elapsed there was not a house which had not been ransacked and plundered of its contents, friends, and foes, the Government suffering to an equal extent. The chief wealth of the citizens however had been carefully buried and secreted in closets which had been ingeniously bricked [up] and plastered over. The Seikhs and others with the Force, very soon learnt the artifice; and a very considerable amount of plunder has been carried off, which will not enrich the Prize Fund.[29]

The amount of loot taken by the Sikh sepoys did cause concern, not from any moral viewpoint, but because it was feared it might set a precedent.

> Already the Seikh soldiers are laden with plunder and some sensible men, who have been long in the Punjab, express an apprehension lest when they return to their homes, their friends among the mountain tribes may have their cupidity excited by the sight of so much silver and gold and of the opportunity of acquiring for themselves, by means less friendly to us a similar booty in this land of gold and silver. [30]

Luckily William Muir's fears were not realised, but rumours of even larger amounts of booty to be had when Lucknow fell certainly attracted the Gurkha troops down from Nepal.

Behind the sepoy looters came the Prize Agents. Charles Saunders reported that

> [they] have since been busily engaged in ransacking the houses of those of the rebels and others who have enjoyed a reputation for wealth, or disloyalty to our Government. It has been considered by the Prize Agents that with regard to loyalty the *onus probandi* [burden of proof] lies with the parties whose property is subjected to search, and that all must be considered to be enemies who cannot satisfactorily prove that they have done anything to show that they are our friends. The Prize Agents and the Army generally were rather anxious to lay it down as a rule that the whole city had become the property of the Army, having been taken by assault and were anxious to dispose of real as well as personal, or moveable property.[31]

The Prize Agents soon learnt what the Sikh sepoys had discovered – that the best place to conceal valuables was behind a false partition. Colonel Dunbar Douglas Muter, a British Army officer, was one of the Prize Agents, and his wife Elizabeth wrote about his work and the excitement of treasure seeking.

> After an early breakfast, he would start, with a troop of coolies, armed with picks, crowbars and measuring lines. A house said to contain treasure would be allotted for the day's proceedings, and the business would commence by a careful survey of the premises … by a careful measurement of the roofs above and the walls below, any concealed space could be detected. Then the walls were broken through, and if there was a secret room or a built up niche or recess it would be discovered, and some large prizes rewarded their search.

14. Sikh troops dividing the spoil taken from mutineers. Lithograph by the London Printing and Publishing Company Ltd.

On one occasion when she was expecting her husband home to lunch with friends, she was told that he had found a large amount of treasure. 'It was late when he came back with thirteen wagons loaded with spoil, and among other valuables, eighty thousands pounds.' She hinted that among the Prize Agents there were some who 'annexed' treasures found, and did not put them into the common pile.[32]

Although cowed into submission outside the city walls, there were a few brave souls prepared to challenge the authorised looting by the Prize Agents. Appeals were made to the Prize Committee, which had been set up to adjudicate in such cases. Lala Kishore Lal had been the banker for the 17th Irregular Cavalry. As such, he would have been allowed back into Delhi during the day, on a day pass, together with traders and shopkeepers. He claimed that his loyalty to the British was never in doubt, that he had given 'active assistance' to distressed British subjects (an important criterion by which people were judged friend or foe), and that he had 'strong certificates of good character' from Major Leprott and Captain Hocken of the regiment. Nevertheless, 'On the 20th October 1857 Captain Grindall and four other officers came to the house, dug it all up and took away all I had to the value of about 22,000 rupees'. Two witnesses were called, Ram Ratan, a lodger in the banker's house, and Ram Sahai, a servant. The latter said he had seen one officer, followed by some others 'come to his Master's house and take a box which he saw opened and which contained ornaments, Rupees and gold mohurs – this box was taken away the officers – a quantity of valuable property was taken away in carts and on an Elephant'. The Prize Committee wrote to Captain Grindall, who had permission from the Prize Agents to search for treasure, and he said he had only got Rs 9,000 from the house. Lala Kishore Lal then told the Committee he had saved the life of an Englishman, Mr Ford, the Collector of Gurgaon, by warning him of the outbreak on the evening of 10 May 1857. Gurgaon was then a small village outside Delhi. The Collector confirmed to the Prize Committee that the banker had indeed warned him of an event taking place some forty miles away, although he does not say how Lala Kishore Lal got this information. Charles Saunders, the Commissioner directed that he should get Rs 9,000 back from the Prize Agents, and the other Rs 13,000 from the Government treasury 'on account of good and loyal service'.[33] The Government however declined to provide its share, saying only that Lala Kishore Lal's advance warning to Mr Ford would be considered.

An even sadder case was considered by the Prize Committee. Umed Singh was one of three brothers living in Delhi, originally from the mercantile class, well-educated citizens, loyal to the Company's government, in fact exactly the kind of people that the British needed to help re-establish confidence after the Uprising. His family had been 'faithful servants of the government for many years', and Umed Singh was described as 'a respectable native gentleman, formerly tutor to Maharaja Holkar'. Because of his connections in Indore, Umed Singh wrote to the Resident, Sir Robert Hamilton, who sent his letter on to the Governor General. If the letter was true, warned Hamilton, it would cast reproach on the British name. Umed Singh, like many other inhabitants of Delhi during the siege, had been doubly punished, once by the rebel sepoys and then by the British. The sepoys had made no distinction between friend or foe on their arrival in Delhi:

> the mercantile classes, the men of substance or those who were friends of order, because they had something to lose, have suffered the most – my own family has been punished more severely by the rebellion than the King of Delhi himself! When the rebels first entered Delhie, about 300 Sepoys attacked and plundered my house, because we were old servants and partisans of the English, and could read their language.[34]

The family fled, but Ramesh Bhai, who had been left in charge of the empty houses, was tortured into paying money when the King's treasury ran short of funds. With the arrival of the British, he went on,

> we thought our miseries will now be over, but no. All the inhabitants who escaped death by bombardment and others who were turned out without a penny worth of property, all the property was plundered. This scene is said to have lasted seven days, and many who could not leave their houses are said to have tasted cold steel! These were, however, not the 'Budmashes', for

> they had fled long ago – the gates of the city were shut, ingress and egress was by a wicket [gate] and the digging of the best houses for hidden property commenced. … Three officers with a few soldiers are said to have come to my once grand house, and having demolished it, are said to have caused I don't know what! Our property in cash, gold and jewels, silver vessels, shawls and furniture, alone was nevertheless it might be more than two lacks [lakhs] – I have got a list of it all – my note 12,000. I have got the numbers, my house worth 50,000 and my money invested in Rewary and 3 others villages was 60,000 rupees, all of which immense wealth is now gone. The labor of a whole life, the accumulation of many long years of all of us, is thus knocked on the head, perhaps never to be retrieved, and the bright visions of independence in the decline of age, which were so vividly formed and so fully described at your last farewell visit at my house are … so entirely passed away.

He begged to be sent 'a letter or certificate at once to recommend protection'. Umed Singh's pathetic letter, written in idiomatic English, prompted the Governor General to ask Charles Saunders to investigate the allegations and this led to the work of the Prize Agents being suspended at the end of November 1857. Saunders then asked William Muir, in Agra, to gather reports on the Prize Agents. It was probably felt that in the frenzied atmosphere of post-siege Delhi an objective opinion might be hard to find in the city.

Muir was in charge of the British Intelligence Department, a highly influential man, a committed Christian, not afraid of voicing his opinions on the information that passed through his hands. He did not hesitate to criticise in strong and sarcastic terms the Prize Agents and their arrogant behaviour at Delhi. He particularly challenged the rules they had laid down for themselves, that 'real property' that is, houses, shops and other buildings, would not be requisitioned, but that the owners of these properties would have to pay a ransom in order to prevent further searches.

> The Officers speak as if having conquered Dehlie, it had become their own property, not the State's and that the State and private individuals must repurchase it from them. That no inhabitant can return to his house till he has given a full consideration for it, and that meanwhile everything valuable about, the treasure which the fugitive people secreted, etc. is being gathered together for the conquerors. An Officer of high rank suggested that the difficulty might be got over if the population could get the services of some millionaires, the Seth or Jotee Pershad, to compound for the ransom and guarantee the payment of an adequate sum, say two lakhs. But the understood idea of ransom is a sum paid by a City to Troops who have assaulted it, in order to save it from plunder. If no ransom is paid, the city is ordinarily given up for one, two or three days plunder. The idea is novel of subjecting a city for above a month to plunder and its inhabitants to temporary exile and then requiring them to pay down the value of their property. For people, or classes of people who have connected themselves with the rebellion, confiscation of property to the State

> is of course a just and reasonable punishment, But the property would be the State's, not that of the Army. There are other loose stories afloat, which it may be well just to mention. For example, that certain *mahajans* [moneylenders] who were not prepared to pay the sum assessed upon them were threatened with execution, and blank cartridges fired or threatened to be fired upon them. It is painful to hear such stories circulated and one is naturally anxious for authority to contradict them.[35]

It was not until the middle of November that Muir could report that 'The ransacking of unransomed houses by the Prize Agency has at length been stopped'. But he added 'with two months licence to dig and hunt for valuables, little can have been spared'.

The Commissioner of Delhi, Charles Saunders had told Muir of the conflict between the civil and military authorities. Having captured Delhi with such loss of life, the army and the engineering corps, led by Colonel Baird-Smith and Captain Alexander Taylor were in no mood to jeopardise security now. Taylor insisted that even though manpower was short, the external defences, that is, the city walls, had to be held, and that it was necessary 'to exclude the mass of the Mahomedan population from whose enmity and fanaticism we have already suffered so greatly'. He said 'their feelings were not sufficiently calmed down to render their return to the city advisable'. While Saunders could understand the military men's view, he knew that the people camping outside the city were certainly not all Muslims and he argued that

> The mass of the Hindoo population being as Merchants, bankers and the like, might have been permitted to return at an earlier date, without much danger, but this view of things was not [taken] by the military Authorities, and it has been with great difficulty that I have succeeded to any extent in preserving the property of staunch adherents of the British Government from plunder ...
>
> I do not think the Prize Agents have any idea now of trying to enforce their doctrine further [he continued], and it appears to be generally conceded that their claims can only extend to moveable property. They do not therefore attempt to ransom household property as such, but they have on the payment down of a certain sum by the inhabitants of a street, ransomed its wealth, or rather, guaranteed it from search and plunder. The Neel ka Kuthra, [katra] the richest quarter in the town, was thus ransomed and guards placed to protect its inhabitants from further molestation, the consequence has been that all the wealth of the city which has escaped the clutches of independent plunderers has been transferred by its owners at night time to their quarter, and the guarantee has been abused. The City has now been so thoroughly ransacked and plundered, that parties are not willing to pay much for their effects still remaining untouched and the sooner the operation of the Prize Agents can be brought to a close, the better it will be.[36]

It was realised, somewhat late in the day, that in depriving the Delhi inhabitants of their property, either by direct plunder, or by holding it to ransom, the Prize Agents were, in effect, robbing people who were supposedly under British protection. As John Walker Sherer, the Fatehpur Magistrate put it, there had been a slight failure of logic. The rebellion was being put down, he argued on the ground that the country was ours. Reprisals which would have been appropriate against the enemy's property 'were not so advisable against the property of our own subjects. The enemy was the Sepoy army.'[37] The actions of the Prize Agents were also inhibiting trade and the restoration of normal life. A 'humble petition' to the Governor General from the native *shroffs* (bankers) and merchants of Calcutta, who had branches or *kothis* (houses) in Delhi, spoke of 'a large quantity of Merchandize, jewels and other property to an enormous value' seized from their places of business by the Prize Agents and stored in the Bhowanishankar Neemakh Karani (the Bhowanishankar Salt Factory). The petition was signed by thirteen respectable Hindu *kothiwallahs*, and each signatory was vouched for by a number of important British business firms including Gladstone Wyllie & Co., Gillanders Arbuthnot & Co., Jardine Skinner & Co. and Mackillop Stewart & Co. Delhi trade was not just a local affair, but one that impacted on the prosperity of the Company's subjects elsewhere. Delhi was so symbolically important that it *had* to be shown to be working again, not only to rally the waverers in India but to answer critics at home. The outcome of the Great Uprising was by no means a foregone conclusion in the autumn of 1857 but the capture of Delhi had been an important propaganda victory, as well as a military one. By the end of the year, when sales of seized property had been going on for nearly three months, the Government Agency Committee was established 'to determine what course should be followed to carry out Government orders about property captured by the Delhi Field Force in the city of Delhi'.

The Committee started its work on the last day of December 1857, at 11 a.m., as its Minutes record.[38] There were three Committee members, all army officers, who had been appointed by a retired officer, Major General Perry. Four radical resolutions were put forward from this first meeting. The Prize Agents were to provide an account of what they had done as quickly as possible, showing the amount of money realised in cash or by the sale of captured property. Lists of unsold property and of all government property recovered were to be made. All sales of captured property by public auction (the usual way of disposing of such property) were to be confirmed. Lists of all 'establishments', that is, work gangs, were to handed over, and books were to be opened to register all claims made by Delhi residents for the restoration of their property. Claimants were 'to state clearly the description and nature of each article and the manner in which it is supposed to have been captured, whether by the Prize Agents or by the Soldiery' – details which obviously could not be provided in the majority of cases.

By the third meeting on 22 January 1858 the scale of the problem of restitution was clearer. What property remained still unsold consisted of 'clothing, furniture, paper and other miscellaneous articles of a perishable nature'. It was considered impossible that any former owners would be able to recognise it, or be able to prove their claims to this indiscriminate collection, so it was agreed it should be sold at public auction and the money put in a separate government account. By auctioning the goods, the Committee added helpfully, if speciously, 'they will be displayed to the Public Gaze and should anyone recognise property as his own he could at once put forward his claim and it could be enquired into on the spot and this claim duly recorded'. However, the Committee didn't anticipate many claims 'as the Bulk of the Prize was taken from the houses of Musulmans and their owners being excluded from the Town as outlaws have no opportunity of claiming their property'. Ironically it was the 'native merchants' who had followed the British into Delhi who now made their fortunes by buying up the goods put up for auction by the Prize Agents.

The Committee's conclusion, reported in May 1858, was that nearly all prize property had already been sold (apart from some jewels belonging to the royal family), before the Prize Agents had been ordered to stop their work. There could be no restoration of goods; what was gone, was gone. The best way forward was that the Committee should investigate all claims put before it for lost property, and they would consider the validity of the claims and the amount of compensation due 'according to the pleasure of the Government'. A 'great number of cases' were already before the Committee, but the only one so far to be fully investigated was that of Umed Singh and his brothers, whose letter had started the government inquiry. We can only hope that the old man did receive some compensation for the loss of his lifetime's work.

Prize could be found in all kinds of places, and where Prize Agents were not appointed, the responsibility for its safe-keeping devolved on a senior officer, who would get it escorted to a cantonment town like Allahabad or Cawnpore. Only treasure of exceptional quality went down to Calcutta to be lodged in the treasury at Fort William. This is where the jewels of Zeenat Mahal, wife of Bahadur Shah Zafar were sent, the only prize property not auctioned in Delhi. Over the Christmas period of 1857 the Royal Engineers, directed by Lieutenant Malcolm, were busy retrieving treasures from the wells at Bithur, a large village some twelve miles north of Cawnpore on the river Ganges. This was where the Nana Sahib had lived in the oddly-named Shanivar Kothi (popularly known as the Saturday House but better translated as the House of Saturn), built by his adoptive father Baji Rao II, and called after a larger palace of the same name, left behind in Poona. Nana Sahib had been chased out of Bithur by General Havelock in July 1857, after the General's fruitless dash to save the captives at Cawnpore. In December of that year Nana Sahib had returned to Bithur in an attempt to recover his treasure, which had been thrown down the wells for safe-keeping at the first alarm. General Hope Grant's troops caught up with him and the remains of his army, and the Nana was forced to flee into Awadh and then Nepal, leaving his treasure behind.

Ninety Royal Engineers and two divers gathered at the Bithur wells. A local blacksmith was ordered to provide a grapple, a spear-like object of ten feet, with a barb on one side, and set into a bamboo handle forty-five feet in length. With this the engineers began poking about. At first only the rubble dumped by the fleeing Gwalior Contingent came up – timbers, wheels, buckets and ropes. Attempts were made to drain the Persian wells using a chain of leather buckets attached to bullock traces, but it was not until a fatigue party of 200 men was organised that the well could be drained effectively. Engineers then let themselves down and brought up a basket of forty-four pieces of silver plate, *paan* boxes, 'squirts' and lamps. On Christmas Day seventy-one pieces of gold were brought up and 182 silver articles.[39] Although the treasure was of immense intrinsic value, because it was solid and of very pure gold and silver, artistically it left a lot to be desired, being described as 'trays and bowls of the rudest shape'. It was escorted to Cawnpore and then down to Allahabad.

After the disputes, petitions, claims and attempts at restoration of property in Delhi, we might imagine that things would have been handled more professionally on the recapture of Lucknow. Not only was it a larger city than Delhi, but a richer city too, because although it didn't have the trading houses of Delhi, it did have the wealthiest ruling family in India, the Nawabs. Some of the treasure had accompanied Wajid Ali Shah down to Calcutta, on his abortive journey to England. As much, if not more, had been taken by the British into the Residency from the Qaisarbagh Palace shortly before the siege. But there was still an enormous amount left. The many palaces were crammed full, not just with over 700 relatives and dependants, but with the treasures of immensely wealthy men collected over the past century. Although the recapture of Lucknow had been planned over the winter of 1857/58 and had even been delayed until March while extra troops were being collected, it soon became painfully obvious that no plans had been made to deal with the treasure that would inevitably fall into the victors' hands. 'The soil of Lucknow is a mint of money' exclaimed one delighted correspondent on unearthing a dirty box which turned out to contain rubies, diamonds, pearls etc to the value of Rs 100,000 (£10,000).[40]

The descriptions of the looting of the Qaisarbagh Palace, written by *The Times* correspondent William Russell, are well known. He reported seeing men smash their way into the rooms so recently vacated by Begam Hazrat Mahal and her relatives and servants.

> From the broken portals issue soldiers laden with loot or plunder. Shawls, rich tapestry, gold and silver brocade, caskets of jewels, arms, splendid dresses. The

> men are wild with fury and lust for gold – literally drunk with plunder. Some come out with china vases or mirrors, dash them to pieces on the ground, and return to seek more valuable booty.[41]

Arthur Moffat Lang, an engineer officer who was one of the first to enter the palace on the morning of 14 March when the Sikhs had pushed forward so quickly, confirmed the story.

> Such jolly gardens, with marble honeycomed arbours, marble canals and high bridges, and such loot – jewellery, and shawls, gold and silks! I was knee deep in valuables ... one officer in the tent next to mine has upwards of 500,000 rupees worth of diamonds, pearls and rubies! I never saw such precious stones as I have here.[42]

A sergeant of the 93rd Regiment, William Forbes-Mitchell wrote his account of the looting of Lucknow more than half a century after it took place, but it was still vivid in his mind.

> The city was in the hands of plunderers; Europeans and Sikhs, Goorkhas, and camp-followers of every class, aided by the scum of the native population ... The Sikhs and Goorkhas were by far the most proficient plunderers, because they instinctively knew where to look for the most valuable loot. The European soldiers did not understand the business, and articles that might have proved a fortune to many were readily parted with for a few rupees in cash and a bottle of grog. But the gratuitous destruction of valuable property that could not be carried off was appalling. Colour-Sergeant Graham ... rescued from the fire a bundle of Government of India promissory notes to the value of over a lakh of rupees.[43]

How frustrating it must have been for James Gibbon, the young officer in camp on the north bank of the Gomti. He told his mother,

> There has been a great deal of plundering, and many people have made good bags for themselves, we had something else to do – however, we hope that there will [be] sufficient left to give us a decent share of prize money. There is a sale of prize property daily and many good prices have been got. I have not bought anything – not having had the opportunity nor do I think you would care for what is to be got. Shawls are the principal attractions, but they may turn out to be Paisley instead of Kashmir, and none but a good judge can tell the difference. India is only desirable when there is plenty of money to be got.[44]

Gibbon also confirmed that

> [W. H.] Russell's letters were very good – his stories about all the jewels etc. were not at all exaggerated. I believe there were bushels of pearls taken by the men – we on the other side, who had to watch the bridges and stick to our work, of course, got nothing – but I was very glad of it, as it greatly

> demoralizes discipline, and besides is not fair or just where there is to be a general division of prize property. Somebody was in fault but no one knows exactly how. Many people here made large sums of money – all the better for them but all the worse for us, whose prejudice will be dismissed accordingly, though the share of each will not suffer materially.

There was undoubtedly someone at fault, and that was the Commander-in-Chief, Sir Colin Campbell, who had the authority to place armed guards throughout the city to prevent indiscriminate looting. But he failed to act for several crucial days. It was not until 18 March that some kind of order was restored when Prize Agents were nominated and guards appointed to intercept the plunderers and camp followers, who were forced 'to disgorge their plunder, nominally for the public good or the benefit of the army', as Forbes-Mitchell reported. As a sergeant, he stood in fear of no one and he was prepared to say what many others were not, namely that some officers got so much plunder from the city that they were able to redeem their mortgaged estates in the British Isles with their 'snug fishing and shooting-boxes in every game-haunted and salmon-frequented angle of the world. … I could myself name one deeply-encumbered estate which was cleared of mortgage to the tune of £180,000 within two years of the plunder of Lucknow.'[45] Even the Prize Agents were accused by him of carrying undeclared loot home in their uniform cases.

Although nothing appears in official records, it is almost certain that there was a gentleman's agreement that Jang Bahadur's Gurkha troops would get their chance of plunder before the Prize Agents took over. The agreement was probably between the Governor General and the Nepalese leader. The latter, from the ruling Rana family, had become thoroughly anglicised, and was a 'sensation' in London during his visit in 1852. He had the curious habit of wearing goggles, as protection against the sun, which were virtually unknown in India at the time. The Commander-in-Chief had wanted to advance on Lucknow in the middle of February, but had been persuaded by Canning to wait for Jang Bahadur. 'It would drive him wild to find himself jockeyed out of all share in the great campaign,' wrote the Governor General, which is probably the nearest we will get to an admission of the inducements held out to him and his troops.[46] As it was, British officers and surgeons, whose expenses were met by the Company, had been sent to accompany the Gurkha army and chivvy it along.

On the Monday 15 March, the day after the Qaisarbagh Palace was stormed and immediately after Begam Hazrat Mahal had left, Sir James Outram, now reinstalled as Chief Commissioner of Awadh issued a proclamation 'to the Inhabitants of the City of Lucknow'.[47] Measures had already been taken, he told them, to prevent the city being plundered and sacked by the troops. This was so patently untrue that the remainder of his words had little or no effect, other than to produce a surreal atmosphere. He called on the moneylenders and shopkeepers to open their shops and carry on their usual trade. Those who hadn't reopened within three days would then be prevented from doing so until they had been strictly investigated and enquiries made. It was the duty of influential and respectable inhabitants to support the British authorities in restoring order and tranquillity, he added. Six people were named whose help was expected. Using a carrot-and-stick approach, he told the assembled crowd: 'It is the wish of the Commander-in-Chief to spare the City, but if the inhabitants do not drive out the rebels, he will be compelled to bombard it.'

Clearly this had little effect in restoring confidence for Outram had to issue instructions 'for the protection and management of the city' a week later. By now the Prize Agents were in full swing, and their activities were so damaging to Outram's standing that he got his secretary to write a letter of complaint to Colin Campbell.

> Notwithstanding the issue of proclamations for the return of the inhabitants of Lucknow to their houses, scarcely any of the respectable inhabitants have returned, and on enquiry the reason assigned is that the Prize Agents continue actively to deprive parties returning of the property they bring with them.[48]

He pointed out that the city had been in the possession of the British for more than fifteen days, and demanded that some limit must be put on the proceedings of the Prize Agents, and their work ended. As a compromise, Outram suggested that the Prize Agents could keep the Qaisarbagh and other palaces occupied by the troops.

The following day, Outram ordered his Deputy Commissioner 'to put a stop to indiscriminate ransacking and confusion by furnishing tickets to all residents not criminal, which were to be affixed to their houses, to protect them from plunder and molestation'.[49] The Deputy Commissioner agreed and said that the responsible heads of such houses would be registered. Lists would quickly be made of all government property and all houses belonging to 'notorious rebels and mutineers'. If moveable property, defined as prize under the orders of 29 January 1858, remained in such houses, then they should be made over to the Prize Agents. The Judicial Commissioner expressed concern on hearing that people who wanted to come back into Lucknow were deterred from doing so by being plundered as they entered (by the Prize Agents) and he too called on the hapless Deputy Commissioner to issue orders 'prohibiting the molestation of all inhabitants of the City' who were not rebels or mutineers. What this all adds up to is confusion and chaos on a grand scale. The army's Prize Agents were robbing people as they attempted to obey the civilian Chief Commissioner's orders.

Matters came to a head on 15 April, when Captain Forster, one of the Prize Agents and his gang of European soldiers, surrounded the house of Mir Wajid Ali, ready to search it for prize. Outram was furious when he learnt of this. First of all there was the undeniable, witnessed fact that two Englishwomen, Mrs Orr and Miss Jackson, had been rescued from the clutches of the mutineers, mainly due to help and information from Mir Wajid Ali. The kind man had also rescued eight begams, ladies attached to the former Nawab's court, and he had taken them all off to the safety of the Gurkha camp, where he was 'handsomely received' by Jang Bahadur himself, who gave the begams a thousand rupees. From here the Mir was escorted to Sir James Outram, who received him equally cordially and allowed him to sit down in his presence. Outram put the eight ladies under British protection, ordered a guard for their safety, and gave the Mir permission to take them back into the city. Captain Alexander Orr, who witnessed this, and was a relative of one of the rescued English ladies, stated that Outram authorised the Mir to collect all the ex-Nawab's begams and to keep them with him.

The Prize Agents countered by saying that Mir Wajid Ali had exceeded his remit granted by Outram. He had not only taken over some buildings adjacent to his own house, but had been going round collecting 'native ladies', and also, it was alleged, had been charging them for the privilege. He was further accused by the Prize Agents of having 'much valuable property unduly concealed on his premises' which the begams had brought with them. The Deputy Commissioner was instructed to settle the affair by getting the Mir to deposit 'any valuable property in the possession of those under him'. As for Outram, on the highest of high horses, and unable to step down to resolve the matter sensibly, he wrote: 'as His Excellency the Commander in Chief has not yet thought fit to put a stop to the search for prize ... the Chief Commissioner feels it beyond his competency to prohibit the proceedings of the Prize Agents'.

A letter followed the next day to the Governor General. 'A very important question in connection with the right of search for Prize property has arisen, which the Chief Commissioner considers can only be settled authoritatively by the Governor General himself.' Outram demanded a decision from Canning on four points:

> 1. What is to be the limit to search for prize?
> 2. Is property taken from the city and now brought back again liable to be seized as prize?
> 3. Are the women from the king's palace, Begams and others to be treated as rebels?
> 4. On whose authority is search for prize to be made in houses once protected?
>
> It is now a month since the British Army obtained a footing in Lucknow [Outram continued]. For the first few days and even weeks, whilst a place which has been taken by storm is essentially held by Military force, all property found may be looked upon as found in course of capture. But now that the invading army has been broken, a garrison settled in the town and the Civil

> power introduced, the essentially military occupation may be considered at an end. And once a proclamation is issued inviting all peaceable and loyal citizens to return to their homes and occupations there is surely a guarantee implied, that all who comply with the invitation shall be free from molestation. It were in vain to talk of restoring confidence and repopulating a town if the citizens are only enticed back to be plundered.[50]

Outram said the city should be declared to be 'freed from this state of capture and to be like every other Town under Civil Government'. He believed that property brought back by citizens should be recognised as their own, but also that anything found in their houses that had 'escaped the notice of the Prize Agents' should also be considered as their own. There the matter rested.

Bad though the situation was for the inhabitants of Lucknow, it was about to get much worse, as wholesale demolitions began. Outram was deemed to have failed as Commissioner, and he was replaced in April by Sir Robert Montgomery, who had been Judicial Commissioner in Lahore. As late as July 1858 Montgomery reported that his enquiries showed there was no effective authority in Lucknow: 'anyone and everyone issues orders. The police amount to a thousand men, the canaille and off-scouring of people. Any man who chooses places a badge on his arm and plunders on his own account.'[51] Large-scale military demolitions were in progress, search parties were looking for caches of arms and fugitive rebels. Hordes of unemployed and desperate men roamed the city for food or treasure, and bands of soldiers plundered and terrorised those inhabitants who had not fled into the countryside for safety.

And at the end of it all, what did the soldiers get from the Prize Agents, on whose behalf they had nominally been working so hard? On 27 January 1860 two questions were asked in Parliament. In the House of Lords the Earl of Ellenborough wanted to know if the captured property (prize) had been distributed, and was answered by the Duke of Argyll who told the House that 'The Indian Government had not yet been enabled to compute the value of property captured at Delhi and in other parts of India, but the information was expected by every mail'. The same question was asked in the House of Commons and Sir Charles Wood, the Secretary of State for India, announced that 'steps were being taken' for the distribution of prize money from the capture of Lucknow, but that more information was required from India before distribution of the Delhi prize money could take place.[52] Shortly afterwards, on 3 February, Sir Charles Wood announced that the Lucknow prize money was £146,000 and was in the process of being distributed. The amount was extraordinarily low, given the wealth of the city. *The Times* had confidently announced in May 1858 that the plunder accumulated by the Prize Agents in Lucknow was estimated at over £600,000, and it was reported to have reached over a million pounds shortly afterwards. Where had it all gone, one wonders? A clue appears in the records of the Royal Military Association which negotiated on behalf of the Royal Hospital Chelsea for a share of the money because the hospital was caring for soldiers wounded in the Uprising.[53] The costs of putting down the revolt swallowed up much more, the lion's share going to the government. The payout for private soldiers was a mean Rs 17.8 per man, a British man that is. Indian sepoys received half that amount. Prize was calculated on the scale of the daily pay for each man, so an ordinary British soldier got one share, but a major general got seventy-six shares. It is not surprising that seasoned soldiers stuffed their knapsacks with treasure from the Qaisarbagh, knowing how little they would benefit from, and how long they were expected to wait for, the prize money.

While it took the Government of India two years to compute the value of the Lucknow prize money, it took them only months to deal with the treasure taken from the Qaisarbagh Palace in June 1857 that went into the Residency during the siege, and was brought out in the November rescue. By February 1858 the treasure had been moved down to Allahabad and lodged in the Treasury. It was agreed with Calcutta that it should be listed and repacked in something stronger than the 'shaky barrels' in which it had been brought out of Lucknow. The Deputy Collector at Allahabad was charged with this task and by July the Lucknow jewels and the treasure found in the Nana's palace at Bithur was repacked in 'strong timber boxes' and labelled 'Thirteen boxes marked 1–13L containing the Lucknow jewels and 14 marked 1–14B the Bithoor property, all boxes locked with English locks and secured with iron bands'. The new inventory prepared in Allahabad took up thirteen pages of foolscap paper and makes mouth-watering reading. Typical entries read:

> One gold tinsel crown decorated with diamonds, pearls and rubies, 4 King's hats, a lot of tinsel, silver armlet with large flat diamonds, 1 silver tinsel crown with valuable diamond aigrette and one very large drop pearl, 1 turban with 7 diamond broaches and with large emerald pendant and six pearl broaches and with large emerald pendant and one very large emerald pendant in front Tinsel puft on top with pearls, emeralds and one ruby, one jasper tray jewelled with rubies and diamonds, a lot of very old tinsel crowns, a rosary of very large rubies, large topaz on gold head band, silver buckles with diamonds. ...[54]

Rather touchingly, given their treatment by the British, there were '3 miniature pictures, one of George IV set in gold with Turquoise and pearls and a miniature of Warren Hastings set in diamonds and rubies'. The loot from Bithur Palace was less exciting, and included embroidered pyjamas, gold embroidered *alams* (religious standards), shawls, ivory knife handles, pearl necklaces, six telescopes and one quadrant. The boxes containing the treasure were put into locked cabins on board the *Koel*, a steamer going down to Calcutta in September 1858, and on their arrival, were stowed away in the treasury at Fort William. The promissory notes had already been sent to the treasury. The following year, the Nawab, Wajid Ali Shah applied to have restored to him 'the jewels which had been taken on annexation, which were then in deposit in the general treasury at Calcutta'. They were apparently not regarded as prize, nor state property, although the difference between these items and similar treasures seized later from the same palace by the Prize Agents is not clear. The jewels were delivered to Wajid Ali Shah by his British Political Agent, Major Herbert, early in 1860. An odd little note, written fifty years later, in 1917, states that there was no proof that the jewels had subsequently passed out of the custody of the Nawab or his family, and that none of his property had been sent to England after annexation.[55] Although Wajid Ali Shah was fortunate to recover some of this family treasure, much more had of course entered Britain illegally, as loot.

The Delhi prize money was finally paid out in 1862, the British private soldier each getting ten rupees (£1.00). The Banda and Kirwee prize dispute took even longer to resolve and the final payments were not made until 1868. The ex-officer waiting for his share of the Banda and Kirwee money became something of a stock figure of fun in Victorian England, one of 'the Indian army of martyrs'. When the prize eventually came however, it was in the region of £78 for British officers. This was the most generous payment of all from the Great Uprising but the wealth of Banda and Kirwee, both small towns in Bundelkhand, could not compare with that of Delhi and Lucknow. Had the prize money from here been paid without deductions to the soldiers who captured the two cities, their share would certainly have surpassed this. The Naval Prize Act of 1864 went some way to regularising the chaotic system on land as well as sea, and was followed by the Prize Courts Act of 1894, defining rights of appeal and what constituted a Prize Court. The concept of prize (booty captured in conflicts) continued well into the twentieth century and Parliamentary Acts were passed at the beginning of both the First and Second World Wars defining these 'spoils of war'.

Five

'HUNG IN PERPETUAL CHAINS'

THE GREAT UPRISING presented the British Government in India with its first major challenge in dealing with widespread unrest. Mutinies in the Company's army were by no means uncommon, as we have seen, and there had been mutinies by European as well as Indian officers and men in the preceding two centuries. Often they were sparked by perceived or real injustices over pay, allowances and overseas postings. The most recent mutiny, before the Great Uprising, had taken place in 1855 in Bolarum, the cantonment at Hyderabad, when a religious clash led to Brigadier General Colin Mackenzie, Commander of the Hyderabad Contingent, being left for dead.[1] What made the Uprising of 1857/58 so significantly different was the speed at which the revolt moved from the military (the sepoys) to the civilian rebels. This time, too, the targets were no longer only Company officers who had failed to deal justly with their men, but all Europeans, anyone with a white face, including many who had no conceivable link with the army. It was the first (and last) time that large numbers of white women and children in India were killed in barbaric circumstances, inadvertently drawn into the theatre of war. As such it was nearer the wars of the twentieth century where blameless civilians are as much targets as fighting men. Much of the shock that ran through Britain in the summer of 1857 was not because the Bengal Army had mutinied, again, but because this time British women and children had been killed.

While there were well-established regulations to deal with mutinous soldiers, and even mutinous regiments, there were few precedents the British could follow in tackling mass civilian revolt. Part of the problem was that the East India Company had only acquired many of its Indian possessions fairly recently, through Dalhousie's aggressive annexation policies. Although the Company was able to put administrative structures in place rapidly, as it had done immediately after the annexation of Awadh, there seemed to be little consciousness of the implications of taking on the enormous task of ruling half of India. The mindset of earlier years had not yet caught up with the reality of India in the mid-nineteenth century and the Company was still prone to react to disturbances as it had done fifty or sixty years earlier, when its remit ran over an infinitely smaller area of land. In those days the help of local rulers could often be sought to punish wrong-doers who threatened the Company's possessions or its staff. Troops could be borrowed from a friendly raja or nawab, who would certainly have armed men at his disposal. But in 1857 there was no British strategy in place that could deal with large-scale civilian unrest, because it had not happened before. Calling out the army to deal with the mob was not an option because the army itself was part of the problem, as were many of the police who had left their posts. The British response to the Uprising was therefore an ad hoc one of both panic and lethargy. It had not previously been necessary to punish civilians en masse and initially it was the demon of revenge that guided the East India Company in dealing with its rebellious subjects. How this demon was eventually reined in, but cruelly refined, is the subject of this chapter.

Even before the news of the worst civilian outrages, the Cawnpore massacres of 12 June, 27 June and 15 July were known, an 'army of retribution' was on the march in northern India. It was composed of certain battalions, most notably, in the early part of Uprising, that of the 1st Madras European Fusiliers, led by Colonel James Neill. Neill was the Victorian militant Christian personified, who believed that God had chosen him to take part in suppressing the revolt. Indeed, he looked like a figure from the Old Testament, with his flowing white hair and moustaches, although he was only forty-seven at the time of his death in 1857. Born in Ayr, in Scotland, he was educated at the University of Glasgow, and had been a soldier all his life. Much of his career had been spent in India, but he had served in the Crimea too, which gave him an edge over the old India hands. Neill had been summoned from southern India with his Fusiliers, to assist what remained of the loyal Bengal Army and its British officers at a desperate point in the revolt. Every day brought reports of more mutinies, more towns sacked, treasuries robbed, prisoners released, cantonments fired, and sepoys heading for Delhi.

Neill arrived by ship at Calcutta, and was to go upcountry by train to the railhead at Raniganj before turning and marching to Allahabad through Benares. At the newly opened Howrah station he found the railway staff were not prepared to hold the train until his troops had all arrived and embarked. Neill was told that although he might command his battalion, he did not command the railway, upon which he promptly arrested the stationmaster, the engineer and the stoker, and held them until his men were all safely on board. He called the railway staff 'traitors and rebels, and loudly regretted it was not in his power to hang them'.[2] There were to be plenty of opportunities later on for hanging the real rebels. On his arrival in Benares he found the sepoys there on the verge of mutiny and presided over the disarming of the 37th Bengal Native Infantry. This was to be a repeat of the disarming at Barrackpore in 1824 and a number of sepoys were mown down by Neill's troops, including some of the hitherto loyal Sikhs and cavalry troops.

Before he marched on to Allahabad, a number of lynch mobs had been set up and 'volunteer hanging parties' went out from Benares in search of anyone who looked like a rebel. Those caught were strung up, indiscriminately, from makeshift gallows, and the executions were known as 'Colonel Neill's hangings'. He was greeted with open arms at Allahabad on his arrival there on 11 June, and within a week had cleared the town of rebels, although the Maulvi Liaquat Ali Khan, who had, for a brief five days, set up his own 'government', managed to escape. Neill's feat was all the more remarkable as he was, at this point, ill and exhausted. He managed to keep going by drinking champagne and water for several days, as he told his wife. Instead of moving swiftly on to relieve the Europeans at Cawnpore, who were being besieged by Nana Sahib's men, Neill set up a reign of terror in Allahabad which so successfully cowed the remaining inhabitants that the town was safe enough for the forward British headquarters to be set up there during the summer of 1857. Allahabad is strategically placed at the confluence of the Jumna and the Ganges, and is on the Grand Trunk Road. Lord Canning and his staff moved up from Calcutta, and the Intelligence Department was established here. Refugees and treasure passed through on their way down to the safety of Calcutta, and officers and men came up through Allahabad to quell the uprisings in Awadh and Rohilkhand.

Six thousand Indian men, women and children are estimated to have been killed in and around Allahabad in June, following Neill's arrival. Many were killed in the most brutal manner – burnt alive in their villages, mown down by grapeshot fired from a steamer on the Jumna, on its way up to Cawnpore, or simply shot like wild animals as they broke cover. Killing Indians became a blood sport and was described in sporting language. 'To "bag a nigger" had become a favourite phrase of the military sportsmen of that day. "Pea-fowls, partridges, and Pandies rose together, but the latter gave the best sport."'[3] When Neill sent a detachment to relieve Cawnpore, under Major Renaud, the major was instructed to clear the way from Allahabad by attacking and destroying all the places held by the enemy en route. At the same time, he was to encourage the inhabitants to return and to 'instill confidence' in them that the British would succeed in reimposing their authority. These two aims were so mutually incompatible that Renaud simply carried out the first order and hanged pretty well anyone he could lay hands on. Twelve men were hanged simply because they were looking the wrong way when the detachment passed them. Observers noted that the lower limbs of the hanged corpses were eaten by wild animals, while the smoke from burning villages drifted over the fields. Not surprisingly, Renaud and his men found difficulty in getting supplies as they marched through the terror-stricken countryside. Villagers were simply too frightened to approach them.

On 30 June Brigadier General Henry Havelock arrived in Allahabad to take over command from Neill and to lead the combined relief force to Cawnpore. He attempted to halt Renaud and his murderous troops, instructing them not to burn any more villages unless they found rebels actually living in them. It took two and a half weeks for Havelock to fight his way into Cawnpore (Renaud was killed in a minor encounter with rebels on the way), but by the time the General and his troops arrived, it was too late. Nearly 200 European women and children had been slaughtered by Nana Sahib's men thirty-six hours earlier.[4] Some of the women had seen their husbands killed in the Satichaura Ghat massacre on 27 June when, reacting to a false promise of safe conduct by Nana Sahib, they had been shot or drowned on the banks of the Ganges. The women and children who survived were taken back up the sandy path from the river and imprisoned in the Bibighar, a house which had served as a zenana for an Indian mistress, a *bibi*, in happier times. As Havelock and his fearsome Highland troops advanced, a decision was taken to kill the remaining women and children. This was carried out by Sarwar Khan, one of Nana Sahib's bodyguards, who was the Anglo-Indian son of a Pathan prostitute and a British soldier. He brought with him butchers and men armed with *talwars* (swords) and the killing commenced. By the next morning, 17 July, only three women and three little boys were still alive. Nana Sahib, who had established his headquarters in Mahomed's Hotel, only a hundred yards from the Bibighar, ordered them to be 'disposed of' and they were thrown alive into a dry well where some of the other European corpses had been put by the sweepers.[5]

There was widespread disbelief at first as the dreadful news spread. This was made worse by the way information was released in a slow trickle. It was not until the middle of September 1857, two months after the massacre, that the newspapers in Britain began to carry the story. Even then, the lists of the dead were not complete, giving false hopes to families who believed their relatives might have survived but who were to learn later that none had escaped. On 25 September the *Illustrated London News* carried a short but graphic report from an officer who had been with Havelock's force as a cavalry volunteer, his own regiment having mutinied:

> Camp Cawnpore 22 July 1857. I have been to see the place where the poor women and children were imprisoned and afterwards butchered. It is a small bungalow close to the road. There were all sorts of articles of women and children's clothing, ladies' hair evidently cut off with a sword, back combs, etc. There were also part of religious works. Where the massacre took place it is covered with blood like a butchers slaughter-house. One would fancy that nothing could be worse than this, but in the well at the back of the house are the bodies and limbs of the poor things. I looked down and saw such a sight as I hope never to see again. The whole of the bodies were naked, and the limbs had been separated. I thought of the two Mrs ... and the three poor girls and

> felt very sad. By all accounts the women were so ill-treated that death, even such a death, must have been welcome to them. I will not enter into more details, I have told you enough to cause you to make allowances if I write savagely. I have looked upon death in every form, but I could not look down that well again.'[6]

The description of the dismembered bodies was bad enough, but the idea that the women may have been raped before their deaths was even worse. How this rumour arose is not known, but it was pervasive, sending men literally mad with rage and more eager than before to kill every Indian they met, guilty and innocent alike. Graffiti appeared on the walls of the Bibighar calling for revenge on the savages who had ravished both young and old before killing them.

Charles Saunders, the Commissioner of Delhi, warned that the atrocities which had been committed during the Uprising were 'quite sufficiently appalling' without the need of any exaggeration, which the newspapers of the 'blood and scalp' school found necessary to introduce, 'with a view to inflame the feelings of our country men and turn them into fiends'. But it was too late to call for reason. Many of the British soldiers and volunteers had, at least temporarily, become fiends, led by officers like Neill. If things had been bad before, they were a hundred times worse after the gruesome discovery in the Cawnpore well. It was, the modern historian, Rudrangshu Mukherjee, has written, as if Satan had been let loose on earth. The very mention of the word 'Cawnpore' on Indian lips was enough to have the speaker killed.

Neill, who had been left in Allahabad, was now ordered up to Cawnpore and promoted to the rank of Brigadier General. At the same time, General Havelock and his men started out towards Lucknow in an abortive attempt to relieve the Europeans besieged inside the Residency there. Both generals disliked each other. There was little of Christian brotherhood between these two deeply religious men and even less for people of other faiths. On his arrival in Cawnpore Neill ordered a unique and horrible punishment for prisoners found guilty of the murders of the European women and children, or those found guilty by association. They were taken into the blood-stained Bibighar by a sweeper and made to crouch down and lick clean a square foot of the floor before being taken out and hanged. The blood had of course long since dried into flakes, but was moistened with water, and the prisoners were lashed until they obeyed. Neill's order was dated 25 July and remained in force for over three months until Sir Colin's Campbell's arrival in Cawnpore on 3 November that year, when he rescinded it as being unworthy of 'a Christian Government'.

Direct punishment by death of the rebels, or those suspected to be rebels, took many forms. At Peshawar where eight potentially mutinous regiments were stationed, forty sepoys were tied to cannon and blown away. This peculiarly horrible form of death dated back to the days of the first Mughal Emperors, but it had been refined by the British. It was always carried out in front of spectators, not only other sepoys, whom it was designed to frighten, but also British officers and occasionally British women too whose crinolines were spattered with gore. Also at Peshawar 192 sepoys from the mutinious 51st Bengal Native Infantry were rounded up, tried at a drumhead court-martial (where a drum is placed on the ground and used as a table), all found guilty, and all shot by firing parties. The 26th Bengal Native Infantry mutinied at Lahore at the end of June and was captured by the Deputy Commissioner, Frederick Cooper, as its 500 men fled towards Amritsar. One hundred and fifty were shot dead, forty drowned in the river Ravi, and 282 surrendered and were locked up for the night in Ajnala police station. The following morning they were brought out in batches of ten and shot by Cooper's Sikhs. Sixty-six men from the same regiment had been imprisoned in an adjacent mud-brick tower during one of the hottest nights of the year. The next day forty-five of them were found dead from heat and suffocation. 'Unconsciously the tragedy of Holwell's Black Hole [of Calcutta] had been re-enacted' explained Cooper in an attempt to vindicate his actions.[7]

Neither rank, nor position, nor age, protected those accused of revolt, and many others who had no sympathy with the rebels, but who were also killed. Two sons and a grandson of Bahadur Shah Zafar were shot by Captain William Hodson at a Delhi gateway, still known today as the Khuni Darwaza or Bloody Gate. Hodson had volunteered to go down to Humayun's tomb with his cavalry troops (named Hodson's Horse), and bring back the King of Delhi and his wife Begam Zeenat Mahal. This had been successfully accomplished and the following day he set off again to round up the princes, who surrendered after seeing that their father and grandfather had not been harmed. As he approached the Delhi Gate Hodson claimed he was forced to shoot the unarmed princes because he feared the crowd was about to attack him and his party of 100 armed Sikhs.[8] The naked bodies of the princes were exposed in front of the Kotwali in Chandni Chowk, where European victims had been dragged and slaughtered, and their bodies similarly exposed. (This was also the place where the body of the Sikh leader Guru Tegh Bahadur, a victim of the Mughal Emperor, had been exposed some 200 years earlier, so there was a certain resonance for the Sikhs in the turn of events.) The British would certainly have been justified in trying the princes for their part in the revolt, and indeed the princes themselves thought this would happen, and that there would be 'a proper investigation . . . in the proper court', but Hodson's precipitate action pre-empted this. Although he was to be criticised later, for the moment Hodson basked in the congratulations of his fellow officers. Sir Robert Montgomery, Judicial Commissioner of the Punjab and a devout Christian who thought that God had personally intervened on Britain's side during the Uprising, hoped that Hodson would 'bag' many more sons of the King of Delhi. The editor of the *Illustrated London News* supported Hodson too, writing on 14 November:

> In the one case a captive King and Queen (*de facto* at least for a few months) are objects of that clemency which spared old age and womanhood while prompt and martial justice is done on the recreant Princes, who, unequal to the stern example of Tippoo Saib, preferred to be seized as coward fugitives from the city the rule of which they had usurped, to dying in its defence.

Hodson himself thought he deserved the Victoria Cross, and might well have got it, had he not been killed in the recapture of Lucknow the following March. His widow was however granted a permanent 'grace and favour' residence at Hampton Court Palace by the Queen.

General Archdale Wilson had ordered that the women and children of Delhi were to be spared during its recapture, but his ruling was met with some criticism. 'This is a stretch of mercy I should not have been prepared to make, had I a voice in the matter', wrote an anonymous officer. It was 'these fiends in female form' who had looted European houses in Delhi during the siege. 'However, it is the General's *hookum* that they should be spared, and I hope he won't rue it.' The same writer, whose views were published in a letter in *The Bombay Telegraph* in September 1857 went on

> All the city people found within the walls, when our troops entered, were bayoneted on the spot, and the number was considerable, as you may suppose, when I tell you that in some houses forty and fifty people were hiding. These were not mutineers, but residents of the city, who trusted to our well-known mild rule for pardon. I am glad to say they were disappointed.[9]

Cecil Beadon, Secretary to Government, received a message through the electric telegraph from an official in Allahabad, acknowledging that 'it is impossible for us to retaliate upon women and children, but I do wish Supreme Government would solemnly pledge itself that for every Christian woman and child maltreated at Lucknow, ten Oude Nobles should be hanged'.[10] Others put the rate at an impractical thousand rebels for each Christian man, woman and child murdered.

But the threat of punishment was not always sufficient to deter the rebels. Major William Orr, commanding the Hyderabad Contingent at Raghogarh, in the Central Provinces, tried to frighten out the inhabitants from the Fort with a warning. In a letter translated into Urdu, so there would be no misunderstanding, he told the Thakur Sahib, 'If the Army of the Company Bahadur of Englishmen enters . . . you had better present yourselves and lay down your arms, otherwise you will be subjected to punishment'. The reasonable reply came back that the inhabitants of the Raghogarh Fort had not caused any damage to the government, nor killed anyone. 'The Government has laid siege to our house,' wrote Thakur Saket Singh, 'and now you are summoning us for a meeting.' Taking this response as a refusal to surrender, Orr began bombarding the Fort, while its inmates fired back using a collection of antique weapons including zumburrooks, small wall pieces and matchlocks. After several hours of this unmatched contest, the Fort's inhabitants decided they did want to surrender and they sent out an emissary to negotiate. But Orr decided they were playing for time until it grew dark enough so they could escape. 'I therefore ordered a Detachment of Infantry to make an entrance by forcing the Gate' he reported. 'This was most gallantly done, the Fort was entered and all those of the insurgents found in it killed, resisting to the last.'[11]

When suspected rebels were given the courtesy of a trial, although they were invariably found guilty, hanging was frequently used, either from trees or from sturdy wooden gallows erected in strategic places. There was particular emphasis on the symbolic placing of the gallows – it had to be at a public site, but it also had to be a site of significance to the rebels. In Delhi the gallows were placed in the centre of the main street, the Chandni Chowk, at the Kotwali. The 'hideous erection of wood' was reportedly the only undamaged structure in the ruined street, 'where hundreds were hung, rajas, nawabs, and common men alike'.[12] In Meerut the gallows were erected near the cantonment cemetery where the victims of the first massacre lay. At Lucknow four gallows were built in the central gardens of the Qaisarbagh Palace where Begam Hazrat Mahal had directed operations in the last frantic days before it was taken in March 1858. Just to make the point clear, another gallows was erected on the lawn behind Barowen, at Musa Bagh, where the Begam had made her final stand against the recapture of Lucknow.

Contemporary reports throughout the summer of 1857 show great tracts of land where the rule of (British) law had broken down. In rural areas the old feudal patterns re-emerged, which in some places had never been very far below the surface of village life. In towns there were brief attempts to re-establish the old administrative patterns. During Maulvi Liaquat Ali's brief rule in Allahabad, he had 'set up a Government' with *thanas* (police stations) and *chowkis* (lock-ups) in the city. Time would no doubt have seen the re-establishment of the *qazi*, the Sharia judge and other officers, whose roles had developed during the Mughal administration.

British India was a highly regulated society, which made the descent into apparent lawlessness all the more shocking. In 1834 the East India Company had given up its India trade, the original purpose of the Company, and, in agreement with the British Government, now took on the role of local political agent for the Crown. As a sweetener, apart from the large amount of money paid to it, the Company was given legislative powers, including the right to propose and implement Acts relevant to India. The Governor General became Governor General for the whole of India, not just Bengal,

15. The execution of two rebels. Photograph by Felice Beato, 1858.

and he had the power to over-rule his colleagues. The six relevant Acts passed by the Legislative Council of India during 1857 reflect the extent of the crisis (in June new Acts were being passed weekly), and the punitive measures to be imposed once military control was regained.[13]

Act XI passed on 30 May 1857 made it an offence to rebel or wage war against the Queen or the government of the East India Company, or to conspire to rebel. This was refined in Act XIV (6 June) when it was found necessary to make further provision for the trial and punishment of 'persons who endeavour to excite mutiny and sedition among the Forces of the East India Company'. The act of 'seducing officers or soldiers' in the Company's army from their allegiance to the British government was a punishable offence, as was any attempt to 'excite or stir up any such officer or soldier'.

Canning's attempt to define this Act and to point out that there was a difference between sepoys who had mutinied and killed, and sepoys who had only mutinied, was leaked to the press amid howls of outrage. Had he been Nana Sahib himself, he could hardly have attracted more anger. The Queen received a petition from 'a number of Christian inhabitants of Calcutta' asking for Canning to be recalled. 'All the calamities, the results of the spread of the mutiny are directly attributable to the blindness, weakness and incapacity of the local Government of India, of which the present Governor General is the responsible head.'[14] *The Times* sarcastically named him 'Clemency Canning', a name that was to stick, but his friends defended him. William Muir wrote that 'the nick name . . . with which our people used to abuse him, was in effect the highest praise that could have marked his just and noble life'. In defending himself, Canning pointed out that he felt ashamed of his fellow countrymen, who imagined that it was right, not to mention practical, to kill every mutinous sepoy. He vowed he would not govern in anger, and his principled stand was backed by Queen Victoria.

Act XVI (13 June) set out a list of 'heinous offences' in certain districts, including murder, rape, maiming, dacoity, breaking and entering, arson, stealing property 'provided for the conveyance or subsistence of troops' and 'all crimes committed with the intention of assisting those who are waging war against the State or forwarding their designs'. Because the judicial system had broken down in the very places where it was most needed, with judges killed, prisons emptied and destroyed, and court-houses burnt, temporary commissioners were appointed to deal with civilian prisoners. There was no presumption of innocence, the Act stating clearly that 'every person guilty of murder' or the heinous offences listed above, was to be tried by court-martial or by the commissioners. The Governor General had the right to extend the Act into any district not already covered by martial law, and this meant that anyone convicted in these areas was liable 'to the punishment of death' or transportation for life, or imprisonment with hard labour for a term not exceeding fourteen years and the forfeiture of all their property and effects. It was explicitly stated that the Act did not apply to any of Queen Victoria's 'natural-born subjects' or their children.

The so-called Gagging Act (Act XV 13 June) caused uproar because it was designed to control the press which had been unrestricted for more than twenty years. Printing presses now had to be licensed by the Governor General himself or by the Executive Government of the Presidency. Magistrates were given powers to search any house or building where they suspected unlicensed presses might be operating. All newspapers had to carry the printer's name and place of publication, and certain newspapers could be banned outright. One might imagine that this Act was aimed specifically at the vernacular press, but as the historian P. J. O. Taylor has pointed out, it was the English-language newspapers, with English proprietors, who were most affected.[15] The *Friend of India*, which later developed into today's *Statesman*, was chastised when it violently attacked the East India Company for its greed. The government's letter of protest to the editor was published, with satirical comments, and this nearly got the paper closed down because vulnerable governments cannot handle satire. The *Bengal Hurkaru* (Bengal Messenger) was closed down when it urged the destruction of mosques in retaliation for churches destroyed and followed this up with a personal attack on Canning for being soft on the rebels.

By the third week of June rural landholders were ordered to inform the authorities about their tenants. Act XVII (20 June) required all zamindars and taluqdars to 'make early communication of intelligence' about those guilty of mutiny or desertion on their estates. This was designed to catch sepoys returning home to their villages after running away, although these were clearly less of a problem than sepoys who had stayed on to fight under rebel leaders.

It took Benjamin Disraeli, a man of Jewish parentage, but himself a Christian, to endeavour to change public opinion in England. Then out of office, and unable to resist a dig at his political rivals 'he regretted that persons in authority had spoken of vengeance on the Indian mutineers, and he trusted that as a Christian nation, we should think of nothing of the kind'.[16] It was indeed a difficult time to be a Christian, when one's inclinations were polarised between the Old and New Testaments, not knowing whether to demand an eye for an eye or to turn the other cheek. Exeter Hall, a large meeting house on the Strand in London, was the embodiment of Evangelical England and its congregation was sharply criticised for referring to 'our dear Indian brethren' in their prayers.

In happier times, one of the major successes of the East India Company had been the elimination of *thuggee*, that uniquely Indian cult whose devotees strangled and robbed travellers supposedly in the name of the goddess Kali, but also for financial gain. (The English word 'thug' is derived from the followers of thuggee.) Sir William Sleeman, who disliked everything about the old Awadh regime, had been so influential in suppressing the movement that he was nicknamed 'Thuggee Sleeman'. The success of his campaign, which started in the 1830s, was based on sound intelligence from informants, pre-empting murderous attacks and the executions of captured thugs. The Thuggee and Dacoity Department was set up, followed by dedicated thug and dacoity jails like the small one in the Residency complex at Lucknow, where Sleeman was Resident for five years. Unlike the abolition by the British of *sati* (widow-burning), which was seen in some quarters as interfering with time-honoured traditions, no one mourned the end of the thugs.

It was the Commissioner of Benares, Mr H. C. Tucker who recommended in January 1858 'the organisation of a Department similar to that for the extirpation of Thuggee, for the express purpose of the apprehension and punishment of mutineers'. His letter was passed up to the Governor General from the Government of the Central Provinces, who felt the creation of such a department would be premature and unworkable until the police forces had been reformed and could provide 'the usual support' to the civilian administrators. (Many of the police, as well as the sepoys, had turned mutinous, which had exacerbated the unrest.) Tucker, who was a liberal and rational man, qualities he managed to maintain during the Uprising, thought that:

> The present machinery of apathetic Military and spasmodic Civil action will never succeed in finding out and punishing the worst mutineers. An occasional

> Sepoy ... may fall into the hands of the magistrate, but without systematic effort, all deserters and mutineers are technically liable to capital punishment. I hardly suppose that Government will dispose in that way of the many thousands of sepoys who may escape death in the battle field and endeavour to mix themselves up with the general population. It is necessary to use some degree of discrimination, to ascertain the worst Regiments and the worst mutineers, especially all who have had any hand in atrocities, and to hunt them to the death. This can only be done by a Commission extending its agency over the whole country.[17]

This was almost exactly along the lines that Canning had been thinking, and he over-ruled the caveats of the Central Government. By the middle of February the Governor General was writing to just the man to head such a commission – John Cracroft Wilson of the Bengal Civil Service, magistrate and keen farmer, with an estate in Kashmir. Wilson had been born in India, sent home to study at Haileybury and Oxford, and returned to India to work as Assistant Commissioner under Sleeman, earning almost equal praise in putting down thuggee. This was hugely in his favour, but he had distinguished himself further while magistrate at Moradabad, during the Uprising. Acting with the increased powers granted him by the Lieutenant Governor, he had successfully prevented outbreaks of trouble and had gone on to superintend the Agra District as Commissioner on Special Duty after the death of the Lieutenant Governor, John Russell Colvin.

Wilson was asked if he could take up the new role of superintending the detection and apprehension of mutineers over the whole of the North-West Provinces, and if he agreed, what would he need to do the job effectively. Wilson did not hesitate. He was in the fortunate position of being able to dictate his own terms to the Company. In a long letter from 'Camp Allahabad' he laid down his conditions. He needed authority for himself and his subordinates to act in Bihar 'which supplied thousands of recruits for our late Army' as well as in the Bengal Presidency. He wanted the right to sanction extra staff, month by month, as they were needed, anticipating increased work once Awadh and Rohilkhand were settled. The power to sanction rewards for the capture of mutineers up to a thousand rupees should, he thought, be conferred on him, as well as free travel by any Government conveyance, 'Rail, Mail Cart, or Van' exclusive of his fixed travelling allowance of Rs 150 a month.

Correct identification of the rebellious sepoys was paramount. The master copies of the Muster Rolls, that is, the lists of officers and sepoys in each of the Bengal Native Infantry regiments, were held in Calcutta, but Wilson said they contained 'many false entries as to the names of Recruits and still more as to their Castes, etc.'. Muster Rolls held in the regimental headquarters of the cantonments that had mutinied had invariably been burnt, together with the Kindred Roll books, which held details of the sepoy's kin, his wife, parents, and siblings, which could have made identification easier. So new lists were to be prepared by assembling all the sepoys from each regiment who had remained 'firm and loyal' at Wilson's headquarters, and who, he thought, 'would be ready to act as Witnesses against their Rebel Brethren in arms when arrested'.

All of Wilson's conditions were met, including the reinstatement of a higher salary for his Deputy Commissioner, which had been mistakenly reduced. His remit was to cover Awadh, Central India, Bengal and the North-West Provinces. (Confusingly, the latter had nothing to do with the North-West Frontier Province, a later designation for the Punjab/Afghan border. It referred in the late 1850s to areas north-west of Calcutta, including Agra.) District officers and commissioners were instructed to supply Wilson with 'all documentary evidence against Mutineers and Rebels which may come into their possession' and to provide him with 'full and regular lists of the convictions and execution of Mutineers, or rebels, which may be carried out under their direction'. He was also to get from the military authorities whatever Muster Rolls and regimental books that had survived. Since Wilson's requests had been granted without hesitation, even the financial demands, he felt able to suggest the names of staff he wanted too. Brevet Captain Gowan, who had escaped from Bareilly at the beginning of the Uprising and had described the awful havoc in the countryside, was to be one of Wilson's deputies. Gowan had lost everything he possessed, Wilson wrote, but had managed to recruit '150 Hindu tribesmen from Rohilkhand' who would be useful in tracing and punishing mutineers and rebels. Wilson's second choice was an interesting one – he recommended Wilayat Hossain Khan, son of a former Chief Minister of Awadh, who had stood in as magistrate in Moradabad, when Wilson had been on two years' sick leave. Wilayat Hossain Khan was 'an irreproachable character' whose services would be invaluable not only to the local authorities of Rohilkhand, but to Wilson personally. 'He did not desert us when called upon to assist us in our time of trouble. I beg that he may be restored to his old position and rank without detriment to his pension.' This Canning agreed to, overlooking a past offence of Wilayat Hossein Khan, when there had been an unfortunate incident with a *taziah* (a Shi'a model tomb) in Moradabad.[18]

By the third week of March 1858 Wilson was fully organised. He had set up ten areas or divisions of jurisdiction, and the names of officers and sepoys from the 'grand list or muster roll' would be extrapolated and sent to the local authorities in each area. Each name was to carry additional information, giving the soldier's caste, army rank and company, village, *pargana* (district), province, and the dates he was on leave, whether he had remained loyal, and if he had mutinied, the date on which this occurred. 'In this way,' Wilson reported, 'the work of tracing and seizing mutineers will be carried on by a hundred individuals at one and the same time.' When a number of such men had been collected, Wilson or his deputies would travel to the area 'with a body of approvers, and the necessary identification will be furnished'. He had already prepared a list, with their castes and places of abode, of more than 500 mutineers of the 29th Regiment, Bengal Native Infantry, who had mutinied at Moradabad, and he was working on a similar list for the 11th Regiment. Wilson had dropped the idea of getting every loyal sepoy, who hadn't mutinied, to turn up at his headquarters when it was pointed out to him by the Military Department Secretary that this could amount to a thousand or so men. He agreed to select personally five faithful men from each corps, to act as 'approvers', that is to testify to the disloyalty of their fellow sepoys. Interestingly, in the course of his work during the summer of 1858, he became convinced that there had been a plan behind the separate mutinies, and that the date originally fixed for the Great Uprising was 31 May 1857. This of course had been pre-empted by the Meerut rising on 10 May, which was precipitated by the fettering of the eighty-five sepoys who had refused the greasy cartridges.

As Wilson's men went to work, and the numbers of sepoys found guilty of mutiny increased, the question arose of what to do with those who were to be imprisoned and not hanged. Jails had been a particular target of the sepoys – for good reason, since in some cases their comrades had been unjustly imprisoned in them. In other cases the release of felons, murderers and lunatics had added to the general mayhem. Burning the town jail was a rite of passage in spreading the urban revolt. Act XI passed by the Legislative Council on 4 April 1858 acknowledged that 'the destruction of the Jails in many parts of India' had led to a lack of 'means for the confinement of convicts and of the due enforcement of prison-discipline'. The Act authorised magistrates to order corporal punishment as an alternative to a jail sentence – 'thirty stripes with a rattan [cane] for burglary, theft, receiving stolen property and injury to property'. The only exceptions were to apply to Europeans, Americans and females, none of whom was to be chastised with physical punishment.

The need to jail men outside the areas from which they came was recognised, especially after a number of rebel zamindars had been liberated from Gaya Fort by fellow rebels. It had long been Company practice to exile defeated or difficult rulers far away from their ancestral homes. This is why Nana Sahib's adoptive father, the Peshwa, had been sent from Poona to Bithur, why the descendants of Tipu Sultan, killed at Seringapatam in 1799, had been sent to Benares and Calcutta, and why Bahadur Shah Zafar and his wife were ultimately to go to Rangoon. (Members of the Burmese royal family were, in turn, to be sent to Ratnagiri, in the Bombay Presidency, after the Third Anglo-Burmese war of 1885–86.) The Andaman Islands lie well south of Burma and the Bay of Bengal, and form a spine-like chain that runs into the Nicobar Islands. The Andamans were initially opened up as a penal colony by the East India Company in the winter of 1788, but were

16. Delhi street near Mori Gate, 1858. Photograph by Dr John Murray. National Army Museum.

abandoned eight years later because of the cost of getting supplies to this remote region, and the high mortality rate of the jailers. Lord Canning had sent out a Commission late in 1857, headed by the energetic Dr Mouat, one-time surgeon and later Secretary to the Bengal Committee of Education, to examine the islands and report back on whether they might be suitable, more than half a century on, for a penal colony. The doctor reported favourably and transportation of convicted prisoners started early in 1858. With delightful irony some of the smaller outcrops of the Andamans were named after the British heroes of the Uprising, so there was John Lawrence Island, Henry Lawrence Island, Outram Island, Havelock Island, Neill Island and Sir Hugh Rose Island.

In May 1858 there was a mass outbreak, and the superintendent, Dr James Walker, who had previously been in charge of the Central Jail at Agra, hanged eighty-one of the men who had tried unsuccessfully to escape from Port Blair. In fact, as some of the prisoners had discovered, escape was impossible. The islands were inhabited by a number of Stone-Age tribes, of possibly African origin, including the savage Jarawa whose specialities were hunting with poison arrows and cannibalism. It is estimated that as many as 3,000 convicted mutineers were sent to the Andamans, never to return home.

A more humane solution had been proposed in October 1857 by the enterprising Mr Neville Warren, Agent of the Scinde Railway. This had been inspired by the Governor of Bombay's comments on the current problem of making the punishment fit the crime. John Elphinstone, like Lord Canning, was anxious to differentiate between the degrees of guilt of the mutinous sepoys and he discussed this at some length with Sir Bartle Frere, Commissioner of Sind (known previously as Scinde). The worst regiments, who had committed 'heinous crimes' were to be punished 'with the most exemplary severity'. Sepoys from other regiments were condemned to transportation and imprisonment with hard labour in irons for longer or shorter periods. At the end of their term they were to be discharged as unworthy to serve. (The implication is that they were still soldiers while undergoing punishment.) This still, however, left a number of regiments 'whose behaviour has been rather undecided than positively bad' or who had shown some redeeming features. It would not be just nor politic to treat these regiments in the same way as those who had murdered their own officers or the assassins who had murdered the women and children at Cawnpore, argued Elphinstone. 'I would be glad if some *locus penitentiae* [place of penance] could be found – some means by which they might expiate their offences and be restored to the favour of Government.'[19] Neville Warren, in a 'Memorandum on the Native Infantry Regiments and Indian Railways' with particular reference to the Punjab Railway running through Sind, had suggested such men might be employed in building the new railway lines, which were being speedily pushed forward in case another uprising took place.[20]

The Railway Company would pay the Government for the hire of the disgraced sepoys at a rate per 100 cubic feet of stone or material used. He suggested that one day a week should be kept aside for regimental drills 'to preserve some degree of military habit'. The advantages were obvious, he pointed out – the railways would be 'much advanced', the regiments would undergo a 'real punishment', and the sepoys would ultimately become better soldiers. Elphinstone pondered this, reasoning that since the majority of sepoys came from the agricultural classes, they should not consider it a disgrace to work digging trenches or building embankments. 'Throughout the Roman Empire', he wrote, 'the roads were made by the legions', and at later periods British soldiers had been employed upon similar works where the climate was suitable.

Bartle Frere had a more imaginative solution. He thought many of the convicted sepoys could be employed on harbour works and fortifications at Karachi and Aden, while Lord Canning favoured Perim (in today's South Yemen) where they could work in building, levelling and constructing reservoirs. If there were large numbers of sepoys to be transported then they could even be settled on the north coast of Australia, where the climate was considered unsuitable for European colonisation. In fact Frere thought a sepoy colony might well be established in Australia, which could become the nucleus for an Indian penal settlement. He foresaw that this arrangement 'would develop the resources of tropical Australia and extend the limits of our Colonial Empire in the East'. This idea came to nothing. The West Indies was also suggested as a place where 'these misguided men, dangerous in their own country, would in due course of time become useful members of the community – it would also address the severe manpower shortage on British sugar plantations'.[21] But in the end the Andaman Islands remained the only place for transported sepoys. Objections had been raised to Mr Warren's railway plan, because the convicted men could not be readmitted into the army when their sentence was finished.

While this rather arcane debate was going on, the Chief Commissioner for Awadh, Sir James Outram was engaged in more practical matters at Camp Alambagh, south of Lucknow. He was still Commissioner in exile in January 1858 when he wrote to Lord Canning with his views on how to punish the mass of sepoys who would inevitably fall into British hands when the recapture of Lucknow began. Outram was certain that once Lucknow fell then the whole of Awadh would be rapidly subdued and that planning for this event should start immediately. He was concerned that an outright war of extermination against the defeated rebels and sepoys would become counterproductive and that the men, faced with no alternative but death, would become dacoits 'in a country where the forests and vast tracts of jungle make that occupation so congenial to every armed Asiatic, comparatively safe and easy'. Only a huge British force, involving an enormous sacrifice of European life, could deal with this kind of guerrilla warfare, where the unseen enemy was 'ever able to move two miles to our one' and proceedings would be dragged out for months, if not years. There was the danger too that the villagers might start to sympathise with the hunted fugitives and in aiding them to escape, would themselves become liable to extreme punishment. Outram thought that even the most bloodthirsty, who called 'for the blood of every sepoy, would hardly be prepared to advocate the extermination of every soul who … should venture to harbour them'. He condemned those who preached 'a bloody crusade against the miserable and abject wretches'.[22]

But this raised the question of how to punish the guilty and how to vary the degrees of punishment. Sitting in the then isolated Alambagh Palace during cold winter days and nights, and fighting off sustained, though ultimately unsuccessful, rebel attempts, Outram thought that if the rebels could be taught a severe lesson on the reoccupation of the city, as they had in the Sikanderbagh, when 2,000 had been killed, then that might suffice. If the ringleaders were given up, 'these men might be hung in perpetual chains on the scenes of the atrocities'. The sepoys who had been spared death would, the Chief Commissioner thought, be able to provide valuable information about the origin of the rebellion and its chief perpetrators. It was these rebels who should be targeted, not the 'blind, credulous and ignorant agents of their crimes'. Outram was also a proponent of architectural revenge, the desire to demolish towns where uprisings had taken place. This would naturally be a severe punishment to the inhabitants, but the arguments for demolition went further than this. In some cases they seemed to be directed against the very buildings themselves, as if their continued existence, silent witnesses to the horrors of revolt, were a standing reproach. Outram thought that Delhi should have been levelled to the ground after it fell to the British.

> A stroke like that would have been a beacon and a warning to the whole of India. And a heavy blow to the Mohamedan religion. It is now too late however, but the Chief Commissioner sees no reason why that fate should not befall Lucknow. There ought to be some place which the mutineers may recognise and point to as the monument of their own crimes and of our retribution ... only such buildings should be preserved as may be requisite for our own military or other purposes. No mosque or temple should be spared.[23]

At the same time, and quite illogically, Outram proposed a series of 'flying columns' accompanied by civil officers of 'capacity, temper and experience who will reassure the bewildered population'. Although Outram's suggestion of razing Lucknow entirely to the ground was not accepted by the Governor General, a huge amount of demolition did subsequently take place under the direction of Colonel Robert Napier of the Bengal Engineers. Much was made of the military necessity for doing so, and the need to drive broad military roads through the most crowded areas. But particular buildings of emotive significance were singled out, like the Qaisarbagh Palace 'where our chief enemies have resided during the rebellion and whence they have issued their proclamations and orders against us'. The palace was partially demolished when a new road was driven through it. The Sikanderbagh, where so many lives, British and Indian, had been lost, suffered the same fate, and remains today straddling both sides of the main road. The Chattar Manzil palaces were similarly separated by a road, and the isolated Barowen Palace at Musa Bagh, scene of the last battle in the recapture of Lucknow, seems to have been partially demolished shortly after 1858.

Before the news of the recapture of Delhi reached London, the Prime Minister, Lord Palmerston, then in his seventies, had demanded that the whole of the city should be demolished. 'Every civil building connected with the Mahomedan religion should be levelled with the ground, without regard to antiquarian veneration and artistic predilections.'[24] Lord Canning had initially agreed with Palmerston, adding he wanted the Red Fort demolished too, except for the Diwan-i-Khas, which had been taken over as army headquarters by General Archdale Wilson. Even more radical proposals were made to demolish the Jama Masjid and build a cathedral on its site. It was Sir John Lawrence, newly arrived from the Punjab, who spoke out strongly against this, and by the beginning of January 1858, Canning had come round to his point of view, declaring that 'there were reasons of policy and justice against an immediate levelling of the town [of Delhi] to say nothing of other more pressing work on hand elsewhere'. Lawrence had sensibly pointed out that the 'military utility' of the Red Fort and the city walls were essential keys to holding Delhi, and, in the argument he knew would most appeal to the Governor General, it would cost too much to demolish anyway. The recommendations of the military engineers to clear substantial areas around the Red Fort and the Jama Masjid were carried out, and the interesting mass of houses that lay between the Lahore Gate of the Red Fort and the beginning of Chandni Chowk, was swept away. The Jama Masjid stands, even today, aloof and isolated from the city it serves. Within the Red Fort, numerous pavilions that had stood in small gardens were demolished, and ugly British barracks in a peculiarly unsympathetic grey stone were erected that still stand today.

Where buildings did survive, they were often badly treated. A mosque at Allahabad was turned into a British barracks as a 'punishment', both for its former worshippers and for the building itself, one imagines. The Great Imambara at Lucknow, the largest Shi'a monument in the city, became a field hospital for wounded British soldiers, and the adjoining Jama Masjid was used to store ammunition. In Delhi, the handsome College was converted into barracks, and a number of popular bazaars demolished.[25]

The financial cost of the Uprising for the British was enormous, estimated at some £42 million.[26] This figure included the unusual expenses of shipping in soldiers from Britain to fight, the extra hospitals for the wounded, imported ammunition, extra labour costs for moving men and equipment around the country, repairing the electric telegraph and much else. It also included the loss of anticipated revenue because of the chaotic situation. Land revenue in northern India had not been paid because the records in the *tehsils* (the sub-district offices) had been destroyed, often deliberately, and there were few officials to collect the revenue anyway. Pursuing small farmers for unpaid sums of money took a very low priority when the revenue collectors were themselves targets because they worked for the British. Customs duties on certain goods passing through different states could not be imposed, because the customs officials had run away or been killed. Tolls imposed at river crossings and on road travellers were not paid, for the same reason. The first act of the rebel sepoys from Meerut, on reaching Delhi on 11 May, was to loot and burn the toll house on the far side of the Bridge of Boats, killing the toll keeper. Cantonment treasuries were an obvious target for the rebels and badmashes. £170,000 was stolen from the Allahabad Treasury alone, and throughout the summer of 1857, thousands of pounds were brought into Delhi by rebel sepoys as a token of their loyalty to Bahadur Shah Zafar. The Government of India's finances were controlled by the Governor General and Council, through the Accountant General, who put up statements from the various departments of the East India Company, like the Military Department, the Judicial Department, the Public Works Department, and the Board of Revenue. There was still a deficit of £7 million in the government treasury in the financial year 1859–60, after the British government had assumed direct control of India.

It was therefore logical that those who had revolted, or were sympathetic to the rebel cause, should be made to pay dearly. Several Gujar villages around Delhi had already paid their land revenue tax for the first half of 1857 direct to the King of Delhi. William Muir thought they should be charged again, and if they deserted their villages because they could no longer afford to live in them, 'it will be a good riddance!' Similarly, villagers around Cawnpore had paid their revenue to Nana Sahib's collectors, as representatives of the new ruler, and they were now having to pay the British again, as were the citizens of Aligarh, who had paid the rebel leader Ghous Mahomed.[27] (Prize money, to pay for the army's expenses, and ransom money for civil reconstruction have already been mentioned.) Act X of 1858 authorised the confiscation of whole villages and the imposition of fines where crimes had been committed by the villagers 'or members of tribes', or the landholders who had neglected 'to assist in suppression or rebellion or apprehending rebels'. If fines were not paid, then the villages could be sold to a new owner.

Land belonging to convicted rebels was automatically confiscated, but this presented a problem where it was owned jointly by family members. J. P. Grant, Lieutenant Governor of the Central Provinces, thought that 'where a family, in the persons of its active members and representatives, has rebelled, the family should suffer as such'. It seemed to him that this was mere commonsense 'and I am sure that this would appear mere justice in native eyes',[28] but he was over-ruled and the difficult task of determining which parts of jointly-owned land belonged to the rebels, and which to innocent members of their families, was begun. The stopping of pensions was another way to punish people financially. Lord Canning had issued an order on 10 July 1857 proclaiming that any military pensioner who concealed a mutinous sepoy or a deserter, or who failed to inform the civil or military authorities 'of any mutinous or rebellious designs of which he may become cognizant', would forfeit his government pension, in addition to any lawful punishment he might receive. This was such a wide definition that it could be applied to almost anyone who had overheard bazaar gossip and had not reported it. The onus for proving their loyalty was put on the old and invalid sepoys, who were told that if they didn't present themselves at the pensions office within the prescribed period of payment, or failed 'to establish a reasonable ground for believing that they have not only not joined in the rebellion, but that they have, according to their opportunities, taken part with the Government, will forfeit their pensions'.

If the pensioner was not sufficiently frightened by this order, and still arrived at the pension office, he would be faced with a 'Committee of Officers' who would institute a rigorous inquiry as to whether he should forfeit his pension. The proceedings of the Committee of Officers would be sent to the Military Department for its opinion, leading, of course, to innumerable delays and voluminous correspondence. The only exemptions to the loss of pension was for 'cripples, [men] infirm from great age or the effects of disease, or the heirs of native officers and soldiers'. Insane pensioners, women and children, and widows of the holders of the 'Order of Merit' were also exempted.

How quickly this became unworkable was shown by a report from the Collector of Allahabad, Mr M. H. Court, who was approached by a pensioner who was 'unable to specify any act of his in favour of Government either at, or after, the rebellion'. Court wrote that he could not 'withhold payment of the sum pledged to [him] for life, and there is in this case no ground of suspicion against the applicant'. But the Lieutenant Governor of the Central Provinces overruled the Collector, pointing out that a military pension was held as a matter of grace, not a matter of right, and that the government 'may strike a pensioner off its roll at its pleasure'.[29] Not all pensioners were ex-soldiers. Some were civilians, whose payments were handled by government officials, and these included families who had been granted pensions, sometimes fifty years earlier, in lieu of land rights which they had surrendered. These pensions, no matter how long established, were still liable to forfeit if the present pensioner had supported the rebels. When the widows of loyal sepoys from the Malwa Bheel Corps, killed in action at Indore in July 1857, applied to the government for pensions, it was suggested 'that the States whose troops caused the Casualties, be made to pay whatever pension or donation his Lordship [Canning] may be pleased to assign', thus neatly providing for the widows and punishing the rebellious states at the same time.

Perenially short of money, even before the Uprising and the expense of putting it down, the East India Company had, for many years, been issuing government bonds, on which interest was paid, and which were redeemable after a fixed period. These bonds were a secure and modern way of putting one's money to work, without having to go to the traditional *shroff*, or banker, and were, as it turned out, considerably safer than burying one's cash in the garden or the house. It was not realised for some time that because anyone with sufficient funds, British or Indian, could invest in the bonds, they might unwittingly have been issued to prominent rebels. An urgent telegram from the Governor General went out to the Home, Foreign and Military Departments asking 'for the Names of any Parties convicted of rebellion or notoriously concerned in it who may be likely to be holders of Government securities'. The names were to be sent to him by telegraph, with a copy to be sent in the post, as soon as possible.[30] Surprisingly perhaps, the list was headed by Nana Sahib. Promissory notes were slightly different, and more like a form of paper currency. They usually carried no date of maturity, and could be sold, but could also be cancelled by the government. Another list of rebel names was issued, and the public was warned not to buy promissory notes that had belonged to the Maulvi of Faizabad, the Nawab of Ballabgarh and several other prominent people involved in the revolt. This meant that men or women considered guilty of revolt, and who had invested in government bonds or acquired promissory notes, could have their assets seized by the government and be made bankrupt. It also meant that the heirs who had inherited the estates of deceased rebels were also punished.

There were other, more subtle forms of punishment, some of them petty in the extreme. The Commissioner of Nagpur, for example, the irascible Mr George Plowden, had received a number of anonymous letters through the post during the summer of 1858, and as a result, ordered the removal of eight letter boxes in the city.[31] This was strenuously objected to by the Deputy Postmaster, J. J. McBride, who complained to the Postmaster General. Closing the letter boxes, McBride said, 'will tease and cause a good deal of annoyance to merchants and other peaceably inclined persons'. It would not stop the anonymous letters, because there were other letter boxes at different post offices, which couldn't be closed at night, but it would inconvenience the population of 100,000 who would have to walk between one and four miles to post their letters.

In another annoying incident, the Political Agent at Bharatpur, Captain J. P. Nixon, noted to the Government Secretary of the North-West Provinces that the coinage of the state

> has hitherto borne the impression of the late Emperor of Delhi's name on the rupee – I have directed this to be discontinued henceforth, and the substitution of the name of the British Government in heir [*sic*] for that of the Archtraitor of Delhi ... the matter may be one that has escaped your notice.

It was found that other states too, including Dholpur, were still coining money in the same way, as though the cataclysmic events of 1857 had not happened.[32]

On 1 November 1858 the Government of India was formally transferred from the East India Company to the Crown. A proclamation was read out in every major town on behalf of Queen Victoria. It stated that the Queen placed especial trust and confidence in Lord Canning, who now became the first Viceroy of India. The Queen pledged that all former treaties made with the Company would remain in place, and that there would be no more territorial expansion, nor any further objections to adoptions by childless rulers. Just as importantly, a two-month amnesty was offered to all offenders, except those who had been convicted of taking part in the murder of British subjects, because for such people 'the demands of justice forbid the exercise of mercy'. The new Viceroy was directed to hold out 'the expectation of pardons' in Awadh on certain terms, but to punish those 'whose crimes place them beyond the reach of forgiveness'. It was a generous and bold move, given the weight of British public opinion against it, and an olive branch was held out to 'those whose crimes may appear to have originated in a too credulous acceptance of the false reports circulated by designing men'.[33]

The government was not unaware of the advantages of rewarding certain people who had helped it during the Uprising and whose help would be needed in the future. Mindful however of financial pressures, rewards had to be devised that would not cost too much, and accordingly some recycling of land went on. With the government fully in control again, lists of those who had assisted British subjects during the Uprising or provided military support were drawn up. Top of the list was Jang Bahadur, the de facto ruler of Nepal who had brought his Gurkha troops down into India at the end of 1857 and joined the British at Lucknow. On his return to Nepal the following year, heavily weighed down with Indian loot, he had been helpful in rooting out the rebels who had taken refuge in his territory. By February 1860 he had handed over to the British 3,000 refugee rebel sepoys and twenty-eight rebel chiefs and according to the *Illustrated London News* received a 'magnificent acknowledgement from our Government – territory 240 miles long and 40 miles broad'.[34] What the magazine did not mention was that the land had in fact originally belonged to Nepal, but had been ceded to the East India Company after the Anglo-Gurkha war of 1814–16. In other places, estates and villages which had been confiscated because the landholder or the villagers couldn't pay the fines imposed on them, were handed out as rewards to men who had been loyal to the British. Thus Raja Tej Singh lost his title and estates 'for disloyalty' and his lands were given to Rao Bhowani Singh of Mainpuri. The Government Secretaries of Bengal, the North-West Provinces, Madras and Bombay were all asked to nominate 'persons who have done good service' and 'who may have distinguished themselves in aiding the British Government during the late disturbances'. Land grants would be conferred by written deed, but it was to be made clear that the continuance of the grant depended on the good conduct of the grantee and his successors, and it could be revoked.

The bestowal of titles and honours on friendly rulers was a common way of rewarding people where land was not given. The Raja Jai Prakash Singh of Deo, in Bihar, got a personal award from the Governor General of 'the title of Maharaja, and a *khillat* . . . as an acknowledgement of his steady devotion to the Government and of the services rendered by him during the late disturbance. A *sunnud* [a formal charter or deed] conferring the title of Maharaja is herewith enclosed.' A *khillat* was not a single robe of honour, as it is often translated, but was made up of different pieces, including a pearl necklace, a *jeegah sirpesh* (turban ornament), a silver mounted stick, an embroidered sword belt and a shield with a silk cloth. The award to the new maharaja is couched in the language of the Mughals, whose last representative, even as it was being bestowed in August 1858, was on his way to exile and death in Burma. The continued use of Mughal language and customs even after the end of the Great Uprising is perhaps surprising – the last vestige of that brief, happy period when mutual respect between British and Indians had led to the incorporation into Company administration of traditional courtesies. Now the intention was to show that the Governor General, soon to become the Viceroy, had indeed assumed the mantle of the last Emperor.

Thus, for example, on the fall of Delhi in September 1857 a *kharita*, that is, a formal letter from one great man to another, was sent by Canning to thirty-seven chiefs, including the Maharao of Kotah, the Nizam and various rajas. Dated 6 October, in its English translation, the kharita began:

> I have the gratification of announcing to your Highness that Delhi, the focus of the treason and revolt which for four months have harassed Hindostan, and the stronghold in which the Mutinous Army of Bengal has sought to concentrate its power, has been wrested from the rebels.

This was a significant honour for the recipients, the sharing of information between seemingly equal men of rank. The fact that the kharita was seen as a reward to loyal chiefs was emphasised by the Secretary's letter to Canning's agent in Rajputana, Brigadier General Lawrence. He was told that because the Governor General had some doubts about the conduct of the Maharaja of Jaipur, the Bharatpur Durbar (Court) and the Nawab of Tonk, discretion should be used 'in delivering or with-holding the accompanying Khureetas – to the Chiefs named above'. If Lawrence did decide to withhold a kharita from a particular chief, he was 'to report fully upon the conduct of the chief in question, and await further orders'.[35]

Humbler people than the chiefs were also recognised and rewarded for acts of support. Subedar Mathura Prasad of the 4th Company, 22nd Regiment Bombay Native Infantry, who had alerted his Adjutant, Captain Jones, and Captain Scott, to a complicated plot being hatched against the British by the Maharaja of Satara, was awarded the Order of British India decoration, consisting of a ribbon and medal. Bubboo, the *ayah* (nursemaid or nanny) to the late Mr Thriepland, the Deputy Collector of Jaunpur, was awarded a pension of Rs 5 per month, for saving the lives of two of his children. Both the Thrieplands had been killed in their house during the Uprising.

Europeans were also recognised and rewarded. Apart from military honours, like the Victoria Cross, which was first awarded in 1857 to Crimean heroes, grants of land were made, jobs created and financial awards given.

William Peppé, who had emigrated in 1843 from Aberdeenshire, in Scotland, to set up a sugar-processing factory in Gorakhpur District, got a grant of land 'for Mutiny services', which remained in his family until 1960, when Prime Minister Jawarharlal Nehru nationalised all remaining zamindaris. Captain George Forrest, VC, one of the men who had defended, then blown up, the magazine in Delhi on 11 May 1857 when the city fell into rebel hands, got a *jagir* (piece of land) at Dehra Dun. Mr Francis Cohen, an elderly Eurasian of German descent, whose full name was Franz Gottlieb Cohen, has recently been identified by William Dalrymple as a poet writing in Urdu and Persian under the *takhallus* (pen-name) 'Farasu'.[36] The Cohens lived at Harchandpur, near Meerut and they had been particularly helpful towards a number of European refugees fleeing from Delhi, including Captain Forrest. The two grandsons of 'Fransoo Sahib', George Cohen Peche and John Cohen Peche, were found jobs in the administrative service, while the old man got the zamindari of three villages bestowed on him.[37]

Thomas Kavanagh, the Irish soldier who had volunteered for the dangerous task of taking a message from the besieged Lucknow Residency to Sir Colin Campbell and his relief force, got not only the Victoria Cross, but a huge financial reward of £20,000.[38] However, Kavanagh, riding on a wave of newly found popularity as one of the heroes of the Uprising, and who was to publish a book modestly entitled *How I Won the VC*, presumed too much on the goodwill of the Company. He requested a year's leave in England and asked that 'some indulgence may be allowed him as regards salary, while he is absent'. This was indignantly rejected, the Chief Commissioner saying that the 'munificent donation' which Kavanagh had received made it quite unnecessary for him to receive a higher amount of salary during his leave, while the Governor General thought his request 'comes with a peculiarly bad grace from him . . . and greatly surprised him'. Kavanagh's fellow Europeans who survived the siege of the Residency were also rewarded. The civilian defenders were made honorary soldiers, because they had engaged in military duties and 'were authorized to draw six months *batta* [allowance] in accordance with their equivalent military rank'.[39] Although it is not stated implicitly in the order of 22 January 1858, one assumes that it was only European men to whom the authorisation applied.

By 1859 the worst was over, and a spirit of forgiveness and even reconciliation was abroad. Village people no longer feared being burned to death in their huts, gallows were dismantled, and the dreadful hanging trees had given up their corpses. It was possible to walk the streets again without fear of being shot by the British, on a whim, or because an inhabitant had shown insufficient respect. A printed 'Circular' issued from the Government of the North-Western Provinces at Allahabad, which had seen some of the worst punishments carried out by the troops of Neill and Renaud stated that:

> [The] Lieutenant Governor is of opinion that no advantage can arise from pursuing or prosecuting those, who are supposed to have taken a subordinate part in such offences [committed during the disturbances]; that, on the contrary, it will be good policy to invite and encourage such persons to return to their homes, and resume their peaceful occupations.

Furthermore, the advice of the Governor General to the magistrates was to

> discourage by every means in their power, private prosecutions for wrongs done during the rebellion, and also to refrain from pursuing an enquiry on the part of Government into cases attended with murder and plunder, which do not present circumstances of particular aggravation.[40]

The wheel had turned almost full circle … but a huge number of people, guilty and innocent alike, had been mown down in its turning.

Six

MUTINY MEMORIALS

MOST VICTORIAN towns in England of any pretension have a road or terrace named after General Sir Henry Havelock. In London alone there are twelve such thoroughfares, allowing us to date the construction of the houses that line them with some precision. There are also numerous public houses named after this staunch teetotaller, from the haunted Havelock Arms in Darlington in the north of England, to the seaside town of Hastings on the south coast, where the Havelock Arms has a splendid wall panel of Doulton tiles depicting the general on horseback. His statue stands at one corner of Trafalgar Square, in the company of Sir Charles Napier, another Indian officer. General Havelock, dying at the moment of victory (the first relief of Lucknow), epitomised the Victorian hero as much as General Charles George Gordon was to do a generation later. The plinth on which General Havelock stands is a regimental memorial as well, listing the regiments that marched from Cawnpore to relieve the Lucknow Residency. There were Highland regiments among the troops including the 93rd, but there was also a Sikh regiment too, of whom the General said they were the bravest men he had ever had the privilege to command.[1]

In October 1943 at the height of the Second World War, the Rani of Jhansi Brigade was formed by Subhas Chandra Bose, the leader of the Indian National Army, fighting with the Japanese against the British. The brigade was a women's combat army unit, made up of Indian civilians in Japanese-occupied Burma and Malaya. The Rani's compatriot, the Nana Sahib, is commemorated in the Nana Rao Ghat at Cawnpore, which was known to the British as Satichaura or Massacre Ghat, and in the Nana Rao Park, the former Memorial Gardens to the victims of 1857. Raja Kanwar Singh, the Raja of Jagdishpur is commemorated in the Vir Kunwar Singh University at Arrah, in Bihar. It was recently announced that Rs 25 lakhs are to be allocated to a girls' degree college in Lucknow, to be known as the Begam Hazrat Mahal College.

The power of a famous name is a potent symbol, a reminder of the past, and an inspiration for the present. Memorials act as a permanent reminder to the victorious, as a permanent irritation to the losers, and as a marker for future generations. Britain, as eventual victor, had two different things to commemorate – those who had lost their lives through violence, by massacre or in battle, and the heroic deeds that had enabled the rebels to be put down. India, it seemed, had far less to commemorate, although the Uprising had led directly to the abolition of the East India Company.

There were immediate problems of disposing of the dead during the Uprising, depending on the circumstances in which they were killed. While Delhi was still in rebel hands, Hindu funeral pyres were reported nightly on the banks of the Jumna, and the Muslim dead were buried in cemeteries within the walled city. Where sepoys and their supporters were killed fighting the British, their bodies were unceremoniously dumped into defensive ditches or pits and covered with earth. Britons killed by the rebels were usually left to rot where they had fallen or, as happened at Cawnpore, thrown down a well. Other Britons were buried in individual or mass graves by their fellow countrymen where this was possible, although some such graves were disinterred later by rebels. Where lone Britons were buried in an ad hoc manner, usually under a tree, a marker was put on the tree – sometimes the initials of the deceased, sometimes a cross, was carved into the bark, to show that a Christian lay nearby.

Captain Augustus Mayne was killed during the relief of Lucknow on 14 November, the peculiar manner of his death being witnessed by William Forbes-Mitchell, a sergeant of the 93rd Highlanders. Just outside La Martiniere College to the south-east of the city, a group of Company officers and men came across a naked *sadhu* (holy man) 'with his head closely shaven except for the tuft on his crown, and his face all streaked in a hideous manner with white and red paint, his body smeared with ashes. He was sitting on a leopardskin, counting a rosary of beads.' A soldier with the group said he would like to 'try my bayonet on that painted scoundrel', but he was stopped by Captain Mayne, who said 'Oh, don't touch him; these fellows are harmless Hindoo yogis, and won't hurt us'. Immediately the sadhu pulled out a blunderbuss from under his leopardskin and fired straight at the captain's chest, killing him instantly. The murderer was promptly bayoneted to death, and Mayne's body was put on a *dooli* (a stretcher). It was recovered the following day by Lieutenant Frederick Roberts and his Adjutant, Arthur Bunny. Roberts described what happened next:

> We decided to bury the poor fellow at once. I chose a spot close by for his grave, which was dug with the help of some gunners, and then Bunny and I, aided by two or three brother officers, laid our friend in it just as he was, in his blue frock-coat and long boots, his eyeglass in his eye as he always carried it. The only thing I took away was his sword, which I eventually made over to his family. It was a sad little ceremony. Overhanging the grave was a young tree,

> upon which I cut the initials 'A. O. M.' [Augustus Otway Mayne] – not very deep, for there was little time; they were quite distinct however, and remained so long enough for the grave to be traced by Mayne's friends, who erected the stone now to be seen.[2]

The isolated grave (a term used for any grave not in a cemetery) was subsequently surrounded by a low brick wall and iron railings. It lies today adjacent to La Martiniere College golf course, and is maintained by the college. Mayne's colleagues were fortunate in that his body remained intact for burial. In several other places where Britons were killed, only bones or fragmentary pieces were subsequently found and buried.

Hissar is a town bordering the Bikaner desert which was brought under British control in 1803. Although technically in Haryana it has more in common with its Rajasthani neighbour. For some reason East India Company officials had assessed the land revenue at an extraordinarily high rate for a semi-desert area. It was the task of the unfortunate Collector and Magistrate, John Wedderburn, to enforce payment. When the Hariana Light Infantry and the 14th Irregular Cavalry mutinied on 29 May 1857, the Wedderburn family were among the first to be struck down. Another eleven Europeans and native Christians were murdered too. John Wedderburn, his wife and infant son had taken refuge in the compound of the little church where they were shot and killed. Also among the dead were the Overseer of the Canal Department, Sergeant Fitzpatrick and his infant child, and Joseph Williams, Superintendent of Customs and his daughter. The site of the massacre was marked by a stone tablet, and the bones of the Wedderburns that could be recovered were buried in the new graveyard. A memorial in the shape of a Gothic plinth with a stone cross was erected in the Company Bagh (garden), off Church Road, with the names of the dead and a simple inscription.

A peculiar story was reported some twenty-five years ago connected with this memorial. The plinth was mistaken by an elderly villager for the tomb of a *pir*, a Muslim saint, and she offered up a prayer at the plinth that her son would be acquitted in a forthcoming criminal case. When the acquittal took place she brought offerings of fruit and wine to the memorial and lit a *deepak* (earthenware lamp) at its base. Her gifts were quickly replicated by others, hoping for the blessings of the Wedderburn pir, and small bottles of whisky and eggs soon appeared, in the belief that this was what the British liked best. The memorial became known as 'Pir John Wedderburn Sahib ka Maqbara' (tomb), though in fact it did not mark the site of the grave. The caretaker of the adjoining church was interviewed at the time, and he said 'I have told people on many occasions that Mr Wedderburn was not a *pir*, but a member of the Bengal Civil Service. However, this has not deterred the devotees from praying.'[3]

A similar event was reported in 2002 at the grave of Captain Frederick

Wale, just outside Lucknow. This highly respectable man, the eighth son of General Sir Charles Wale, was captain of the 48th Bengal Native Infantry and he subsequently commanded the 1st Sikh Irregular Cavalry. He was killed in the last action of the British in the recapture of Lucknow, at the country palace of Barowen (Musa Bagh), to which Begam Hazrat Mahal had retreated. Offerings of fruit, flowers, bottles of beer and cigarettes began to be left at his tomb, which stands in an isolated garden. Extempore hymns and prayers were composed by villagers in Wale's honour, and he was referred to as Captain Baba or the Gora Bhagwan (White God). A local self-appointed guardian of his tomb said that the captain's help was particularly sought by barren women, and that Thursday was considered as the most auspicious day to visit his tomb.[4] We may snigger at the credulous behaviour of these villagers, but there is something genuinely moving in their belief, their careful offerings of alcohol and tobacco, to which they are not addicted, and the power of a mutiny memorial to speak to people today.

Not all British victims of the Uprising in Lucknow were as fortunate as Captain Wale. During the siege of the Residency the dead were buried in individual or mass graves in the garden around the church. It had not previously been used as a cemetery, because it was considered unhealthy to bury the dead in a residential area. But the circumstances of the siege made this inevitable, and there are many sad accounts of burial parties going out at night to dig fresh graves for those killed by the besiegers, or who had died from illness. The Residency graveyard today is a place of great tranquillity, green with small plants, a haunt of butterflies, and well maintained by the Archaeological Survey of India. (The whole of the Residency complex is a protected site.) But the dead who were hurriedly placed here during those desperate four and a half months between July and November 1857 did not rest in peace. Following the second relief of the Residency and the withdrawal of British troops to form a token force at Alambagh, the ad hoc cemetery was thoroughly excavated by the town's badmashes in a mad search for treasure which might have been buried with the corpses. It is thought that the disinterred bodies were subsequently thrown into the river Gomti. Thus the simple grave of Sir Henry Lawrence, Chief Commissioner of Awadh, surrounded by iron railings until well into the 1970s, but now stolen, may be more a symbolic rather than an actual burial site. The graves of officers and men who died in the fierce fighting for the Sikanderbagh were similarly dug up. 'We found [they] had been desecrated and torn up by the niggers,' reported Captain Herford.[5]

The problem of the upkeep of graves of victims was raised at Sialkot, an ancient town in northern Punjab, which had been annexed by the British after the Anglo-Sikh war of 1849. There were no British troops here when two sepoy regiments mutinied on 9 July 1857. Some of the Europeans from the cantonment, which had been built only five years earlier, managed to get to the old fort while the treasury was ransacked and general looting took place, but others were not so fortunate and were killed. A number of officers had been buried on land belonging to a group of faqirs, rather than in the new cemetery. The government decided that instead of moving the bodies, it would make a grant, backdated from 1 May 1858, to one Boodhoo Fukeer and his successors

> on the condition that he will keep in order the tombs of certain officers who were murdered during the mutiny at Sealkote in July last and buried within the land attached to the Fukeers 'Tukeea' [hermitage] and around whose graves trees and flowers have been planted.

The sum of Rs 3.8 was to be paid monthly to the faqir.[6]

The largest British mass grave was the well at Cawnpore, into which the bodies of nearly 200 women and children had been thrown by the rebels on the morning of 16 July 1857. By the time General Havelock and his troops arrived the following day, the naked and dismembered corpses were already putrefying in the heat and there was simply no question of a proper burial. John Sherer, the Magistrate and Collector from Fatehpur who had accompanied the officers to Cawnpore, wrote to Cecil Beadon in Calcutta that the terrible sight of the contents of the well had deadened his nerves with horror. 'I am going this very moment to fill the well up – and cover its mouth with a mound. Let us mention the subject no more – silence and prayer alone seem fitting.'[7] Of course silence could not be maintained and in time the well at Cawnpore became the most iconic image of the Uprising, together with the shattered walls of the Lucknow Residency – tragedy and victory together in two photographs. The covering of earth that Sherer had put over the mouth of the well proved inadequate, and a brick and mortar cap had to be built. A small monument in the shape of a cross was erected in front of the well, with the simple inscription 'I believe in the resurrection of the body'.

The Bibighar, the building in which the killings had taken place, was demolished after it had been photographed, and the area was cleared of trees. Lord Canning had ordered that all the ruined buildings surrounding the well were to be cleared, and it was his wife, Charlotte, Lady Canning, who suggested a memorial should be placed over the site, rather than a new church that some had suggested. On her death in 1860 the project was taken over by her husband, and her relatives and friends who formed a small committee.[8] The sculptor Baron Carlo Marochetti, a boyhood friend of Lady Canning, was approached. Marochetti was reluctant at first to take on the commission and suggested that designs from other sculptors should be submitted before a final decision was made. A sketch sent in by another sculptor horrified the gentle Canning because it showed a female figure leaning against a cross, and pierced by a sword. At her feet were the bodies of dead children. This was, of course, near the truth of what had happened, but in the spirit of

17. The Angel of the Resurrection over the Bibighar Well at Cawnpore. Statue by Carlo Marochetti, commissioned by Lord and Lady Canning.

reconciliation that now prevailed, it would not have been a tactful memorial. Canning wrote to the Earl of Granville, one of the committee members, saying he wanted a figure of good taste and one that would not remind the indigenous population, in the future, of the horrors of 1857. Marochetti then produced a design showing the figure of Britannia, which Lord Canning said simply reminded him of a halfpenny rather than a monument suitable for a Christian grave. The patient sculptor finally came up with a version based on his Scutari Angel, made in 1856 to celebrate the heroes of the Crimean War. The Angel of the Resurrection, a marble figure holding palm fronds and standing in front of a cross, was placed at the centre of a finely worked

Gothic screen, designed by Colonel Henry Yule of the Bengal Engineers. The angel was slightly damaged during celebrations to mark Independence in 1947 and it was agreed to move the figure and the screen to the grounds of All Souls' Memorial Church, for its future safety, the cost being met by the state government. (The Canning family had paid for the statue.) The original inscription on the pedestal, which was subsequently lost, read simply:

> Sacred to the perpetual memory of a great company of Christian people, chiefly women and children, who, near this spot, were cruelly massacred by the followers of the rebel Nana Dhoondo Punt, of Bithoor, and cast, the dying with the dead, into the well below on the XVth day of July, MDCCCLVII.

The massacre at Jhansi led to the erection of a smaller memorial to the British men, women and children killed there on 8 June 1857. The exact number killed is not known, but it is estimated to be between fifty-five and sixty-five people. The battered tin notice at the entrance to the memorial compound gives the figure of 166, but this includes officers and men killed in the subsequent siege. On the annexation of Jhansi in 1853, the 12th Bengal Native Infantry was garrisoned in the main fort which stands on an outcrop of rock. Captain Alexander Skene was the Political Officer, and Captain Dunlop commanded the garrison. Both men were to be killed during the revolt. Trouble had started on 6 June when part of the 12th BNI broke into the Star Fort, which held the magazine and the treasury. Four and a half lakhs of rupees were stolen, and the sepoys barricaded themselves into the smaller fort and put two guns in position. Calls for help were sent by express letters to Cawnpore and Gwalior as Skene led the Europeans from the cantonment into Jhansi Fort. It appears that no food supplies went into the main fort, which had its own water supply and tank within its walls. The Europeans may have felt their retreat was only a temporary measure, and an investigation carried out in 1858 found that in fact servants had been allowed on the first day to take food into the fort for their British masters and mistresses, as had also been done at Agra Fort.

On the following day, however, after two officers, including Captain Dunlop, were shot and killed, the fort was blockaded. Captain Skene opened negotiations with the rebellious sepoys, and was assured, in writing, and with much swearing of oaths, that the British were free to leave. But on coming out of the fort, the group were surrounded by sepoys and rebels who led them to the Jhokun Bagh, a so-called garden, but in reality a large open area, dotted with Hindu memorial temples. Here the whole party was massacred, the murderers being led by the jail *daroga* (superintendent), Bakhsh Ali. The corpses were left exposed for three days, until a large common pit was dug, into which they were flung. The role of the Rani of Jhansi in this event has been closely scrutinised, and evidence produced by historians like R. C. Majumdar and Surendranath Sen appears to exonerate her. In fact the Rani

18. The Memorial Well at Jhansi, built to commemorate the Europeans killed at the Jhokun Bagh in June 1857.

seemed, in the summer of 1857, to be as much a victim of the rebellious sepoys as the British. The Jhansi memorial erected to the British dead is a chaste monument of red sandstone, described as an octagon structure with four entrances, standing on a stepped plinth. The dome is topped with a cross. In front of the memorial stood a fountain and within were inscriptions bearing the names of the dead, but these have been moved to the cantonment cemetery at Sadr Bazar and are now lodged in the gatehouse of the cemetery. The garden which surrounded the memorial in British days no longer exists.

The long siege of Delhi, followed by its recapture, resulted in a huge demand for Christian burial spaces. A new cemetery was opened by the Kashmir Gate, which is known today as the Nicholson Cemetery, after its most famous, some would say infamous, incumbent. The name however is comparatively recent, and it was known simply as the Kashmir Gate Cemetery until well into the early part of the last century. Brigadier General John Nicholson, who lies beneath a slab of marble taken from the Red Fort, was one of the first people to be buried here, and a contemporary photograph shows the solitary grave in what was then a wilderness. Intensely fierce fighting had reduced houses to rubble, and not a tree seemed to survive the need for firewood. The lush greenery of the site today is in complete contrast. Near the Nicholson grave is a plaque to a brother and sister, both killed during the Uprising – Miss M. Clifford, one of the first victims, was visiting the Reverend Jennings in the Delhi Palace where he lived when she and others were struck down on 11 May 1857. Her brother Wigram Clifford, a Bengal civil servant, was killed during an attack on a Mewati outpost in the Gurgaon District in September of the same year. Recent restoration of the Nicholson Cemetery and its 're-opening' in October 2006 led to a spate of criticism in newspapers both in Britain and India. People felt that the work done to beautify the cemetery was to condone the behaviour of the man after whom it is known today. In fact many other people are buried here too, the majority of them local Christians. But the furore clearly demonstrates the emotive pull of 'mutiny memorials' even 150 years after the event.

The majority of the graves of British victims lie in the Rajpura Cemetery, near Delhi University, which has been heavily encroached by squatters and petty traders in the last quarter of a century. Little of the wall that once surrounded the three-acre site remains today. St James' Church (Skinner's Church) contains a large number of memorial tablets to victims whose bodies were not found.[9] They make sad reading, especially that of the Beresford family, father, mother and five daughters, all killed in the Delhi Bank on 11 May. Remains said to be theirs were not buried until the end of 1858. Also memorialised here is the Christian convert, Dr Chaman Lal who fell 'a martyr to his faith' on the same day. On the tablet to officers of the 74th

Regiment, who died at Cawnpore, Saugor, Jhansi and Delhi are the bleak words from Psalm 79:

> O God, the heathen are come into thine inheritance; thy holy temple have they defiled, and made Jerusalem an heap of stones. The dead bodies of thy servants have they given to be meat unto the fowls of the air, and the flesh of thy saints unto the beasts of the land. Their blood have they shed like water on every side of Jerusalem; and there was no man to bury them.

These were public expressions of grief, but individual graves tell their own stories too. Major John Jacob came from an Armenian family. His father, Colonel Jacob Petruse had worked for the Maharaja of Gwalior for many years, as commander of the ruler's 1st Brigade and this is where Major Jacob served too. On his father's death, the major moved from Gwalior to Agra, and he had evidently prospered, because he built himself a very fine house there. During the Uprising at Agra when the Europeans had fled into the fort, Jacob refused to go with them, maintaining that his many friends in the town would see that he and his family came to no harm. He volunteered to fight with the British militia under the incompetent Brigadier Polwhele and survived the battle of Sasia on 5 July 1857 in which 140 men were killed. The following day Jacob himself was killed 'by people who he had trusted'. He was buried under a handsome Mughal-style pavilion directly in front of the portico to his house.[10] The marble inscription gives his age as forty-five. His widow and daughter had inscribed underneath the single line 'It is better to trust in the Lord than to put any confidence in man' – a clear reference to the manner in which he met his death.

'Mutiny' inscriptions, whether on memorial tablets or graves, had to be finely judged. They had to record details of the deceased, who had often died in horrible circumstances; officers who were almost invariably mourned by their regimental friends; nurses and servants who were always faithful; children who were always innocent. But at the same time anger and grief were expressed too, often in Biblical language. This was entirely acceptable in Christian cemeteries and churches, in fact it would have seemed odd not to draw attention to the circumstances in which a loved one had met his or her death. There are plenty of references to mutineers, massacres and murders. But more caution was used for the wording of public monuments, which would be seen by Indian and British passersby.

A case in point is the delicately worded memorial to Sir Mountstuart Jackson and others murdered in Lucknow in poignant circumstances. Jackson, with his two sisters, Madeleine and Georgina, had arrived recently in India and was stationed at Sitapur, fifty miles north of Lucknow. When three regiments and the military police mutinied there at the beginning of June, the Jacksons and others, including Sergeant Morton, the quartermaster of the 10th Oude Irregular Infantry, managed to escape. They sought shelter with a supposedly friendly raja, Loni Singh of Mitauli, whose actions towards the refugees were distinctly ambiguous. He was already sheltering another small group of British refugees, but kept the two groups separate, telling them it would be safer for them. A message was sent by a servant to Sir Henry Lawrence, who instructed the Raja to escort all the Britons to Lucknow. But with the defeat of Lawrence's troops at the battle of Chinhat on 30 June and increasing signs that the British were on the run, the Raja was not inclined to accept an order from the Chief Commissioner. He told the fugitives to leave, without making any provision for them.

The Awadh administration, now headed by Begam Hazrat Mahal, had been informed by Loni Singh about the small British group, and had asked the Raja's *vakeel* to bring them to Lucknow.[11] The vakeel agreed to do so, and asked if they were to be brought in alive or just the heads. They were to be brought in alive, he was told. The group was marched, or driven on carts, to Lucknow, the men having had fetters put around their ankles by a blacksmith. On arrival they were imprisoned in the Qaisarbagh Palace and though their fetters were subsequently removed, they remained in a pitiable state. The story is now taken up by 'the Madras boy' – a Christian camp follower who had come into Lucknow with General Havelock during the first, failed, relief in September. Songeness Madrasi had seen General Neill killed under the Sher Darwaza gateway which had frightened him badly. He said that in 'endeavouring to escape with other Natives, he rushed unwittingly as did many others into a house held by Sepoys who seized him. At once he was plundered, and said he was a sweeper' and by implication a person who could be given menial and dirty tasks.[12]

Songeness told a Court of Inquiry that when Sir Colin Campbell entered Lucknow on 16 November to effect the final relief, the three male prisoners from the group, including Mountstuart Jackson, were taken out of their Qaisarbagh jail and shot by sepoys from the rebellious 71st Bengal Native Infantry. The sepoys were supposed to be acting on the orders of Ahmadullah Shah, the Faizabad Maulvi. The three bodies, said Songeness, were then left lying about a hundred yards outside one of the Qaisarbagh gateways, facing towards Hazratganj, the main street. Songeness and other prisoners of the sepoys were brought out to bury the three men but this could only be done after Campbell and his troops had left Lucknow with the people rescued from the Residency. It had been too dangerous for anyone to approach the bodies while British soldiers were on the loose.

The boy reported that the three men had been tied arm to arm before their execution. One body, that of a short man, had a prayer book in his waistcoat pocket, another had a bullet in his left side. There was no doubt they were Europeans, from their clothes, shoes and a leather helmet hat, although at first glance Songeness had thought they were Indians, because their faces and hands were 'perfectly black – from corruption'. A convenient trench was near by and the burial party untied the corpses and placed them in it, one on top of the other. 'I put the hat and book in with them', Songeness said. He also reported the behaviour of the jostling sepoys who were standing looking on, saying to each other '"Who are these men?" "They must be great men, Governors perhaps?" to which the reply over and over repeated was, "Oh yes, this man's Governor of Indore, that of Bombay and that of Bengal!"'

When Lucknow was recaptured, Songeness was taken out by Captain Hutchinson, the Military Secretary, to see if he could identify the burial place, somewhere between the Qaisarbagh and the Chattar Manzil palaces. He was unable to do so, because the great defensive ditch dug around the Qaisarbagh had swallowed up everything.

> I would suggest [wrote Hutchinson to Calcutta] that a plain, but well proportioned monument be erected on the spot, which I feel sure is within fifty yards of their last resting place. This monument should be enclosed by an iron railing as the site is at the junction of two or three new roads. For inscription, as it does not appear desirable in so public a place to put up any words tending to perpetuate the ill-feeling between the white man and the black, so it cannot be that our grievous wrong should be entirely unnoticed, and I would therefore propose that the names of the fallen be inscribed with the date as near as can be given, and the simple remark 'Victims of 1857'.[13]

The triangular monument still exists today, in a pleasant park, although it has lost its iron railings. The inscription reads: 'Sacred to the Memory of Mountstuart Jackson, Captain Patrick Orr, Lieut. G. J. H. Burnes Bombay European Fusiliers, Sergeant Major Morton. Victims of 1857.' The inscription on the other side of the monument reads 'Sacred to the Memory of C. R. Carew, Esq. Mrs Greene, Miss Jackson and others European and Natives – faithful servants of Government. Victims of 1857.' In the panic of the escape from Sitapur, the two Jackson sisters had been separated. Georgina was brought to Lucknow in another small group and killed. Her sister Madeleine, together with Mrs Orr, the widow of Captain Patrick Orr, and her daughter Louisa, were kept as prisoners too, but they were rescued by Mir Wajid Ali who got them safely to the British camp (see Chapter Four, page 150) When the Raja, Loni Singh, was eventually captured by the British, it was found that he had 'sold' the refugees to Begam Hazrat Mahal for Rs 8,000. He was transported for life, and his property confiscated by the government.

Many British victims were never found, but were commemorated, as we have seen, in memorial tablets in churches in India. All Souls' Church in Cawnpore was erected in 1862 as a giant memorial to those who had died in the massacres, and it was filled with individual or group tablets. Some comfort was given to the families of the victims in Britain by erecting their own memorials in parish churches. Seven members of the prominent Thornhill family were killed in 1857. Robert Bensley Thornhill was the Magistrate at Fatehgarh, above Cawnpore, and when trouble broke out there, boatloads of British refugees took to the river Ganges in the hope of finding safety at Cawnpore, only to be killed on their arrival. Robert Thornhill had escaped with his wife, Mary, their two small children, Charles Cudbert and Mary Catherine, and 'their faithful nurse Mary Long'. An inscription above a little stoup at Liston church, in the village of Foxearth, Essex, records that they were all 'cruelly massacred on the 15th June 1857 at Cawnpore where they had gone seeking help'.[14] Thornhill was shot near the town's assembly rooms and his wife, children and nurse were killed in the Bibighar. His brother, Henry Bensley Thornhill, had been caught at Sitapur where he was 'ruthlessly murdered' together with his wife, their infant daughter, also named Catherine, and their 'faithful nurse' Eliza Jennings, on 3 June by rebellious sepoys. (This was the incident from which Sir Mountstuart Jackson and his party had escaped.)

A memorial at Haileybury School in Hertford bears the names of forty members of the Indian Civil Service 'sometime students at Old Haileybury College, who lost their lives in the active discharge of their duty, during the outbreak of mutiny and insurrection throughout India in the years 1857 to 1859'. Both the Thornhill brothers are named here, together with John Wedderburn, Sir Mountstuart Jackson (here given as 'Mountsteuart'), Simon Fraser, the Commissioner of Delhi, Manaton Collingwood Ommaney, Judicial Commissioner at Lucknow, and others. It is not surprising to find so many familiar names here, because Haileybury College was established to train civil officers for the East India Company, Addiscombe College being its military counterpart. Recognition of the former Haileybury students was tardy, and it was not until the 1890s that the handsome white marble memorial was erected. The inscription was written by Sir Alfred Comyns Lyall, Lieutenant Governor of the North-West Provinces in the 1880s, who had been a student himself at the college from 1853 to 1855.[15]

Also memorialised here are two men from among the twenty-one Europeans who were killed at Hamirpur on 13 June 1857 when the 53rd Bengal Native Infantry mutinied. This Hamirpur lies on the river Jumna, fifty miles or so south of Cawnpore. Its Collector, Thomas Kirkland Lloyd, had taken decisive action on learning of the wave of mutinies spreading like some dreadful waterborne disease down the river. He contacted the local chiefs of Charkheri, Barhi and Baoni and they agreed to supply him with 500 new recruits, whose task was to guard the small number of Europeans at the station. However, on the rising of the 53th BNI these men simply joined the mutineers and took part in the usual looting and plundering. Three boatloads of unarmed sepoys, who were going to their homes after being disarmed at Agra and had the bad luck to be passing Hamirpur at this time, were mown down and plundered by the rebels. Thomas Lloyd, and another Englishman,

Donald Grant, hid themselves in the reed beds of the Jumna for several days but they were then betrayed, taken out and executed in the town.

An imaginative memorial was erected in Jedburgh, Scotland, which had celebrated the news of the recapture of Delhi with a bonfire and fireworks. The town had responded generously to the India Relief Fund, but there was a feeling, voiced by the founder of the first local newspaper *The Teviotdale Record*, that something more permanent should be done to mark the events of 1857. Two local families had lost relatives in the Uprising, and they are thought to have suggested the erection of a fountain, to be put over an existing stream and topped with a cross. In due course this was built and named the Inchbonny Memorial Fountain, popularly known as the Memorial Well, after the Cawnpore Well, and even more popularly as the 'Dribbly Well'. It was described in the late 1990s as a 'rather sad monument consisting of a leaking stone chalice protruding two feet above a carpet of soft leaves, and, under a veil of bramble and ivy, a faded sandstone panel which is inscribed to "The Women and Children who suffered in India during the Sepoy Mutiny 1857."'[16] A more successful memorial is that erected on the Dover seafront to officers and men of the 1st Battalion 60th King's Royal Rifle Corps, who had been part of the Delhi Field Force and who died between 1857 and 1859 in the mutiny. The memorial was erected in 1861, and it bears the Regimental motto 'Celer et Audax' ('Swift and Bold') together with the names of the battles around Delhi, and 'in Oude and Rohilcund'. It was this battalion which was the first to be equipped with the Enfield rifle.[17] The regiment returned to Dover in 1860 where it spent a year, before moving to Aldershot.

So far we have been examining British memorials, but these tell only one side of the story. Only after Independence in 1947 were Indians able to reclaim their own mutiny history. When Begam Hazrat Mahal left Lucknow in March 1858 she retreated towards the Nepalese border along with other rebel leaders. By June 1858 it was reported that:

> The rebels [from Oude] still 6,000 strong, are in terrible distress. A light force which recently penetrated into the hills found the road strewed with the dead, and dying, women imploring mercy, and bearded men still scowling with the old hatred of the Kaffir. Almost all their animals are dead, and their plunder is wasting away under the necessity of paying for all the food they take from the Nepaulese. The Nana, the Begam, and and Bala Rao, brother to the Nana Sahib, are the only three leaders of note remaining, and they are deserted day by day by parties of their followers. According to a leader who recently surrendered, they have ceased to hope since the publication of the amnesty, though they still endeavour to open correspondence with most Indian princes.[18]

Jang Bahadur had been persuaded to hand over a number of rebels and their followers, in return for substantial sums of money. His attitude towards the

Begam and her son Birjis Qadr, however, was ambivalent, to say the least. A plea for help from the crowned 'king' to the Nepalese ruler was met with a firm rebuttal, on the excuse of the latter's enduring friendship with the British. But Jang Bahadur refused to expel the Begam and her remaining sepoys, thus keeping British troops tied up on the frontier. Sir Colin Campbell particularly disliked him and he wrote to Cecil Beadon that 'We have been far too civil to Mr Jung Bahadoor'.[19] In the end Jang Bahadur did grant asylum to the Begam and her son and she settled down in Kathmandu. She had managed to bring with her sufficient jewels and treasure, and their sale allowed her to lead a comfortable life in exile. She funded the building of a mosque in her new home, which was called the Hindustani Masjid. It was in the grounds of this mosque that the Begam was buried on her death in April 1879. Her tomb was a modest rectangle near a main road. Over the course of time, all but one minaret of her mosque was demolished, and her tomb became wedged in between shacks and a petrol pump. A large new mosque, the Kashmiri Jama Masjid was built on the site, and in 2002 the Begam's tomb was restored and protected. However, recent rioting in the capital apparently caused damage to the Jama Masjid, and the present condition of the tomb is unknown. As for Birjis Qadr, the boy king, he married a grand-daughter of Bahadur Shah Zafar, and was finally allowed by the British government to return to India where he died in 1893, the victim of accidental or deliberate poisoning at Calcutta.

A large square stone platform in the Muslim portion of Père Lachaise Cemetery, in Paris, marks the last resting place of the Queen Mother of Awadh, Janab Alia Begam, who died in Paris on 23 January 1858, aged fifty-three, on her way home to India. She was joined in death by her son General Mirza, who died in London in March of the same year and whose body was taken to Paris, to lie in the same grave. The unmarked tomb was identified in 2000, with the help of Mme Françoise de Valence, after the publication of my story of Janab Alia Begam's visit to Europe.[20] Any superstructure or inscription that may have marked the tomb in the mid-nineteenth century has long disappeared, and the slabs which topped the structure have been replaced with an unsatisfactory mosaic of red tiles. After some correspondence, a painting of the area about 1857 was erected in a small frame at one corner of the grave, together with a short notice on the queen and prince who lie there. Unfortunately the notice is full of mistakes, describing Janab Alia Begam as the 'Queen of Oude', mis-spelling her titles, mis-spelling the name of her son, who is incorrectly shown as the heir to the throne, and claiming that the last Nawab, Wajid Ali Shah died during the Sepoy Uprising of 1857. (The Nawab, in fact, died in 1887 in Calcutta.) The story of the queen mother who went to England, in spite of her failing health, to plead with Queen Victoria for the annexation of Awadh to be reversed is sad enough, without any embroidery or misinformation.

The tomb of Bahadur Shah Zafar in Rangoon, where he was exiled after his 'trial', has recently been described by William Dalrymple in his authoritative biography of the last king of Delhi. Deliberate policy by British officials had prevented any kind of marker being put up at the time of his death in 1862 and the site was returfed so its exact location would be quickly forgotten. But a shrine was known to exist by the 1920s, above or near the grave of the old man, and it received some attention during the Second World War, when supporters of the Indian National Army, under their leader Subhas Chandra Bose, were stationed there. The King's skeleton, lying within a brick-lined grave, was discovered in 1991 by workmen digging a drain, some twenty-five feet from the shrine.[21] The grave is 'now located in a sort of crypt below, and to one side of the old shrine' and has become a place of pilgrimage for people seeking blessings or favours, though the offerings will be different from those given to English pirs killed during the mutiny in India.

After the dead of the Uprising had been buried, British attention turned to commemorating its victories and its fallen heroes. Contrary to the usual belief, it was not the British government that ordered statues of Mutiny heroes to be placed at prominent sites as a perpetual reminder to the indigenous population. The majority of such statues were commissioned by local committees in India, who raised money by public subscriptions and chose the sites. Donations came mainly from Britons although there were some Indian benefactors too. In some cases a regiment would contribute funds, and in the case of the Angel of the Resurrection at Cawnpore, as we have seen, it was the Cannings who paid for the statue. Of the six Mutiny statues discussed below, none were funded by government.

The history of British statuary in India is a fascinating subject and one that has been unjustly ignored by its historians.[22] The first statue to be sent out was that of Charles, Marquess Cornwallis, Governor General and Commander in Chief. It was paid for by public subscription and was erected in Fort St George, Madras, in 1800, the first of many. All but one of the colonial statues in the Indian subcontinent today were commissioned from sculptors working in Europe, and usually in Britain itself. The exception, by a sculptor working in India, was the aluminium statue of Queen Victoria erected at Sarsaiya Ghat in Cawnpore. It was the work of a local firm that advertised itself as 'Practical European Monumental & Architectural Sculptors, Modellers and Founders'. Sadly, this statue no longer remains in place. But the misconception that, since Independence, the majority of statues to Britons has been lost, is untrue. One hundred and seventy such statues were found in the Indian subcontinent and a few places in South-East Asia during a recent survey. (In addition, three statues and a bust have been erected, by Indians to Englishmen since 1947.)[23] Some of the colonial statues have been removed from their original sites and have become private rather than public works of art. A few went abroad and a few more have been vandalised or split up where there were groups of figures.

Captain Alexander Taylor of the Bengal Engineers, together with Colonel Baird-Smith, was one of the two men responsible for the practical work of recapturing Delhi in the autumn of 1857. Taylor, who was later knighted and became a general, had been working on the restoration of the Grand Trunk Road between Lahore and Peshawar, before being summoned to Delhi. Engineers, like statues, seldom get an honorable mention in histories of the Uprising, but their work was essential. Every time we read of troops crossing a river in pursuit of rebels, or entrenchments being dug, or fort doors blown open, or pontoon bridges built, or wells excavated, or gun emplacements erected, even if we do not fully grasp the practical implications, it was the Engineers who made this possible. When Brigadier General Archdale Wilson hesitated during the capture of Delhi, it was Baird-Smith and Taylor who urged him on, supported by the dying John Nicholson, who, true to form, threatened to shoot him if he retreated. The Engineers' careful surveys during the months of the siege enabled the officers and men to capture strategic areas, to scale the city walls, albeit with dreadful loss of life on both sides, and to blow open the Kashmir Gate, which was the key to entering Delhi.

Not surprisingly then, a statue was raised to Taylor outside the Delhi walls, to mark his part in securing the city for the British. Lord Roberts, who as Lieutenant Frederick Roberts had known Taylor in the Delhi days, headed the statue committee and the figure was erected outside the Mori Gate, two years after Taylor's death. It shows him in characteristic pose, a sword hanging from his belt, and a telescope under his arm. In January 1956, with the centenary of the Uprising approaching, the Indian government took the decision to remove it for fear of possible repercussions during the celebrations. The statue was repatriated to Britain, free of charge, by the P&O Steam Navigation Company, and after some dithering, it was re-erected at Coopers Hill, in Egham, near London, the site of the former Royal Indian Engineering College, and now, appropriately, part of Brunel University. (Colonel Baird-Smith is commemorated in his own village of Lasswade, in Scotland, by a Celtic cross memorial inset with bronze panels.)

Another statue which left India at the same time as General Sir Alexander Taylor's, was that of Brigadier General John Nicholson, one of the leaders of the assault on Delhi. A plaque marks the spot where he fell fatally wounded, between the Kabul and Lahore city gates, and we have noted his burial in the Kashmir Gate cemetery. The funds for Nicholson's statue were raised 'by his surviving comrades', who possibly had mixed feelings about the man recently described by Dalrymple as 'near-psychopathic'. Nevertheless, the money was collected and Thomas Brock RA was commissioned to make a bronze portrait statue. It is a striking, indeed noble, piece of work. Nicholson is pictured gazing out from the top of a high pedestal, which is inscribed simply with his name. The statue stood near the Kashmir Gate, adjacent to that of Taylor. For the same reason, although possibly with more justification, the Government of India had it removed as well in 1956. Because both statues were of British origin, the late Brigadier Perry of the Commonwealth War Graves Commission was invited to be present as they were removed. Perry later noted in his diary that a large number of police and workmen were standing round the statue of Nicholson. When he asked the Superintendent of Police why his men were gathered there, the officer replied 'rather sheepishly that "Jan Nikalsayn" had been a very "zubberdust" [fierce] man, and that they could not be sure that his spirit would not return to haunt those who disturbed him'.[24] The Superintendent may have been joking, but Brigadier Perry didn't think so.

After its removal the statue was initially stored in the grounds of the British High Commission in Delhi. Later, through the intervention of a missionary whose nephew was on the Board of Governors of the Royal School, Dungannon, County Tyrone, in Ireland, it was offered a home there. The Old Boys Association raised the money for its transport, and it was officially unveiled by the late Lord Mountbatten on 13 April 1960. Its inscription reads

> Brigadier John Nicholson, born 11 December 1822, a pupil of Dungannon Royal School 1834–1838. He led the assault at Delhi but fell in the hour of victory mortally wounded and died 23 September 1857, aged 34. Fortes Creantur Fortibus [The Strong are created by the Strong].

Brigadier General James Neill, another ruthless officer, is memorialised in a similar bronze portrait statue, funded by public subscription. It was completed in 1860, and stood in Connemara Circle, Madras, because Neill had been commanding part of the Madras Army on his deathly forays through northern India in 1857. Unusually, this was one statue that was removed before Independence, in 1937, due, it seems, to attempts to disfigure it. It remains in the Madras Museum today, one hand pointing towards the wall of a store-room, and with a manic expression on the face. Lieutenant General Sir James Outram's statue in Calcutta has fared better, possibly because he was seen as a more rational man, willing to admit that there might be more than one point of view, during his term as Chief Commissioner of Awadh. It is a bronze equestrian statue, full of expression and vigour, and like the others, it was funded by public subscription. It stood originally near the junction of Chowringhee and Park Street, but was subsequently moved to the grounds of the Victoria Memorial.

Two statues of Sir John Lawrence, later known as Baron Lawrence of the Punjab, stood in undivided India. The first, by Thomas Woolner RA, was a bronze portrait statue, funded by public subscription in Calcutta and

19. Statue of the Rani of Jhansi, in Jhansi.

originally placed south of Government House. It was later moved to Barrackpore. The second statue, by Joseph Edgar Boehm RA, had originally been erected in London, but it was not a popular image. It showed the man who had pleaded for the activities of the Delhi Prize Agents to be reined in, brandishing a pen in one hand and a sword in the other, with the inscription 'Will you be governed by the pen or the sword?' 'Pen', would have been Lawrence's answer. After much criticism, the sculptor offered the statue to the Municipality of Lahore. Free freight was provided for its shipment, and it stood on the Mall, between the cathedral and the Chief Court Buildings. Equally unpopular in Lahore it was removed in 1962 and was presented to Foyle College, Londonderry, Northern Ireland, where Lawrence had been a pupil.[25]

'Clemency' Canning, Lord Canning, was commemorated by a bronze equestrian statue, funded by public subscription, that stood in Eden Gardens, Calcutta, where he had spent most of his time as Governor General. When the Calcutta Municipality removed a number of British statues in the 1970s, it sensitively sent Canning's to Barrackpore, where, in what is now the Police Hospital Grounds, he faces the tomb of his dearly loved wife, Charlotte.

Surprisingly, given India's wealth of sculptors, there appears to be no tradition of secular sculpture by indigenous artists before or during the British period. The art of casting bronze statues had to be learnt by India's new generation of artists after Independence in 1947. When an equestrian statue of the first Prime Minister, Pandit Jawarharlal Nehru was required, the young sculptor was told to model it on that of Sir Harcourt Butler, at Lucknow. More embarrassingly, the equestrian statue of Subhas Chandra Bose in Calcutta is a variant of that of Sir James Outram by John Henry Foley.[26] But heroic secular sculptures have now been refined, and most towns in northern India can boast an equestrian Rani of Jhansi, a Begam Hazrat Mahal, or a Nana Sahib. As the popularity of portrait sculpture of any artistic merit has declined in Britain to vanishing point, it is to India that we now have to look for contemporary works of art of the kind that used to dot our Victorian streets. The statue of the great Hindu reformer, Raja Ram Mohun Roy, recently erected in Bristol, where he died in 1833, was made in India and exported to Britain.

In the early 1970s, a bust appeared in the Sikanderbagh in Lucknow, of a rather squat figure on a pedestal. Painted, as many new busts are today in India, it showed a sari-clad woman, and an inscription that named her as an unknown heroine of the fierce fighting that took place here during the first relief of the city. There is more than one account of this armed woman, who was sitting in a large peepul tree in the walled enclosure, picking off the Highlanders as they came into the garden and within her range. A number of bodies was observed piling up under the tree, and a sergeant was ordered to shoot into the branches. This he did, and a body fell to the ground, its bodice opening to reveal a woman soldier. But she was not Indian. The dead woman was one of Wajid Ali Shah's 'amazons', a group of African women brought in as slaves who formed part of the Nawab's retinue. They were dressed in mens' uniform and rode on horseback to accompany their master. Little more is known about them, but we do know that Africans were being imported into Lucknow certainly from the end of the eighteenth century. One of the most skilful of the rebels besieging the Residency was nicknamed 'Bob the Nailer' by the British, in reluctant acknowledgement of his unerring aim. He was an African eunuch who was stationed in a house overlooking the site. Another was noted in the Latkan Darwaza, the clocktower outside the Bailey Guard gate. A third, dressed in a handsome yellow gown, was noted at a window in La Martiniere, shooting at British soldiers. These men and women are likely to have been soldiers from the Nawab's Habshiyan (Negro) Regiment, commanded by Ali Naqi Khan.[27] The Nawab's African retinue was described by Lieutenant Colonel William Gordon-Alexander, who was present during the fighting at Sikanderbagh. He noted

> even a few amazon negresses, amongst the slain. These Amazons, having no religious prejudices against the use of greased cartridges, whether of pigs' or other animal fat, although doubtless professed Muhammadans, were armed with rifles, while the Hindu and Muhammadan East Indian rebels were all armed with muskets; they fought like wild cats and it was not till after they were killed that their sex was even suspected.[28]

It says a lot for the skill of these women and the respect in which they were held that they got the best weapons. The unknown warrior of Sikanderbagh was one of the earliest monuments put up to commemorate those who fought against the British. Since the 1970s, numerous statues have been erected. In addition to those of the Rani of Jhansi, Tantia Tope is commemorated at the site of his execution in Shivpura town, and Raja Kanwar Singh at Ballia, and at Jagdishpur Fort, near Arrah. At the entrance to the Meerut Cantonment stands a large statue of a rebel sepoy, still in his Company uniform and shako, ready to fire his musket, while behind him a peasant farmer is unsheathing his sword. As in Britain, there appears to be no comprehensive listing of mutiny memorials and statues in India, which is surely a worthwhile survey waiting to be carried out.

The commemoration of battle sites does not feature heavily among British memorials of the Uprising. The days when opposing armies would march out and meet each other on the field as happened at Plassey or Buxar, had gone. Much of the fighting had been street by street, in the narrow alleys of the old towns, in the cantonments, or concentrated on hill-top forts. There were a few significant rural encounters, of which Badli-ki-Serai, on the Grand Trunk Road, north of Delhi, is one of the most important. It was the defeat of some 3,000 sepoys here, by the combined British forces from Meerut and Karnal, that enabled the new Commander-in-Chief, Major General Sir Henry Barnard, to reoccupy the cantonment on the Ridge, and from here to plan the recapture of the Mughal capital. During the visit of King George V and Queen Mary to the Delhi Durbar of 1911, a military tattoo took place on the parade ground near Badli-ki-Serai with an estimated 50,000 troops marching past the King-Emperor and Queen-Empress, as they were titled. A British memorial cross was erected on top of a mound, a few minutes' drive away from the two remaining Mughal gateways that mark the serai. The mound and the memorial stand today next to a wholesale vegetable market together with a single stone marking the grave of Lieutenant Alfred Harrison of Her Majesty's 75th Regiment 'who fell in action while gallantly leading the charge on this mound on 8 June 1857, aged 27'.

An equally important site is at Chinhat on the Faizabad Road, some six miles east of Lucknow. Like Badli-ki-Serai, now subsumed into the Delhi suburbs, Chinhat, too, has become part of greater Lucknow, and it is hard to appreciate the significance of this once small village, which, as its name implies, was a market for locally produced chinaware. The Faizabad Road was considered particularly dangerous because of the dacoits that haunted it, and well within living memory this jungle-fringed path was greatly feared. The production of good chinaware is still carried on at Chinhat, but there appears to be no sign today of the memorial that marked the defeat of Sir Henry Lawrence's troops on 30 June 1857 and, more importantly, his retreat into the Lucknow Residency and the beginning of the siege which led to his death. Neither is there any memorial to the Indian soldiers who won a significant victory here which gave them the confidence to surround the Residency for so long.

It was important to the mid-nineteenth-century Briton that particular buildings associated with acts of heroism, victory or defeat during the Uprising should be permanently marked. There was a reverence for such places amounting to an almost religious feeling, closely bound in with associations of Christian martyrdom, of gallant soldiers engaged in honorable warfare, and of brave civilians rising beyond the normal call of duty. Apart from specific memorials like the Angel of the Resurrection, the area of Wheeler's Entrenchment at Cawnpore, where the wretched Europeans held out during June 1857 before meeting their deaths, was preserved, with brick markers showing the boundaries of the site. The ravine along which the Europeans were marched to be transported downstream to the safety of Allahabad, as they vainly hoped, still exists at Cawnpore, as does the ghat, from where they were picked off, to be shot and drowned.

In Lucknow, the site of the Residency and its surrounding buildings has been preserved very much as it was in 1858 on the recapture of the city. Indeed, this is the largest and most awesome memorial to the Uprising in the subcontinent, a site of thirty-three acres, frozen in time, the holes made by bullets and cannonballs still plainly visible on the battered walls. A fireplace still stands at first floor level in the main building, and in the *tyekhana*, or basement (now a museum), it is not difficult to imagine the chaplain's wife, Mrs Harris, visiting the poor families with words of comfort. Outside, the lawn has resumed the tranquil appearance it had when Lawrence held his durbar here in May 1857, in an unsuccessful attempt to calm the rising storm. Not much remains of the house of Martin Gubbins, where he and his guests enjoyed their wine and rice puddings during the siege, although wine-bottle tops have been found in recent archaeological excavations, together with prettily-patterned Worcestershire china fragments, and a couple of pistols.[29] The grounds are heavy with regimental memorials in the form of crosses, and one of the guns from HMS *Shannon*, so laboriously brought from Calcutta. Outside, in the town, although much has been destroyed, both by the British after 1858, and its inhabitants since Independence, the Shah Najaf still stands and some of the Sikanderbagh walls and the gatehouse.

Delhi has suffered more demolitions, and there is no single site here, like the Residency at Lucknow, where one can stroll quietly and get a sense of the past. To be quiet in old Delhi is indeed almost impossible, but the Kashmir Gate can be walked around, and through, with its memorial inscription still *in situ*. The moat in front of the gate has been covered over, although a glimpse down an open manhole shows that water is still running swiftly several feet below. The sandstone plaque at the gateway names the eleven men, six British, and five Indian, who were killed when the right-hand leaf of the gate was blown open, allowing the British troops into the city. General Lord Napier, a former Royal Engineer, paid for the memorial here. An obelisk which stood until recently in front of the present Telegraph Office commemorated William Brendish and I. W. Pilkington, the two young Anglo-Indian signallers who remained on duty on 11 May 1857 and alerted staff in the Punjab to the first news of the Uprising. The entrance gate and one tower of the Delhi Magazine stand opposite, on a road island, marked by a tablet commemorating the 'nine resolute Englishmen' who held it for more than four hours against impossible odds. Here, unusually, the then Government of India paid for the memorial.

On the Delhi Ridge stands the Mutiny Memorial, an enormous four-tiered structure of red sandstone in high Gothic. Its octagonal form contains seven faces, with memorial panels, while the eighth is the foot of the spiral staircase that leads to the two tiers above. This is the second mutiny monument in Delhi that was erected at government expense, and it was built by the Public Works Department. The design of the monument had been hastily approved by the officers who had fought at Delhi, but the workmanship was considered poor, and it was described as looking 'like a telescope badly drawn out'. 'Would any other government than the British have left such a memorial to stand up gaunt and solitary on the end of a mountain ridge, without an attempt to show that honouring and loving hands had charge of it, or have permitted the stone, once marked by the life-blood of our men, to be quarried for railway ballast and the profit of cantonment funds?' asked H. C. Fanshawe, a retired Bengal civil servant, in 1902.[30] The regiments that recaptured Delhi are listed here, British and Indian, with their British officers. A list of actions fought by the Delhi Field Force between the end of May and 20 September is noted, together with the different batteries that made the actual breaches in the city walls in September. Inscriptions in Urdu and Hindi make it clear that the memorial is to all who fought for the Government ('*angrezi aur hindustani afsir aur sipahi . . . unki yadgari ke vaste*'). In 1972, twenty-five years after Independence, the memorial was renamed Ajitgarh, which means the Place of the Unvanquished and a new plaque was added that states:

> The 'enemy' of the inscriptions on this monument were those who rose against colonial rule and fought bravely for national liberation in 1857. In memory of the heroism of these immortal martyrs for Indian freedom, this plaque was unveiled on the 25th anniversary of the nation's attainment of Freedom, 28th August 1972.

Also on the Ridge stands Flagstaff Tower, an interesting round building, which probably dates from the establishment of the cantonment here about 1828. It was in this building, with its spiral staircase, that those Britons who did manage to escape from Delhi on 11 May congregated, and debated their next move. The majority of those who opted to try to reach Meerut, forty miles away, did eventually get there, though there were casualties. It was, however, their only option, and there was no question of defending the tower, because it was far too small.

Not all memorials take the form of buildings, or statues, or inscriptions. Many memories of those who lived through the events of 1857–58, as we have seen, were put down on paper, some immediately, and some many years after. Photographs and photographic albums were another way of reminding people of what had happened. The idea of army photographers had not been established in 1857 and there were no photographers with the Delhi Field Force when it went into the city. Technical limitations on photography at the time meant there could be no 'action' shots, and the only two which might fulfill this criteria are the pictures by Beato, one of the Sikanderbagh dead, which has been discussed, and the other of two Indians hanging from a gallows.

There are however, a number of vivid, impressionistic watercolours by the Swedish artist Egron Lundgren, who was commissioned by Queen Victoria to capture scenes of the Uprising in 1858. Lundgren attached himself to Sir Colin Campbell's force as it was pursuing rebels northwards towards Nepal. Lundgren's battle-sketches at Dondiakera, a fortified jungle encampment where an estimated 7,000 supporters of Raja Beni Madho were routed, are the nearest we can get to seeing the Sikh cavalry streaming past in pursuit of the rebels, and the subsequent melancholy inspection of the battlefield where barefoot sepoys lie dying. Lundgren's own impartial observations, both sketched and written, more truthfully reflect the real horror of war than those of most other commentators.[31] Both Lundgren and Beato met and showed each other their work, and at least one of the artist's sketches is from a photograph by the latter, although his scenes in the British camp, and in battle, are drawn from life – and death.

The majority of photographers were working for themselves, some as professionals, like Beato, and others like Harriet and Captain Robert Tytler, as amateurs. The husband and wife team had been forced to remain on the Ridge during the siege, because Harriet was heavily pregnant. (Her son, born on 21 June 1857 in a covered cart, was given the resounding name of Stanley Delhi Force Tytler.) Captain John Milliken, who photographed Musa Bagh after it had been left by the fleeing Begam Hazrat Mahal, was an officer in the Royal Engineers. He was stationed at Sitapur in the aftermath of the Uprising there, and moved to Lucknow during its recapture. Invaluable though his photographs are to us today, because they are the only record of this elegant building in its prime, they were not taken for work-related purposes, but because Milliken was a keen, and good, photographer.

The Delhi photographs by Beato, particularly those from around the Jama Masjid area, as the historian Narayani Gupta has pointed out, have 'a significance unintended by the photographer – it recovers the area outside the pale, making it the only visual evidence to corroborate details given in some letters and archival records'.[32] From the Ridge, Beato shot 'picket by picket, battery by battery, the camera led on to a blow by blow commentary of the point where the city wall was scaled, the Kashmir Gate was battered open, and the British troops swarmed into the city'. All this had, of course, happened some six months before Beato's arrival in India, but the general public was avid for information, even if it was out of date. The *Illustrated London News* reports, delayed by nearly two months, were usually accompanied by lithographs, and some of these were engraved from photographs which are untraceable today.

Regular albums in the form of guide books were produced, both for people in Britain and for tourists to India. Daroga Abbas Ali, an engineer, published his first book of photographs, entitled *The Lucknow Album containing a series of fifty photographic views of Lucknow and its environs* in 1874. It consists of fifty views in and around the city, concentrating mainly on sites connected with the Uprising. His introduction is telling, that of an anglicised inhabitant of Lucknow, addressing an English-speaking readership:

> This work will not prove an intellectual treat alone ... this Album will bear a sacred interest, and many a tear will fall at the contemplation of some well-

> remembered spot, over which a sort of holy radiance will appear to linger as the book is sorrowfully closed.

As the photographic historian Sophie Gordon has pointed out in a recent article on the work of Daroga Abbas Ali,

> the use of such language, with its religious associations, is designed to appeal directly to a British audience, which considered the city to be a sacred site. Visiting Lucknow had become something of a pilgrimage, something every British tourist in India would undertake as a matter of duty.[33]

The sequence of photographs follows the route that the relieving force took in March 1858, starting at the Alambagh Palace, where Outram had spent the winter, and progressing through the Shah Najaf, the Sikanderbagh, the Chattar Manzil palaces, and Qaisarbagh until the viewer reaches the Residency itself. By 1874, nearly twenty years after the Uprising, parts of the city would have been unrecognisable to the troops who had fought their way past the great walls and embankments. Much demolition had taken place, and buildings once embedded within a mass of small courtyards, corridors and pavilions, had become isolated when these were stripped away. The Residency buildings had now grown romantic coats of ivy, and time had smoothed the rawness of Beato's immediate images.

As for other memorials, let us conclude with three last images. Allan Octavian Hume, a Bengal civil servant, twenty-six years old at the time of the mutiny, was Joint Magistrate at Mainpuri, and Magistrate and Collector at Etawah in the North-West Provinces. When news of the Uprising at Aligarh on 20 May reached Etawah, a detachment of the 9th BNI stationed there also rose, although, unusually, the rebels failed to loot the cantonment treasury. The town was defended by a few Britons, with the help of Rao Bhowani Singh, a cousin of the Raja of Mainpuri, and a small number of sepoys and police. The British women and children had been sent to the Fort at Agra. After two forced withdrawals in the face of the rebels, a group of local men was recruited, known as the Etawah levies. With these untrained soldiers, Hume and the other officers were able to put down the revolt and as Magistrate he ensured that the mutineers who were subsequently captured, were given a fair trial. This was an unusual event in the frenzy of blood-letting, and Hume was criticised, as Lord Canning had been, for his 'excess of leniency'.[34] In 1885 Hume founded the Indian National Congress party, whose initial aim was not to oppose British rule, but to ensure a greater representation for Indians in government. How much this action was tempered by Hume's experiences during the Uprising, we shall probably never know, but it would be good to think that they did affect him profoundly, leading him to realise that the way forward to eventual independence was not through revolt, but in partnership with honest men.

In December 1907, the *Daily Telegraph* gave a 'Golden Commemoration

Christmas Dinner' to all the Mutiny survivors it could find. Surprisingly, nearly 800 men were collected (nothing was said about female survivors). A grand dinner was given at the Royal Albert Hall in Kensington. Lord Roberts, who as young Lieutenant Roberts, had been in the thick of the fighting, took the chair. Marquess Curzon of Kedleston, and a former Viceroy of India (the title that had replaced that of Governor General), proposed the toast and gave a speech.[35] Many British veterans were remarkably long lived, as though the Uprising had tempered those who survived like steel. A handful were still alive in 1939, including the ninety-three-year-old Elizabeth Morton, who had escaped as a child from Mirzapur. Her father, an uncle of Brigadier General John Nicholson, had been warned in advance of the coming revolt by his servants, and had got his family out in time to Calcutta.

I found an ancient, undated, newspaper cutting among the Mutiny Scrapbooks at my old university, the School of Oriental and African Studies, while researching for this book. It is headed 'A Lucknow Relief Veteran' and it reports that Major General George Stewart, CB, had died in 1927, aged eighty-seven, the last surviving officer who took part in the relief of Lucknow. Survivors of the Lucknow Garrison and the relieving force had held a dinner in London every 25 September (the anniversary of the first relief). By 1915 numbers had dwindled and dinner was abandoned. The balance in hand of the Dinner Committee was made over to the Indian Soldiers Fund, which provided comforts for Indian troops serving in the Great War. The remaining veterans lunched quietly together every 25 September for a few more years until only two remained – Major General F. E. A. Chaumier and Major General Stewart, who were left to take tea together by way of commemoration. Major General Chaumier died in 1923.

GLOSSARY

ayah – a children's nurse
batta – field allowance for soldiers
bibi – an Indian mistress
chaprassi – a messenger
chowk – a street, usually with shops at ground level
chowkidar – a watchman
cossid – a spy
daffadar – an Indian military officer
daroga – superintendent, usually of a building
darwan – a gate keeper
deepak – a small pottery lamp
diwan/ dewan – chief minister
diwan-i-khas – private chambers in a palace
dooli – a covered palanquin, also used as a stretcher
faqir – a poorly dressed Muslim holy man
firman – an order or decree
ganj – shopping area often with gateways at each end
gomashtah – a middle man, usually in trade
haveli – courtyard house
hookum/ hukum – an order
jagir – piece of land bestowed on a person (*jagirdar*)
jemadar – a junior Indian military officer
khansama – a domestic/household steward
kharita – a formal invitation or letter
khillat – 'robe of honour' sometimes conferred with jewellery, a shawl and sword
koss – a distance of about two miles in northern India
kotwal – a combination of town mayor and chief police officer, in charge of the police station (*thana*)
kotwali – the *kotwal's* office
kutchery/ kutcheri – a law court
mahajan – moneylender
maidan – large open area, used for riding, or carriage driving
maulvi – a learned man, generally a Muslim
muhalla – a neighbourhood area
munshi – a tutor
nazul – property of the government
nullah – a ditch
pargana – a district of land, subdivided into *tehsils*, smaller administrative areas
pir – Muslim saint
risaldar – an army company commander
ryot – peasant
sadhu – Hindu holy man
sati – a widow burnt on a funeral pyre
sepoy – Indian soldier
shroff – banker
sowar – cavalryman
subahdar – governor of a subah, or province
subedar – a senior Indian military officer
sunnud/ sanad – formal decree
takhallus – a pen name
taluq – same as *tehsil*
taluqdar – person in charge of a *taluq*
talwar – a sword

taziah – a model tomb (Shi'a)
tehsil – a sub-division of a *pargana*
tehsildar – a district officer (see *pargana*)
thana – police station
thuggee – the practice of killing and robbing travellers
tyekhana – basement
vakeel – a lawyer or authorised representative
zamindar – a landholder
zumburrook/ zamburak – small gun or cannon

NOTES

Introduction

1 Lord Frederick Roberts, *Forty-One Years in India* (London: Richard Bentley & Son, 1897), vol. i, pp. 385–86.
2 Lt Gen. S. L. Menezes, *Fidelity and Honour: The Indian Army from the Seventeenth to the Twenty-First Century* (Delhi: Oxford University Press, 2004), p. 10.
3 India Political Consultations, 1 September 1857, No. 20, from Lt Col. Strachey to Cecil Beadon, Secretary to the Government of India. India Office Records, British Library.
4 P. J. O. Taylor, *A Companion to the 'Indian Mutiny' of 1857* (Delhi: Oxford University Press 1996), p. 221.
5 Reverend William Butler, *The Land of the Veda: Being Personal Reminiscences of India; its People, Castes, Thugs and Fakirs; its Religions, Mythology, Principal Monuments, Palaces, and Mausoleums; together with the Incidents of the Great Sepoy Rebellion, and its results to Christianity and Civilisation* (Cincinnati: Walden & Stowe, 1871), p. 15.
6 India Political Consultations, 10 July 1857, No. 42, Col. Sir R. C. Shakespear to G. F. Edmonstone, Secretary to Government of India. India Office Records, British Library.
7 Menezes, *Fidelity and Honour*, pp. 88–9.
8 Home Department, Public Branch, 12 February 1858, Nos. 10–11. A printed list of 'Officers and Servants of the Government of India and other Christians killed from 10 May to 15 December 1857'. National Archives, Delhi.
9 David Harding, 'Arming the East India Company's Forces' and Michael Baldwin, 'Arming the Indian Army, 1857–1947', in *Soldiers of the Raj: The Indian Army 1600–1947*, ed. Alan Guy and Peter Boyden, exhibition catalogue (London: National Army Museum, 1997).
10 Foreign Consultations, 31 July 1857, Nos. 86–9. Printed proclamation sent to G. F. Edmonstone, Secretary to Government of India by M. H. Court, Magistrate of Allahabad 'who got them from Mr Wilcock at Cawnpore'. National Archives, Delhi.
11 P. J. O. Taylor, *What Really Happened during the Mutiny: A Day-by-Day Account of the Major Events of 1857–1859 in India* (Delhi: Oxford University Press 1997).
12 Noah Chick, *Annals of the Indian Rebellion … Containing Narratives of the Outbreaks and Eventful Occurrences, and Stories of Personal Adventure, during the Mutiny 1857–58 etc.* (Calcutta: Sanders, Cones & Co, 1858).
13 Sir John Kaye, *A History of the Sepoy War in India 1857–1858* (London 1864–76), vol. ii, p. 630.
14 Roberts, *Forty-One Years*, p. 198.
15 Captain Fletcher Hayes is a much under-rated man. He was Military Secretary to Sir Henry Lawrence, Chief Commissioner of Awadh and was killed at the start of the

Uprising. He was the liaison officer between the Government of India and members of the royal family who remained in Lucknow. In this role he compiled the detailed list of 768 members who claimed pensions before annexation in 1856, and he advised that the pensions should be continued. He was an erudite man and had built up a fine library. After his death, his books were used to build barricades in the Lucknow Residency, together with other miscellaneous objects, including a harp case belonging to Mrs Colina Brydon.

16 Roberts, *Forty-One Years*, p. 181.

17 Taylor, *What Really Happened*, p. 152.

18 Sir William Hunter, *Imperial Gazetteer of India* (Oxford: Clarendon Press, 1907–9), vol. xxi, p. 371.

19 John Walker Sherer, *Daily Life during the Indian Mutiny: Personal Experiences of 1857* (London: Swan Sonnenschein & Co, 1898), pp. 33–43.

20 Sita Ram, *From Sepoy to Subedar*, translated and first published by Lt Col. Norgate, Bengal Staff Corps, at Lahore, 1873. This edition edited by James Lunt (London: Macmillan, 1988). It took Sita Ram forty-eight years to progress from the rank of sepoy to that of subedar, by which time he was aged sixty-five. He complained that even on reaching the rank of subedar 'I was shouted at by the [British] Adjutant as if I was a bullock, and he a mere boy, young enough to be my grandson' (p. 172).

21 *Press List of Mutiny Papers, being a Collection of the Correspondence of the Mutineers at Delhi, Reports of Spies to English Officials and other Miscellaneous Papers* (Calcutta: Superintendent of Government Printing, 1921). Translations of some of these papers, which were brought together for the trial of Bahadur Shah Zafar, the deposed King of Delhi, were published in Parliamentary Papers in 1859. They are not entirely unknown and were used by Michael Edwardes, who had studied Indian languages, in his book *Red Year: The Indian Rebellion of 1857* (London: Hamish Hamilton, 1973). However, William Dalrymple, in his definitive biography of Bahadur Shah Zafar *The Last Mughal* (London: Bloomsbury, 2006), is absolutely right in pointing out that a systematic study of this treasure has never been made.

22 *Mutiny Papers*, 23 June 1857, Kishen Dayal, subedar to Bakht Khan, Commander-in-Chief. National Archives, Delhi.

23 Mrs Elizabeth Muter, *My Recollections of the Sepoy Revolt 1857–1858* (London: John Long, Ltd. 1911), p. 56.

24 Foreign Department, 31 July 1857, Nos. 84–5, M. H. Court, Magistrate at Allahabad, to G. F. Edmonstone, Secretary to the Government of India. National Archives, Delhi.

25 Dr S. N. Sinha (ed.), *Mutiny Telegrams* (Uttar Pradesh: Department of Cultural Affairs, 1988), p. 56.

26 Chick, *Annals of the Indian Rebellion*, p. 150.

27 Home Department, Public Branch, 8 January 1858, Nos. 82–6, Report on the India Relief Fund. National Archives, Delhi.

28 *New York Daily Tribune*, 29 August 1857. Article written on 14 August by Karl Marx.

29 *New York Daily Tribune*, 16 September 1857. Article written on 4 September by Karl Marx.

30 Edouard de Warren, *L'Inde anglaise avant et après l'Insurrection de 1857*, with a critical study by Françoise de Valence (Paris: Éditions Kailash, 1994), vol. ii, pp. 185–86.

31 Jean Richepin, *Nana-Sahib: Drame en vers en sept tableaux* (Paris: Maurice Dreyfous, 1883), p. 35. I am indebted to Mme de Valence for the loan of this rare book.

32 Edwardes, *Red Year*, p. 163.

33 Ibid.

34 Anon. (subsequently identified as William Ireland), *History of the Siege of Delhi by an Officer who Served There* (Edinburgh, 1861), p. vii.

35 Pavan Varma, *Ghalib: The Man, the Times* (New Delhi: Penguin Books, 1989), p. 142. This biography does not however mention Ghalib's elegant chronogram on the Uprising – *rustkhez-i-beja*. Difficult to translate, its meaning is something like 'misplaced tumult' although *rustkhez* also means the Day of Judgement, or the Last Day, with apocalyptic overtones. Each Urdu letter has a numerical value, and *rustkhez* is equivalent to 1277 *hijri* in the Muslim calendar. *Be* means 'without' or 'minus', *ja* means 'place', so by taking away the numerical value of *ja* which is 4, the date of 1273 is arrived at, equivalent to 1857.

36 See note 24 above.

37 Quoted in Edwardes, *Red Year*, Appendix 4, pp. 174–82.

38 C. A. Bayly (ed.), *The Raj: India and the British, 1600–1947*, exhibition catalogue (London: National Portrait Gallery Publications, 1990), p. 241.

39 Rahaab Allana, 'The Silent Memorial: Life of the Mutiny in Orchha's Lakshmi Temple', in *Sarai Reader 06* (New Delhi: Centre for the Study of Developing Societies, 2006), pp. 271–81.

One: Rebels and Renegades

1 John Walker Sherer, *Daily Life during the Indian Mutiny: Personal Experiences of 1857* (London: Swan Sonnenschein & Co., 1898), p. 57.

2 Noah Chick, *Annals of the Indian Rebellion … Containing Narratives of the Outbreaks and Eventful Occurrences, and Stories of Personal Adventure, during the Mutiny 1857–58 etc.* (Calcutta: Sanders, Cones & Co., 1858), p. xii.

3 Foreign Political Consultations, 31 December 1858, No. 3022, Proclamation issued by Begam Hazrat Mahal in Birjis Qadr's name. National Archives, Delhi.

4 Sir William Muir, *Records of the Intelligence Department of the Government of the North-West Provinces of India during the Mutiny of 1857 including correspondence with the Supreme Government, Delhi, Cawnpore and other places. Preserved by and now arranged under the superintendence of Sir William Muir …* ed. William Coldstream (Edinburgh: T. & T. Clark, 1902), vol. i, p. 374.

5 Eric Stokes, *The Peasant Armed: The Indian Revolt of 1857*, ed C. Bayley (Oxford: Clarendon Press, 1986), p. 145.

6 Lt Gen. S. L. Menezes, *Fidelity and Honour: The Indian Army from the Seventeenth to the Twenty-First Century* (Delhi: Oxford University Press, 2004), p. 101.

7 Chick, *Annals of the Indian Rebellion*, p. 58.

8 George Forrest, *Selections from the Letters, Dispatches and Other State Papers Preserved in the Military Department of the Government of India 1857–1858* (Calcutta: Superintendent of Government Printing, 1893–1912), 4 vols. The first volume contains depositions from the principal witnesses from which the quotations on the following pages are taken.

9 See Rudrangshu Mukherjee's *Mangal Pandey: Brave Martyr or Accidental Hero?* (New Delhi: Penguin Books, 2005), appendix 1, for a summary of the court-martial.

10 Chick, *Annals of the Indian Rebellion*, pp. 132–33.

11 Ibid., p. 65.

12 Ibid., p. 70.

13 See Saul David's *The Indian Mutiny 1857* (London: Viking, 2002), pp. 383–84 for a discussion on the conspiracy theory.
14 Home Department, 30 April 1858, Nos. 355–62, 'List of Persons who have taken a leading part in the present rebellion, prepared from papers on record at the Home Department'. National Archives, Delhi.
15 Home Department, Public Branch, 12 February 1858, Nos. 95/96. National Archives, Delhi.
16 Mutiny Scrapbooks, Box 3, 'List of Bengal Officers by Regiment'. School of Oriental & African Studies, University of London.
17 Omar Khalidi, *The British Residency in Hyderabad: An Outpost of the Raj 1779–1948* (London: British Association for Cemeteries in South Asia, 2005), p. 28.
18 Charles Allen, *God's Terrorists: the Wahhabi Cult and the Hidden Roots of Modern Jihad* (London: Little, Brown, 2006), p. 145.
19 Chick, *Annals of the Indian Rebellion*, p. 163.
20 Ibid., p. vi.
21 Sherer, *Daily Life*, p. 8.
22 India Political Consultations, 19 March 1858, No. 133. India Office Records, British Library.
23. Muir, *Records of the Intelligence Department*, p. 5.
24 Roshan Taqui, *Lucknow 1857: The Two Wars at Lucknow – the Dusk of an Era* (Lucknow: New Royal Book Company, 2001), pp. 53 and 66.
25 Andrew Ward, *Our Bones Are Scattered: The Cawnpore Massacres and the Indian Mutiny of 1857* (London: John Murray, 1996), p. 357.
26 Michael Satow and Ray Desmond, *Railways of the Raj* (London: Scolar Press, 1980), pp. 12–14.
27 India Political Consultations, 18 September 1857, Nos. 43–4. India Office Records, British Library.
28 Mutiny Scrapbooks, Box 2, File A.
29 India Political Consultations, 14 August 1857, No. 10, R. B. Chapman, Officiating Under-Secretary to the Government of India, to Lt P. Stewart, Officiating Superintendent Electric Telegraph. India Office Records, British Library.
30 India Political Consultations, 21 August 1857, No. 14, J. N. Rose, Magistrate at Satara, to A. L. Anderson, Judicial Secretary to the Government of Bombay. India Office Records, British Library.
31 India Political Consultations, 2 October 1857, No. 21, Governor General's Proceedings in Council. India Office Records, British Library.
32 Foreign Department, 31 July 1857, Nos. 84–5, M. H. Court, Magistrate and Collector, Allahabad, to G. F. Edmonstone, Secretary to Government of India, enclosing 'A full and literal translation of a diary of events which occurred at Cawnpoor down to 12th June [1857] obtained from the person of an Opium Gomashtah who was there on leave.' Entries for 8 and 11 June. National Archives, Delhi.
33 Chick, *Annals of the Indian Rebellion*, p. 324.
34 Sir John Kaye, *A History of the Sepoy War in India 1857–1858* (London, 1864–76), vol. iii, p. 100.
35 S. N. Sen, *Eighteen Fifty-Seven*, 3rd edn (New Delhi: Publications Division, Ministry of Information & Broadcasting, Government of India, 1995, first published 1957), p. 5.
36 Sherer, *Daily Life*, p. 30.
37 Mutiny Scrapbooks, Box 1.

38 Ibid., Box 2, File A.
39 Ibid.
40 India Political Consultations, 20 November 1857, No. 232, A. R. Young, Secretary to Government of Bengal, to C. Beadon, Secretary to Government of India. India Office Records, British Library.
41 India Political Consultations, 29 October 1858, No. 349, T. D. Forsyth, Secretary to Chief Commissioner, Ondh, to G. F. Edmonstone, Secretary to Government of India. India Office Records, British Library.
42 John Fraser, 'More Europeans who sided with the Mutineers in India 1857–9', *Journal of the Society for Army Historical Research* 80 (2002), pp. 110–27 at p. 112.
43 Anon, (author identified as William Ireland) *History of the Siege of Delhi by an Officer who Served There* (Edinburgh, 1861), p. 93.
44 Fraser, 'More Europeans', pp. 111–12.
45 Ibid., pp. 119–27.
46 Iris Macfarlane, *Daughters of the Empire* (New Delhi: Oxford University Press, 2006). Letter from Maria Juxon Jones, September 1857, pp. 48–9.
47 P. J. O. Taylor, *A Star Shall Fall: India 1857* (New Delhi: Indus, 1993), pp. 234–37.

Two: The Kotah Residency Murders

1 The name Kotah is probably derived from Koteya, the name of a Bhil chieftain who was killed by a Bundi prince in the thirteenth century. The Bhils were the original occupiers of much territory in present day Rajasthan.
2 Colonel James Tod, *The Annals and Antiquities of Rajasthan* (Calcutta: Indian Publication Society, 1898–99).
3 O[live] Crofton, *List of Inscriptions on Tombs or Monuments in Rajputana and Central India* (Delhi: Manager of Publications, n.d. but *circa* 1934), p. 76.
4 G. H. R. Tillotson, *The Rajput Palaces: The Development of an Architectural Style, 1450–1750* (Delhi: Oxford University Press, 1987), pp. 161–66.
5 George Michell and Antonio Martinelli, *The Royal Palaces of India* (London: Thames & Hudson, 1994), pp. 18–19.
6 See *Chowkidar*, (the journal of the British Association for Cemeteries in South Asia) 9(5), 2002, pp. 97–8 for more on this interesting Irishman.
7 Captain Timothy Ash, 'A Family's Mutiny', *Medal News* (May 1992), pp. 21–2. I owe a great debt to Captain Ash, who first told me about the Kotah Residency murders in 1988, and who has generously shared his research, and enthusiasm, with me.
8 Crofton, *List of Inscriptions*, pp. 73–4.
9 Captain Timothy Ash, 'A Gwalior Star', *Journal of the Orders and Medals Research Society* (Autumn 1995), pp. 158–65.
10 Ash, 'A Family's Mutiny'.
11 Crofton, *List of Inscriptions*, p. 192. Only one family was killed at Neemuch during the first outbreak on 3 June 1857 – Store Sergeant Supple and his family were trapped and massacred in their quarters in the Commissariat Stores.
12 P. J. O. Taylor, *A Companion to the 'Indian Mutiny' of 1857* (Delhi: Oxford University Press, 1996), p. 184.
13. Charles Allen, *God's Terrorists: The Wahhabi Cult and the Hidden Roots of Modern Jihad* (London: Little, Brown, 2006), pp. 123–24. Captain Thomas Rattray was informed by

his Indian second-in-command, Hidayat Ali, in January 1857 that troops at Barrackpore, near Calcutta, were on the verge of mutiny.

14 P. J. O. Taylor, *What Really Happened during the Mutiny: A Day-by-Day Account of the Major Events of 1857–1859 in India* (Delhi: Oxford University Press, 1997), p. 112. In fact there was an isolated incident at Nasirabad, when a trooper of the 1st Bombay Lancers urged his regiment to mutiny, and was quickly dealt with by British officers.

15 Foreign Department, 5 August 1859, Nos. 324–27, Brigadier General George St Patrick Lawrence, Officiating Agent to the Governor General in Rajpootana, to Secretary to Government of India, from Camp Kotah, 17 April 1858. National Archives, Delhi. Much of the remaining material in this chapter is taken from a single large folder in the National Archives, Delhi. The original folios are not numbered, and the reports and statements within are not always in separate files. Letters and depositions will be identified by their writers, where given.

16 Foreign Department, 5 August 1859 Nos. 324–27, Major Burton, Political Agent Harrowtie, to Brigadier General Lawrence, from Neemuch, 9 August 1857. National Archives, Delhi.

17 Ibid.

18 Hugh Davenport, *The Trials and Triumphs of the Mewar Kingdom* (Jaipur: no publisher given, n.d. but *circa* 1975), pp. 79–84.

19 Foreign Department, 5 August 1859, Nos. 324–27, statement from Charles William Burton, 3 April 1858. National Archives, Delhi.

20 This is not the large city of Etawah in Uttar Pradesh, but a smaller town in former Rajputana.

21 Foreign Department, 5 August 1859, Nos. 324–27, undated statement from Sukha Ram Pandit, Tribute (i.e. revenue) Collector. National Archives, Delhi.

22 Foreign Department, 5 August 1859, Nos. 324–27, statement from Mrs Elizabeth Jane Burton, from Neemuch, 4 April 1858. National Archives, Delhi.

23 Ibid., quoting a letter from Major Burton written at Singoli in early October 1857.

24 Nanta is a short distance from Kotah, and contains a palace where the Burtons would have stayed during the day.

25 Foreign Department, 5 August 1859, Nos. 324–27, letter from Francis Burton to his mother from Kotah, 12 October 1857. National Archives, Delhi.

26 Foreign Department, 5 August 1859, Nos. 324–27, letter from Arthur Burton to his mother from Kotah, 14 October 1857. National Archives, Delhi.

27 Foreign Department, 5 August 1859, Nos. 324–27, Charles William Burton, quoting a statement by Natoo, a Residency chaprassi. National Archives, Delhi.

28 Foreign Department, 5 August 1859, Nos. 324–27, statement from Mangal Singh, Jemadar, Kotah, 2 November 1857. National Archives, Delhi.

29 Foreign Department, 5 August 1859, Nos. 324–27, undated statement from Niaz Ali, head munshi at the Kotah Agency, National Archives, Delhi.

30 Ash, 'A Gwalior Star'.

31 Charles William Burton appears to be quoting the camel-driver Komji, who was supposedly the only surviving witness to escape from the upper room, but the words are those of a mid-Victorian Englishman.

32 Foreign Department, 5 August 1859, Nos. 324–27, undated deposition from Louisa Cantem, Kotah. National Archives, Delhi.

33 Although the Maharao said in his statement that he had refused Lala Jai Dayal's request for a pay rise for the troops, the Jemadar Mangal Singh said when he escaped to Bundi he heard that 'the sepoys at Kotah got their arrears of pay, the Purdessees

[*pardesis* – outsiders] Rs 1 and the Daisees [*desis* – natives of the country] 8 annas, in excess of their fixed pay'. The pardesis, troops from Awadh and Bhojpur, received more money because it was considered they had more expenses than men who lived locally.

34 Foreign Department, 5 August 1859 Nos. 324–27, undated deposition of Henry Chriskote. National Archives, Delhi.

35 Louisa Cantem's deposition (see note 32).

36 Secret Consultations, 28 May 1858, Nos. 711–14, report on the recapture of Kotah by Major General H. G. Roberts, dated 7 April 1858. National Archives, Delhi.

37 Foreign Department, 5 August 1859, Nos. 324–7, Elizabeth Burton's statement. National Archives, Delhi.

38 Ash, 'A Gwalior Star'.

39 The inscription plaque on the Burton family tomb was stolen, probably in the 1980s, although the tomb itself was undamaged. An initiative by INTACH (Indian National Trust for Art and Cultural Heritage) and BACSA (British Association for Cemeteries in South Asia), led to a new inscription stone being erected in 2004, bearing the original wording, and the restoration of the whole cemetery.

40 K. R. N. Swamy and Meera Ravi, *British Ghosts and Occult India* (Calcutta: Writers Workshop Greybird Book, 2004), pp. 19–22.

Three: The Great Wall of Lucknow

1 India Political Consultations, 19 March 1858, No. 244. India Office Records, British Library.

2 See the two photographic panoramas by Felice Beato in *Lucknow, City of Illusion*, ed. Rosie Llewellyn-Jones (Munich: Prestel and The Alkazi Collection of Photography, 2006), pp. 64–9 and 90–9.

3 The Oude Blue Book (Parliamentary Papers) 1856, Enclosure 13, No. 4, pp. 291–92.

4 Rosie Llewellyn-Jones, *A Fatal Friendship: The Nawabs, the British and the City of Lucknow* (Delhi: Oxford University Press, 1985).

5 Michael Edwardes, *The Orchid House: Splendours and Miseries of the Kingdom of Oudh 1827–1857* (London: Cassell, 1960), pp. 38–42.

6 William Sleeman's report, which he described as a 'Diary of a Tour through Oude' was an official document, circulated among Company officials, but not published until 1858, two years after the author's death at sea. It is entitled *A Journey through the Kingdom of Oude 1849–1850: with Private Correspondence relative to the Annexation of Oude to British India* (London: Richard Bentley, 1858), 2 vols.

7 See for example Sleeman's letter of complaint in India Political Consultations, 13 June 1851, No. 145. India Office Records, British Library.

8 See Mirza Ali Azhar, *King Wajid Ali Shah of Awadh* (Karachi: Royal Book Company, 1982), Appendices 14, 15, 16, 17 for the draft proclamations.

9 Herbert Edwardes and Herman Merivale, *Life of Sir Henry Lawrence*, 3rd edn (London: Smith Elder & Co., 1873), p. 564.

10 India Political Consultations, 31 March 1857. India Office Records, British Library.

11 Rudrangshu Mukherjee, *Awadh in Revolt 1857–1858: A Study of Popular Resistance*, paperback edn with a new introduction (New Delhi: Permanent Black, 2002), p. 81.

12 John Pemble, *The Raj, the Indian Mutiny and the Kingdom of Oudh 1801–1859* (Hassocks: The Harvester Press, 1977), p. 209.

13 Andrew Ward, *Our Bones Are Scattered: The Cawnpore Massacres and the Indian Mutiny of 1857* (London: John Murray, 1996), p. 67.

14 Noah Chick, *Annals of the Indian Rebellion ... Containing Narratives of the Outbreaks and Eventful Occurrences, and Stories of Personal Adventure, during the Mutiny 1857–58 etc.* (Calcutta: Sanders, Cones & Co., 1858), p. 81.

15 India Political Consultations, 25 June 1858, No. 191, T. D. Forsyth, Secretary to Government Central Provinces, to G. F. Edmonstone, Secretary to Government. India Office Records, British Library.

16 Roshan Taqui, *Lucknow 1857: The Two Wars at Lucknow – the Dusk of an Era* (Lucknow: New Royal Book Company, 2001), p. 88.

17 Colina Brydon, *Diary of the Doctor's Lady*, compiled by Geoffrey Moore (privately printed, 1979). I am grateful to Mr John Cunningham, author of *The Last Man: The Life and Times of Surgeon Major William Brydon CB* (Oxford: New Cherwell Press, 2003), for telling me about Colina Brydon's diary. William Brydon had the extreme misfortune to be one of the few survivors of the retreat from Kabul in 1842, then to be trapped in the Lucknow Residency during the siege with his family.

18 *Illustrated London News*, 26 September 1857.

19 Taqui, *Lucknow 1857*, pp. 107–8.

20 India Political Consultations, 21 August 1857, Tables of Salutes; Salutes for Anniversaries and Native Sovereigns and Chiefs. India Office Records, British Library.

21 Mukherjee, *Awadh in Revolt*, p. 141.

22 R. C. Majumdar, *The Sepoy Mutiny and the Revolt of 1857*, 2nd edn (Calcutta: Firma K. L. Mukhopadhyay, 1963), p. 318.

23 Chick, *Annals of the Indian Rebellion*, p. 24.

24 See, for example, Pemble, *The Raj*, p. 212, where he has confused the Maulvi of Faizabad with a different man of the same name, who was from a Wahhabi family in Patna and a disciple of Syed Ahmad of Rae Bareli. Despite this error, Pemble's analysis of the relationship between Begam Hazrat Mahal and the Maulvi is very astute.

25 Ibid., p. 213.

26 P. J. O. Taylor, *A Companion to the 'Indian Mutiny' of 1857* (Delhi: Oxford University Press, 1996), p. 40 under the entry for Bashiratganj.

27 Taqui, *Lucknow 1857*, p. 292.

28 Anon. [Mrs G. Harris], *A Lady's Diary of the Siege of Lucknow* (London: John Murray, 1858), p. 129. This book was published anonymously 'for the perusal of friends at home' but internal evidence shows it to be by the Reverend Harris's wife. We never learn her first name. The Harris family arrived in Lucknow in March 1857, and Mrs Harris wrote 'I have kept a rough sort of journal during the whole siege, often written under the greatest difficulties – part of the time with a child in my arms, or asleep on my lap.'

29 Ibid., p. 56.

30 *The Times*, 11 February 1857.

31 India Political Consultations, 10 November 1857, No. 57. India Office Records, British Library.

32 S. A. A. Rizvi and M. L. Bhargava, *Freedom Struggle in Uttar Pradesh: Source Material* (Lucknow, 1957), vol. ii, p. 98.

33 Mukherjee, *Awadh in Revolt*, p. 166. In fact the tribal bowmen were very effective in raining arrows down on the British from the parapets of buildings under siege.

34 Martin Gubbins, *An Account of the Mutinies in Oudh and of the Siege of the Lucknow Residency* (London: Richard Bentley, 1858), pp. 238–9.

35 Llewellyn-Jones, *A Fatal Friendship*, pp. 82–4.

36 William Howard Russell, *My Diary in India in the Year 1858–59* (London: Routledge Warne & Routledge, 1860), vol. i, p. 273.

37 Foreign Consultations, 26 February 1858, Nos. 222–23, Lt Col. Strachey, Secretary to Government Central Provinces, to G. F. Edmonstone, Secretary to Government, writing from Allahabad. National Archives, New Delhi.

38 Sir James Hope Grant, *Incidents in the Sepoy War 1857–58, compiled from the Private Journals of General Sir Hope Grant GCB by Henry Knollys* (Edinburgh: William Blackwood & Sons, 1873), p. 243.

39 Foreign Department, Secret Consultations, National Archives, New Delhi. A series of newsletters compiled by Major Carnegie from intelligence brought in by Indian spies over the winter of 1857–58.

40 Pemble, *The Raj*, p. 224.

41 Taqui, *Lucknow 1857*, p. 243.

42 After the fall of Lucknow, the Maulvi roamed about Awadh, still with a considerable body of men, some 8,000 cavalry alone, engaging in sporadic fighting. He was defeated at Shahjahanpur by Sir Colin Campbell, but seeming to lead a charmed life, he again escaped. By now he was calling himself 'King of Hindustan' and there was a price of Rs 50,000 on his head. On 5 June 1858 he attempted to storm the fort of the Raja of Powain, a few miles from Shahjahanpur. He was shot dead, and the Raja immediately cut off his head, and carried it himself, by elephant, to the British Magistrate at Shahjahanpur, who stuck it on a pole at the Kotwali, the main police station. Majumdar, *The Sepoy Mutiny*, pp. 168–69.

43 India Political Consultations, 25 June 1858, No. 191 cited in note 15 above. No escort could be provided in June to take the prisoners from Allahabad to Calcutta, but by December 1858 they had been moved to the Presidency and released.

44 See the article in the *Hindustan Times*, 10 January 2005, by Professor P. C. Little entitled 'British Lens tells Sikandar Bagh's 1857'.

45 The photographic historian Dr Maria Antonella Pelizzari, writing in *Traces of India: Photography, Architecture, and the Politics of Representation, 1850–1900* (Montreal: Canadian Centre for Architecture, 2003), says that Beato's 'decision to rearrange human remains that were chaotically unearthed from their burial place on the site of the former battle is an indication of both the power of photographic media already in existence at that time and of the fiction that photography could introduce into the recording of historical events', p. 43.

46 Harris, *A Lady's Diary*, pp. 162–63.

47 John Fraser, 'Beato's Photograph of the Interior of the Sikanderbagh at Lucknow', *Journal of the Society of Army Historical Research* 59 (1981), pp. 51–5.

Four: The Prize Agents

1 Letter 12, from James Gibbon to his mother, dated 31 March 1858. James Gibbons Letters, Centre for South Asian Studies, University of Cambridge.

2 Foreign Department 17 November 1857, No. 520, Sannat Nana to Sir Robert Hamilton. National Archives, Delhi.

3 Reverend William Butler, *The Land of the Veda: being Personal Reminiscences of India; its People, Castes, Thugs and Fakirs; its Religions, Mythology, Principal Monuments, Palaces, and Mausoleums; together with the Incidents of the Great Sepoy Rebellion, and its results to Christianity and Civilisation* (Cincinnati, Walden & Stowe,1871), p. 15.

4 Anon., *The Case of the Banda and Kirwee Booty: A Sequel to "Prize Money"*, published by the authority of the Prize Agents of Sir G. C. Whitlock's force (London: Harrison, 1864), p. 1.

5 Ibid., p. 4.

6 Ibid., pp. 25–6.

7 Saul David, *The Indian Mutiny 1857* (London: Viking, 2002), pp. 28–9.

8 Lt Gen. S. L. Menezes, *Fidelity and Honour: The Indian Army from the Seventeenth to the Twenty-First Century* (Delhi: Oxford University Press, 2004), p. 85.

9 Charles Dodgson Madden's certificate, Archive of Blaker, Son & Young, Solicitors, East Sussex Record Office, Lewes, Acc2327/36/9.

10 John Walker Sherer, *Daily Life during the Indian Mutiny: Personal Experiences of 1857* (London: Swan Sonnenschein & Co., 1898), p. 24.

11 Foreign Department, 25 November 1859, No. 46/9, Lt Col. de Renzie Brett to the Adjutant General, Bengal Army. National Archives, Delhi.

12 *Illustrated London News*, 12 July 1857

13 Roshan Taqui, *Images of Lucknow* (Lucknow: New Royal Book Company, 2005), p. 11. The Government Census of Oudh, published in 1872, gave the figure of 370,000 inhabitants for Lucknow in 1856, but could not say how this figure was arrived at because the records had been destroyed in the Uprising. However, Roshan Taqui has found the 1856 census details in *Tilism-i-Laknau*, the weekly newspaper published between 1856 and the summer of 1857. The number of houses in each locality are listed, though not the number of inhabitants. Estimating each household to contain eight persons, he has calculated a total population of nearly 700,000 including transient people in the capital.

14 P. J. O. Taylor, *What Really Happened during the Mutiny: A Day-by-Day Account of the Major Events of 1857–1859 in India* (Delhi: Oxford University Press, 1997), pp. 123–26; David, *The Indian Mutiny*, p. 303.

15 *Illustrated London News*, 1 August 1857.

16 Sir William Muir, *Records of the Intelligence Department of the Government of the North-West Provinces of India during the Mutiny of 1857 including correspondence with the Supreme Government, Delhi, Cawnpore and other places. Preserved by and now arranged under the superintendence of Sir William Muir* ..., ed. William Coldstream (Edinburgh: T. & T. Clark, 1902), p. 92.

17 Ibid., p. 125.

18 Foreign Department, Secret Consultations, 27 November 1857, Nos. 80–7, Sir William Muir to G. F. Edmonstone, Secretary to the Government of India, writing on 29 September 1857. National Archives, Delhi.

19 Ibid. William Muir quoting a letter from Major Anson written 21 September to Mrs Muir. National Archives, Delhi.

20 Ibid. Memorandum of Intelligence by William Muir, writing on 27 September 1857 and quoting Colonel Becher's report of 22 September 1857. National Archives, Delhi.

21 *Illustrated London News*, 5 December 1857.

22 Butler, *The Land of the Veda*, pp. 418–19.

23 Home Department, 9 April 1858, Nos. 160–61. The Commissioner of Patna to Cecil Beadon, Secretary to Government. National Archives, Delhi.
24 Muir, *Records of the Intelligence Department*, p. 20.
25 India Political Consultations, 16 April 1858, No. 84, Lt Col. Malcolm, RE, commanding the Shorapur Field Force, To G. F. Edmonstone, Secretary to Government (Foreign Department), writing on 20 February 1858. India Office Records, British Library.
26 Home Department, Public Branch, 10 September 1858, No. 42, from G. F. Edmonstone, Secretary to Government (Foreign Department), to Captain W. Lees, Secretary to the Board of Examiners, writing on 28 August 1858. National Archives, Delhi.
27 Pavan Varma, *Ghalib: The Man, The Times* (Delhi: Penguin Books India), p. 156.
28 Foreign Department, 16 November 1857, No. 524, Charles Saunders, Commissioner of Delhi, to William Muir, Intelligence Department. National Archives, Delhi.
29 Ibid.
30 Foreign Department, 21 October 1857, No. 522, from William Muir to Cecil Beadon. National Archives, Delhi.
31 Foreign Department, 16 November 1857, No. 524, from Charles Saunders, Commissioner of Delhi, to William Muir. National Archives, Delhi.
32 Mrs Elizabeth Muter, *My Recollections of the Sepoy Revolt 1857–1858* (London: John Long Ltd, 1911), pp. 136–40.
33 Home Department, 14 May 1858, No. 97, Case of Lalla Kishore Lal. National Archives, Delhi.
34 Foreign Department, 20 October 1857, No. 520, Umed Singh to Sir Robert Hamilton, Resident of Indore. National Archives, Delhi.
35 Foreign Department, 20 October 1857, No. 524, William Muir, Intelligence Department, to Charles Saunders, Commissioner of Delhi. National Archives, Delhi.
36 Foreign Department, 16 November 1857, No. 524, Charles Saunders, Commissioner of Delhi, to William Muir, Intelligence Department. National Archives, Delhi.
37 Sherer, *Daily Life*, p. 24.
38 Home Department, 14 May 1858, No. 97. National Archives, Delhi.
39 Reports of Engineer Operations 954.1857/8 ENG, Royal Engineers Library, Chatham, Kent.
40 Unidentified newspaper cutting reporting an item from *Allen's India Mail*, April 1858. The Mutiny Scrapbooks, Box 2, School of Oriental and African Studies, University of London.
41 William Howard Russell, *My Diary in India in the Year 1858–59* (London: Routledge Warne & Routledge, 1860), vol. ii, pp. 130–34.
42 David, *The Indian Mutiny*, p. 340.
43 William Forbes-Mitchell, *Reminiscences of the Great Mutiny 1858–59* (London: Macmillan & Co. Ltd, 1910), p. 221.
44 Letter 13 from James Gibbon to his mother, dated 10 April 1858 and Letter 22 dated 22 June 1858. James Gibbon Letters, Centre for South Asian Studies, University of Cambridge.
45 Forbes-Mitchell, *Reminiscences*, p. 228.
46 George Forrest, *Selections from the Letters, Dispatches and Other State Papers Preserved in the Military Department of the Government of India 1857–1858* (Calcutta: Superintendent of Government Printing, 1893–1912), vol. ii, p. 303.
47 Foreign Department, 7 May 1858, No. 109. National Archives, Delhi.

48 Ibid., T. D. Forsyth, Secretary to the Chief Commissioner, Oudh, to Commander-in-Chief, writing on 6 April 1858.
49 Foreign Consultations, 7 May 1858, No. 109, from T. D. Forsyth, Secretary to the Chief Commissioner, Oudh, to G. F. Edmonstone, Secretary to Government of India. National Archives, Delhi.
50 Ibid.
51 Veena Talwar Oldenburg, *The Making of Colonial Lucknow, 1856–1877* (Princeton, NJ: Princeton University Press, 1984), p. 64.
52 House of Lords and House of Commons Reports, 27 January 1860. The Mutiny Scrapbooks, Box 1, File B. School of Oriental and African Studies, University of London.
53 Unclaimed prize money from 1851 to the Royal Military Hospital, Chelsea, 8211/26. National Army Museum, London.
54 Political Proceedings, Volume 10, 10 September 1858, No. 51, from P. B. Reid, Deputy Collector in charge of the Treasury, Allahabad, to C. B. Thornhill, Officiating Commander, Allahabad, writing on 22 July 1858. National Archives, Delhi.
55 Political and Secret Memorandum LPS.18 D225, p. 2. India Office Records, British Library.

Five: 'Hung in Perpetual Chains'

1 Lt Gen. S. L. Menezes, *Fidelity and Honour: The Indian Army from the Seventeenth to the Twenty-First Century* (Delhi: Oxford University Press, 2004), pp. 120–21.
2 Michael Edwardes, *Red Year: The Indian Rebellion of 1857* (London: Hamish Hamilton, 1973), p. 81.
3 Bolanauth Chunder, *The Travels of a Hindoo to Various Parts of Bengal and Upper India* (London: N. Trübner, 1869), vol. i, pp. 103–4.
4 The definitive story of the Cawnpore massacres and what led up to them is told by Andrew Ward in his book *Our Bones Are Scattered: The Cawnpore Massacres and the Indian Mutiny of 1857* (London: John Murray, 1996).
5 In an interview by Andrew Ward with the late Zoë Yalland, the historian of Cawnpore, Zoë recalled a cousin who lived there and who saw the ghosts of two little fair-haired boys running around the well trying to escape. Ward, *Our Bones are Scattered*, p. 551.
6 Letter published in the *Illustrated London News*, 25 September 1857, written by an volunteer cavalry officer with General Havelock's force at Cawnpore. The officer's own regiment had mutinied in Awadh.
7 P. J. O. Taylor, *A Companion to the 'Indian Mutiny' of 1857* (Delhi: Oxford University Press, 1996), p. 334.
8 For an authoritative picture of the Delhi siege and its aftermath, see the recent book by William Dalrymple, *The Last Mughal: The Fall of a Dynasty, Delhi, 1857* (London: Bloomsbury, 2006).
9 The writer of this letter to the *Bombay Telegraph* has not been identified. A printed copy of the letter appears in Box 4 of the Mutiny Scrapbooks, School of Oriental and African Studies, University of London
10 Foreign Department, 25 September 1857, No. 219, C. Chester, Allahabad, to Cecil Beadon, Secretary to Government of India, Calcutta, written on 29 August 1857. National Archives, Delhi.

11 Foreign Department, 18 December 1857, No. 141, Copy of a letter from Major William Orr to Thakur Saket Singh of Raghagarh, written on 25 October 1857. National Archives, Delhi.
12 Mrs Elizabeth Muter, *My Recollections of the Sepoy Revolt 1857–1858* (London: John Long Ltd, 1911), p. 132.
13 India Acts 1854–57 India Office Records, British Library.
14 *Illustrated London News*, 21 November 1857.
15 Taylor, *A Companion*, p. 271.
16 *Illustrated London News*, 3 October 1857.
17 India Political Consultations, 21 May 1858, Nos. 46–47, exchange of letters between Lt Col. R. Strachey, Secretary to Government, Central Provinces, and Cecil Beadon, Secretary to Government of India, Home Department, enclosing correspondence from H. C. Tucker. India Office Records, British Library.
18 Ibid., Nos. 47–58, John Wilson to G. F. Edmonstone, Secretary to the Government of India, Foreign Department.
19 Home Department, 4 February 1859, Nos. 18–19, quoting a Minute by the Governor of Bombay, John Elphinstone, written on 6 October 1857. National Archives, Delhi.
20 Ibid. Memorandum by Mr Neville Warren, Agent of the Scinde Railway.
21. Taylor, *A Companion*, p. 286.
22 Foreign Department, 29 January 1858, No. 361, the Secretary to the Chief Commissioner George Couper to G. F. Edmonstone, Secretary to the Government of India, Foreign Department, written on 18 January 1858 and stating Outram's views. National Archives, Delhi.
23 Ibid.
24 Eric Stokes, *The Peasant Armed: The Indian Revolt of 1857*, ed. C. Bayley (Oxford: Clarendon Press, 1986), p. 92.
25 Pavan Varma, *Ghalib: The Man, The Times* (New Delhi: Penguin Books, 1989), p. 166.
26 Vincent Smith, *The Oxford History of India*, ed. Percival Spear (Oxford: Clarendon Press, 1958). In the 1970 edn, p. 677.
27 Sir William Muir, *Records of the Intelligence Department of the Government of the North-West Provinces of India during the Mutiny of 1857 including correspondence with the Supreme Government, Delhi, Cawnpore and other places. Preserved by and now arranged under the superintendence of Sir William Muir* ..., ed. William Coldstream (Edinburgh: T. & T. Clark, 1902), vol. ii, p. 23.
28 Home Department, 8 February 1858, No. 37, Minute by J. P. Grant, Lieutenant Governor, Central Provinces. National Archives, Delhi.
29 Home Department, 23 April 1858, quoting the Governor General in Council in the Financial Department on 16 January 1858. National Archives, Delhi.
30 India Political Consultations, 9 April 1858, No. 88, telegram from the Governor General. India Office Records, British Library.
31 India Political Consultations, 18 September 1857, No. 43–4, E. Impey, Postmaster General at Bombay, to Cecil Beadon, Secretary to Government of India. India Office Records, British Library.
32 India Political Consultations, 9 April 1858, No. 67, Captain J. P. Nixon, Political Agent Bharatpur, to C. B. Thornhill, Secretary to Government North-Western Provinces. India Office Records, British Library.
33 Queen Victoria's proclamation, reprinted in the *Illustrated London News*, 26 December 1857.
34 *Illustrated London News*, 25 February 1860.

35 India Political Consultations, 9 October 1857, No. 103, G. F. Edmonstone to Colonel George Lawrence, Rajputana Agent to the Governor General. India Office Records, British Library.
36 Dalrymple, *The Last Mughal*, pp. 238–39.
37 Home Department, 4 June 1858, Nos. 28–9, Captain W. Holland's account of his escape from Delhi on 11 May 1857, National Archives, Delhi. Captain Holland was lent a pony by Francis Cohen, and finally reached the safety of Meerut cantonment on 27 May. The Cohen family home at Harchandpur was later plundered by mutineers and the Cohens had to flee to Meerut.
38 India Political Consultations, 23 April 1858, No. 73, From T. D. Forsyth to G. F. Edmonstone. India Office Records, British Library.
39 India Political Consultations, 22 January 1858, No. 61, order from G. H. Lawrence, later Deputy Commissioner of Gondah. India Office Records, British Library.
40 Home Department, 5 August 1859, No. 28, printed circular issued by George Couper, Secretary to the Chief Commissioner, to Government North-Western Provinces, dated 21 July 1859. National Archives, Delhi.

Six: Mutiny Memorials

1 Information from Sir Mark Havelock-Allan QC, great-great-grandson of Brigadier General Sir Henry Havelock.
2 Lord Frederick Roberts, *Forty-One Years in India* (London: Richard Bentley & Son, 1897), vol. i, p. 314.
3 *Chowkidar* (the journal of the British Association for Cemeteries in South Asia), 2 (5), 1982 p. 50.
4 *Chowkidar*, 9 (6), 2002 p. 125.
5 Captain Ivan Herford, *Stirring Times under Canvas*, (London, 1862), p. 129.
6 India Political Consultations, 25 June 1858, Memorandum from the Financial Department, Government of India. India Office Records, British Library.
7 Andrew Ward, *Our Bones Are Scattered: The Cawnpore Massacres and the Indian Mutiny of 1857* (London: John Murray, 1996), p. 436.
8 Mary Ann Steggles, *Statues of the Raj* (London: British Association for Cemeteries in South Asia, 2000), p. 13.
9 Miles Irving, *Indian Monumental Inscriptions* (Lahore: Punjab Government Press, 1910), vol. ii, part I, pp. 20–4.
10 *Chowkidar*, 8 (5), 1999, p. 10.
11 P. J. O. Taylor, *A Star Shall Fall: India 1857* (New Delhi: Indus, 1993), pp. 189 et seq.
12 Foreign Consulations, 10 September 1858, No. 187, Captain G. Hutchinson, Military Secretary, to G. F. Edmonstone, Secretary to Government, writing from Lucknow on 20 August 1858. National Archives, Delhi.
13. Ibid.
14 *Chowkidar*, 10 (2), 2003, p. 29.
15 Information from Mr Toby Parker, Honorary Archivist at Haileybury, who kindly sent me photographs of the memorial.
16 *Chowkidar*, 8 (6), 1999, p. 120.
17 Information kindly provided by Mr Mark Frost, Assistant Curator, Dover Museum.
18 Report from the Calcutta correspondent, *The Times*, 18 June 1858.

19 P. J. O. Taylor, *A Companion to the 'Indian Mutiny' of 1857* (Delhi: Oxford University Press, 1996), p. 176.
20 Rosie Llewellyn-Jones, *Engaging Scoundrels: True Tales of Old Lucknow* (Delhi: Oxford University Press, 2000), pp. 112–21.
21 William Dalrymple, *The Last Mughal: The Fall of a Dynasty, Delhi, 1857* (London: Bloomsbury, 2006), p. 483.
22 Steggles, *Statues of the Raj*. Her book is the first attempt to list and classify British statues exported to India from Britain.
23 The statues are those to Sir Arthur Cotton, the engineer who worked on the Godaveri river project (erected in the 1980s); Sir Robert Stanes, founder of the Stanes School at Coimbatore (erected 2006); Charles Freer Andrews, the priest friend of Mahatma Gandhi, (erected 2006); and the author's late father-in-law, Jack Rust (bust erected in 1984), at Vidya Bhawan School, Udaipur.
24 Steggles, *Statues of the Raj*, p. 147.
25 Ibid., pp. 123–24.
26 Ibid., p. 30.
27 Roshan Taqui, *Lucknow 1857: The Two Wars at Lucknow – the Dusk of an Era* (Lucknow: New Royal Book Company, 2001), p. 15.
28 Lt Col. Gordon-Alexander, *Recollections of a Highland Subaltern* (London: Edward Arnold, 1898), p. 104.
29 Dr R. S. Fonia, *1857 Memorial Museum Residency Lucknow* (Lucknow: Archaelogical Survey of India, 2002), p. 43.
30 H. C. Fanshawe, *Delhi Past and Present* (London: John Murray, 1902), pp. 84–5.
31 Sten Nilsson and Narayani Gupta, *The Painter's Eye: Egron Lundgren and India* (Stockholm: Nationalmuseum, 1992), pp. 113–16.
32 Narayani Gupta, 'Pictorializing the "Mutiny" of 1857', in *Traces of India: Photography, Architecture, and the Politics of Representation, 1850–1900*, ed. Maria Antonella Pelizzari (Montreal: Canadian Centre for Architecture, 2003), pp. 216–39 at p. 230.
33 Sophie Gordon, 'A City of Mourning: The Representation of Lucknow, India in Nineteenth-Century Photography', *History of Photography* 30 (1) (spring 2006), pp. 80–91 at p. 87.
34 Christopher Hibbert, *The Great Mutiny India 1857* (Harmondsworth: Penguin Books, 1980), p. 215.
35 *Illustrated London News*, December 1907. The Mutiny Scrapbooks, File 1B, Box 1, School of Oriental and African Studies, University of London.

BIBLIOGRAPHY

Records

Foreign Consultations, Secret and Public Branches, National Archives, Delhi
Home Department, Public Branch, National Archives, Delhi
India Acts 1854–57, British Library
India Financial Consultations, British Library
India Political Consultations, British Library
James Gibbon Letters, 1858, Centre for South Asian Studies, University of Cambridge
Mutiny Scrapbooks, School of Oriental and African Studies, University of London
Prize Money, National Army Museum, London
Report of Engineering Operations 1857/58, Royal Engineers Library, Chatham, Kent

Books and journals

Allana, Rahaab, 'The Silent Memorial: Life of the Mutiny in Orchha's Laksmi Temple', in *Sarai Reader 06* (New Delhi: Centre for the Study of Developing Societies, 2006), pp. 271–81

Allen, Charles, *God's Terrorists: the Wahhabi Cult and the Hidden Roots of Modern Jihad* (London: Little, Brown, 2006)

Anon. [Mrs G. Harris], *A Lady's Diary of the Siege of Lucknow* (London: John Murray, 1858)

Anon. (subsequently identified as William Ireland), *History of the Siege of Delhi by an Officer who Served There* (Edinburgh, 1861)

Anon., *The Case of the Banda and Kirwee Booty: A Sequel to "Prize Money"*, published by the authority of the Prize Agents of Sir G. C. Whitlock's force. (London: Harrison, 1864)

Ash, Captain Timothy, 'A Family's Mutiny', *Medal News* (May 1992), pp. 21–2

Ash, Captain Timothy, 'A Gwalior Star', *Journal of the Orders and Medals Research Society* (autumn 1995), pp. 158–65

Azhar, Mirza Ali, *King Wajid Ali Shah of Awadh* (Karachi: Royal Book Company, 1982)

Bayly, C. A. (ed.), *The Raj: India and the British, 1600–1947*, exhibition catalogue (London: National Portrait Gallery Publications, 1990)

Brydon, Colina, *Diary of the Doctor's Lady*, compiled by Geoffrey Moore (privately printed, 1979)

Butler, Reverend William, *The Land of the Veda: being Personal Reminiscences of India; its People, Castes, Thugs and Fakirs; its Religions, Mythology, Principal Monuments, Palaces, and Mausoleums; together with the Incidents of the Great Sepoy Rebellion, and its results to Christianity and Civilisation* (Cincinnati, Walden & Stowe, 1871)

Chick, Noah, *Annals of the Indian Rebellion … Containing Narratives of the Outbreaks and Eventful Occurrences, and Stories of Personal Adventure, during the Mutiny 1857–58 etc.* (Calcutta: Sanders, Cones & Co., 1858)

Chunder, Bolanauth, *The Travels of a Hindoo to Various Parts of Bengal and Upper India* (London: N. Trübner, 1869), 2 vols

Crofton, Olive, *List of Inscriptions on Tombs or Monuments in Rajputana and Central India* (Delhi: Manager of Publications, n.d. but *circa* 1934)

Dalrymple, William, *The Last Mughal: The Fall of a Dynasty, Delhi, 1857* (London: Bloomsbury, 2006)

Davenport, Hugh, *The Trials and Triumphs of the Mewar Kingdom* (Jaipur: no publisher given, n.d. but *circa* 1975)

David, Saul, *The Indian Mutiny 1857* (London: Viking, 2002)

de Warren, Edouard, *L'Inde anglaise avant et après l'Insurrection de 1857*, with a critical study by Françoise de Valence (Paris: Éditions Kailash, 1994) 2 vols

Edwardes, Herbert, and Merivale, Herman, *Life of Sir Henry Lawrence*, 3rd edn (London: Smith Elder & Co., 1873)

Edwardes, Michael, *The Orchid House: Splendours and Miseries of the Kingdom of Oudh 1827–1857* (London: Cassell, 1960)

Edwardes, Michael, *Red Year: The Indian Rebellion of 1857* (London: Hamish Hamilton, 1973)

Fanshawe, H. C., *Delhi Past and Present* (London: John Murray, 1902)

Fonia, R. S., *1857 Memorial Museum Residency Lucknow* (Lucknow: Archaelogical Survey of India, 2002)

Forbes-Mitchell, William, *Reminiscences of the Great Mutiny 1858–59* (London: Macmillan & Co. Ltd, 1910)

Forrest, George, *Selections from the Letters, Dispatches and Other State Papers Preserved in the Military Department of the Government of India 1857–1858* (Calcutta: Superintendent of Government Printing, 1893–1912), 4 vols

Fraser, John, 'Beato's Photograph of the Interior of the Sikanderbagh at Lucknow', *Journal of the Society of Army Historical Research* 59 (1981), pp. 51–5

Fraser, John, 'More Europeans who sided with the Mutineers in India 1857–9', *Journal of the Society for Army Historical Research* 80 (2002), pp. 110–27

Gordon, Sophie, 'A City of Mourning: The Representation of Lucknow, India in Nineteenth-Century Photography', *History of Photography* 30 (1) (spring 2006), pp. 80–91

Gordon-Alexander, Lt Col., *Recollections of a Highland Subaltern* (London: Edward Arnold, 1898)

Grant, Sir James Hope, *Incidents in the Sepoy War 1857–58, compiled from the Private Journals of General Sir Hope Grant GCB by Henry Knollys* (Edinburgh: William Blackwood & Sons, 1873)

Gubbins, Martin, *An Account of the Mutinies in Oudh and of the Siege of the Lucknow Residency* (London: Richard Bentley, 1858)

Gupta, Narayani, 'Pictorializing the "Mutiny" of 1857', in *Traces of India: Photography, Architecture, and the Politics of Representation, 1850–1900*, ed. Maria Antonella Pelizzari (Montreal: Canadian Centre for Architecture, 2003), pp. 216–39

Guy, Alan and Bowden, Peter (eds.), *Soldiers of the Raj: The Indian Army 1600–1947*, exhibition catalogue (London: National Army Museum, 1997)

Herford, Captain Ivan, *Stirring Times under Canvas*, (London, 1862)

Hibbert, Christopher, *The Great Mutiny India 1857* (Harmondsworth: Penguin Books, 1980)

Hunter, Sir William, *Imperial Gazetteer of India* (Oxford: Clarendon Press, 1907–9), 13 vols

Irving, Miles, *Indian Monumental Inscriptions* (Lahore: Punjab Government Press, 1910), 2 vols

Kaye, Sir John, *A History of the Sepoy War in India 1857–1858* (London, 1864–76), 3 vols

Llewellyn-Jones, Rosie, *A Fatal Friendship: The Nawabs, the British and the City of Lucknow* (Delhi: Oxford University Press, 1985)

Llewellyn-Jones, Rosie, *Engaging Scoundrels: True Tales of Old Lucknow* (Delhi: Oxford University Press, 2000)

Llewellyn-Jones, Rosie (ed.), *Lucknow, City of Illusion* (Munich: Prestel and The Alkazi Collection of Photography, 2006)

Majumdar, R. C., *The Sepoy Mutiny and the Revolt of 1857*, 2nd edn (Calcutta: Firma K. L. Mukhopadhyay, 1963)

Menezes, Lt Gen. S. L., *Fidelity and Honour: The Indian Army from the Seventeenth to the Twenty-First Century* (Delhi: Oxford University Press, 2004)

Michell, George, and Martinelli, Antonio, *The Royal Palaces of India* (London: Thames & Hudson, 1994)

Muir, Sir William, *Records of the Intelligence Department of the Government of the North-West Provinces of India during the Mutiny of 1857 including correspondence with the Supreme Government, Delhi, Cawnpore and other places. Preserved by and now arranged under the superintendence of Sir William Muir* ..., ed. William Coldstream (Edinburgh: T. & T. Clark, 1902)

Mukherjee, Rudrangshu, *Awadh in Revolt 1857–1858: A Study of Popular Resistance*, paperback edn with a new introduction (New Delhi: Permanent Black, 2002)

Mukherjee, Rudrangshu, *Mangal Pandey: Brave Martyr or Accidental Hero?* (New Delhi: Penguin Books, 2005)

Muter, Mrs Elizabeth, *My Recollections of the Sepoy Revolt 1857–1858* (London: John Long Ltd, 1911)

Nilsson, Sten and Gupta, Narayani, *The Painter's Eye: Egron Lundgren and India* (Stockholm: Nationalmuseum, 1992)

Oldenburg, Veena Talwar, *The Making of Colonial Lucknow, 1856–1877* (Princeton, NJ: Princeton University Press, 1984)

Pemble, John, *The Raj, the Indian Mutiny and the Kingdom of Oudh 1801–1859* (Hassocks: The Harvester Press, 1977)

Press List of Mutiny Papers, being a Collection of the Correspondence of the Mutineers at Delhi, Reports of Spies to English Officials and other Miscellaneous Papers (Calcutta: the Superintendent of Government Printing, 1921)

Richepin, Jean, *Nana-Sahib: Drame en vers en sept tableaux* (Paris: Maurice Dreyfous, 1883)

Rizvi, S. A. A., and Bhargava, M. L., *Freedom Struggle in Uttar Pradesh: Source Material* (Lucknow, 1957), 6 vols

Roberts, Lord Frederick, *Forty-One Years in India* (London: Richard Bentley & Son, 1897), 2 vols

Russell, William Howard, *My Diary in India in the Year 1858–59* (London: Routledge Warne & Routledge, 1860), 2 vols

Satow, Michael and Desmond, Ray, *Railways of the Raj* (London: Scolar Press, 1980)

Sen, S. N., *Eighteen Fifty-Seven*, 3rd edn (New Delhi: Publications Division, Ministry of Information & Broadcasting, Government of India, 1995, first published 1957)

Sherer, John Walker, *Daily Life during the Indian Mutiny: Personal Experiences of 1857* (London: Swan Sonnenschein & Co., 1898)

Sinha, Dr S. N. (ed.), *Mutiny Telegrams* (Uttar Pradesh: Department of Cultural Affairs, 1988)

Sita Ram, *From Sepoy to Subedar*, translated and first published by Lt Col. Norgate, Bengal Staff Corps (Lahore, 1873), ed. James Lunt (London: Macmillan, 1988)

Sleeman, William, *A Journey through the Kingdom of Oude 1849–1850: with Private Correspondence relative to the Annexation of Oude to British India* (London: Richard Bentley, 1858), 2 vols

Smith, Vincent, *The Oxford History of India*, ed. Percival Spear (Oxford: Clarendon Press, 1958)

Steggles, Mary Ann, *Statues of the Raj*, (London: British Association for Cemeteries in South Asia, 2000)

Stokes, Eric, *The Peasant Armed: The Indian Revolt of 1857*, ed C. Bayley (Oxford: Clarendon Press, 1986)

Swamy, K. R. N., and Ravi, Meera, *British Ghosts and Occult India* (Calcutta: Writers Workshop Greybird Book, 2004)

Taqui, Roshan, *Lucknow 1857: The Two Wars at Lucknow – the Dusk of an Era* (Lucknow: New Royal Book Company, 2001)

Taqui, Roshan, *Images of Lucknow* (Lucknow: New Royal Book Company, 2005)

Taylor, P. J. O., *A Star Shall Fall: India 1857* (New Delhi: Indus, 1993)

Taylor, P. J. O., *A Companion to the 'Indian Mutiny' of 1857* (Delhi: Oxford University Press, 1996)

Taylor, P. J. O., *What Really Happened during the Mutiny: A Day-by-Day Account of the Major Events of 1857–1859 in India* (Delhi: Oxford University Press, 1997)

Tillotson, G. H. R., *The Rajput Palaces: The Development of an Architectural Style, 1450–1750* (Delhi: Oxford University Press, 1987)

Tod, Colonel James, *The Annals and Antiquities of Rajasthan* (Calcutta: Indian Publication Society, 1898–99)

Varma, Pavan, *Ghalib: The Man, The Times* (New Delhi: Penguin Books, 1989)

Ward, Andrew, *Our Bones Are Scattered: The Cawnpore Massacres and the Indian Mutiny of 1857* (London: John Murray, 1996)

INDEX